THE JOSHUA GENERATION

The Joshua Generation

ISRAELI OCCUPATION AND THE BIBLE

RACHEL HAVRELOCK

PRINCETON UNIVERSITY PRESS
PRINCETON & OXFORD

Published by Princeton University Press
41 William Street, Princeton, New Jersey 08540
6 Oxford Street, Woodstock, Oxfordshire OX20 1TR

press.princeton.edu

First paperback printing, 2022
Paperback ISBN 9780691235622
Cloth ISBN 9780691198934
ISBN (e-book) 9780691201498
LCCN: 9780691198934

British Library Cataloging-in-Publication Data is available

Editorial: Fred Appel and Jenny Tan
Production Editorial: Debbie Tegarden
Cover Design: Leslie Flis
Production: Erin Suydam
Publicity: Nathalie Levine and Kathryn Stevens
Copyeditor: Hank Southgate

Cover Credit: Mosaic artist Mordechai Yoeli and photographer Kevin Dwarka

This book has been composed in Arno

Dedicated to the memory of Michael Feige, ז״ל

friend and cherished interlocutor

whose life was cut short by a conflict he understood all too well.

CONTENTS

ILLUSTRATIONS

ACKNOWLEDGMENTS

I BEGAN WRITING about Joshua soon after completion of my previous book, *River Jordan: The Mythology of a Dividing Line*. Since then, my research and life have been enriched by many gatherings and experiences. During the same period, I've witnessed shocking things occur in the places relevant to this book, as well as across the globe. Both have influenced the nature of the present volume. I thank all of the people whose consideration of my ideas and dialogue about them shaped this work, and I take full responsibility for any of its missteps.

I dedicate this book to Michael Feige, a friend and colleague who was killed in an act of violence both targeted and random. Prior to his untimely death, Michael and I discussed at great length the biblical texts, archaeologists, and Israeli interpreters covered here. I have vivid memories of our dialogue in Chicago parks, memorials in Washington, DC, Tel Aviv cafes, and—quite by accident—on the Formula 1 racetrack in Jerusalem. Most memorable was a visit Michael arranged for me at the Ben-Gurion archive and the former prime minister's Sde Boker retreat. What turned out to be our final in-person conversation was held in the desert that Ben-Gurion pumped with symbolic meaning. I feel Michael's absence profoundly. Even worse, the academic community has lost one of the few scholars able to face the pitched Israeli-Palestinian conflict with a calm demeanor while entertaining the political positions of its combatants no matter how they clashed with his own.

Archaeologist Zvi Lederman set me on this journey when he leant me his copy of the proceedings on the book of Joshua at Ben-Gurion's home. I thank him for the tip and the extended book loan—finding my own copy constituted a journey within a journey. Laura Levitt, beloved friend and feminist hero, made this book happen in so many ways, not least by leading me through the American Academy of Religion/Society of Biblical Literature book hall in her shining silver cloak. Particular thanks are due to Nasser Mufti, Shai Ginsburg, Yosefa Raz, Seth Sanders, and Kam Shapiro for their attention to the manuscript and key editorial interventions. Nory Peters served as my research assistant early in the process and guided me through vital German texts. Efrat Appel generously sat with me to puzzle through Joshua texts. Often, this left us as the last people sitting in bars and cafes lingering over Hebrew to English translations. I so value her precision, patience, and humor.

My gratitude extends to the conveners and participants in the Borders in Jewish Thought conference at the University of Chicago: Uri Shachar, David Scholen, Paul Mendes-Flohr, Ofri Ilani, Sam Berrin Shonkoff, Hillel Ben Sasson, Israel Yuval, Julie Cooper, and Na'am Rokem; and to the presenters at my Holy War Conference held at the University of Illinois at Chicago (UIC) Institute for the Humanities: William Morrow, Reuven Firestone, James Turner Johnson, Michael Sells, Janaki Bakhle, David Watt, and Mahinda Deegalle. My fellows at the University of Cambridge Centre for Research in Arts, Social Sciences, and Humanities (CRASSH)—Dana Arnold, Lauren Arrington, Naor Ben-Yehoyada, Anders Ekström, Abhijit Gupta, Wilson Jacob, and David Monteyne—advanced my thinking and ensured a pleasurable sabbatical. Jim Aitken made some remarkable Joshua manuscripts available to me, and I also enjoyed time with Gabriel and Michal Rosenbaum in Cambridge. Special thanks are due to Simon Goldhill for running the fellowship at CRASSH and never wavering in the role of consummate host. Thanks to Simon, I have been able to maintain my connection to Cambridge through an Israeli-Palestinian water working group. The group remains an important part of my life, and I have learned much from its participants, including Samer Alatout, Stephen Gasteyer, Sreematti Mitter, Julie Trottier, Dan Rabinowitz, Rami Narte, Itamar Mann, Tamara Lotner Lev, David Brooks, Eran Feitelson, Ezgican Ozdemir, Jauad El Kharraz, Steven Caton, and Sophia Stamatopoulou-Robbins. Dean Astrida Tantillo and a UIC College of Liberal Arts and Sciences Dean's Research Award further supported vital sabbatical inquiries.

As I learned during a fellowship at the UIC Humanities Institute, one doesn't need to travel to be on leave. I thank former director Susan Levine and associate director Linda Vavra as well as Joaquín Chávez, Salome Skvirsky, Rosilie Hernández, Malgorzata Fidelis, Priscilla McCutcheon, Melissa Hibbard, and Saniye Vatansever for the lively conversation and their contributions. Frederick Greenspahn convened a conference around biblical studies and Jewish studies, whose proceedings illuminated the stakes of my arguments. Biblical scholars like Seth Sanders, Yvonne Sherwood, Joel Kaminsky, Erin Runions, Alan Levenson, Eva Mroczek, Mark Leuchter, Alison Joseph, Mark Brett, Tamar Kamionkowski, Marc Zvi Brettler, Rhiannon Graybill,

Abraham Winitzer, Nili Wazana, Stephen Russell, Elizabeth Goldstein, Robert Kawashima, Diana Lipton, Ken Stone, Jeremy Hutton, and Ron Hendel keep the field interesting and vibrant. My fellow Joshua enthusiasts in the Society of Biblical Literature Joshua-Judges section—Zev Farber, Daniel Hawk, Edward Noort, Thomas Dozeman, and Ralph Hawkins—have welcomed my ideas while debating them with seriousness and vigor. I owe much to the friendship, dialogue, and support of Johari Jabir. Among the acts for which I extend gratitude is his convening of a group to read my work as I was preparing to submit it for review. Nasser Mufti, Patrick Schafer, Ellen McClure, Mark Canuel, Joe Tabbi, and Tatjana Gajic offered guidance, along with Johari, at a pivotal juncture.

Yael Zerubavel, Toby Jones, Jonathan Gribetz, Carol Bakhos, Omer Bar Tov, Avner Ben-Amos, Yosefa Raz, Alison Schachter, Roz Schindler, Shai Ginsburg, Eric Meyers, Carol Meyers, Elyse Semerdjian, Eugene Sheppard, David Slucki, Joel Kaminsky, Ofri Ilani, Margaret Olin, and Inamul Haq, among others, welcomed me to their campuses and facilitated productive interactions around my work. I would also like to thank the editors and anonymous reviewers of *Critical Research in Religion* for advancing an early *Joshua Generation* article. Oren Yiftachel introduced me to cartographer Roni Blushtein-Livnon, who drew the maps for this book. Kevin Dwarka photographed the cover image.

Along with those named above, I extend my appreciation to UIC colleagues Lisa Freeman, Ellen McClure, Rama Mantena, Sunil Agnani, Sam Fleischacker, Robin Grey, Junaid Quadri, Jennifer Ashton, Natasha Barnes, Daniel Borzutzky, Nicholas Brown, Ralph Cintron, Peter Coviello, Anna Kornbluh, Raphael Magarik, Walter Benn Michaels, Mary Anne Mohanraj, Robin Reames, Alfred Thomas, Luis Urrea, Mustapha Kamal, Nanno Marinatos, Sultan Tepe, Norma Moruzzi, Nadine Naber, Sandy Sufian, Marina Mogilner, Julia Vaingurt, Judith Gardiner, Jeff Gore, Jennifer Tobin, Karen Underhill, Leon Fink, Beate Geissler, Molly Doane, Ömür Harmanşah, Stephen Engleman, and Teresa Cordoba. Thanks to Mark Canuel for constant support and good advice. Many students have inflected this work, including Abeer Al Jamal, Timothy Oravec, Nicole Krause, Kathleen Blackburn, Justin Raden, Cecilia Villarruel, and Edith Tovar. My gratitude extends also to Corbin Hiday, who jumped on at the end as a graduate research assistant.

I would be remiss without mentioning the support of great friends in the academy and outside of it: Matti Bunzl, Ari Kelman, Marla Segol, David Shneer, Sayed Kashua, Susan Shapiro, Mary Beth Rose, Susanna Heschel,

Andrea Most, Bruce Rosenstock, Rochelle Rubenstein, Caryn Aviv, Brant Rosen, Dean Bell, Kaveh Ehsani, Jason Frank, Jen Jordan, Matan Boord, Elizabeth Yaari, Kevin Dwarka, Jane Lerner, Shira Sargent, Meg West, Virginia Eubanks, Linda Pulik, Denis Weil, Merav Argov, Sasha Earle, Sara Strahan, Andy Hall, Dan Rybicky, Doug Fogelson, Sharif Ezzat, Tobin Belzer, Antonio Lopez, Ethan Michaeli, Todd Hasak-Lowy, and Michael Kaminer. I met Prince Asael and Prince Amiel at a key moment. The Jordanian-Palestinian-Israeli NGO Ecopeace Middle East and its remarkable directors and staff have done more to teach, inspire, and reorient my sense of place than I can articulate. I write this book with the hope that their vision might continue to manifest.

Fred Appel and the staff at Princeton University Press have turned a manuscript into a book with respect and loving care at every turn. I am truly honored to work with them.

My writing on war has been balanced by love. As I reached the end of this project, my father, Dr. Kenneth Havrelock, passed away. He was buried with honor by the US Army, adding a new inflection to my discourse on militarism. I am pleased that Rhoda Stamell, my mother, now lives close and can agonize over my sentence structure in greater proximity. Yuri Lane, my husband, and Delilah Lane, my daughter, have joined me as I pursued Joshua evidence, searched for relics of a 1950s study group, and crossed militarized borders and checkpoints. Delilah even toured the Sorek desalination plant with me on one of the hottest days I have experienced. Both of them have remained agreeable and enthusiastic and opened the space and time for my research and writing. In this book, I make much of the ancient household run by women. In my life, I am blessed to share the responsibilities and comforts of a household with the two of them.

THE JOSHUA GENERATION

INTRODUCTION

Endless War

The Gates of the Promised Land

On March 3, 2015, Israeli Prime Minister Benjamin Netanyahu addressed the United States Congress on the subject of US negotiations over Iran's nuclear capacity. In short, Netanyahu came to oppose the impending agreement between the United States and Iran to slow Iran's nuclear capabilities and lift American sanctions. His emphatic speech reached for existential themes, causing several commentators to suggest the very personal nature of the existential crisis. Netanyahu's political career has been dedicated to decrying the nuclear capacities of Iran, and, at the time, the Democratic President Barack Obama and Secretary of State John Kerry stood on the verge of a new approach to Iran and its nuclear program.

The Republican Party took up Netanyahu's passionate opposition and allied with him against the American president. This unprecedented level of affiliation between a single American political party and the leader of a foreign country led Speaker of the House John Boehner to invite Netanyahu to Congress without consulting the White House, a clear violation of protocol. Defying President Obama had become both a sport and purpose among the Republican Party, so the Netanyahu invitation aimed to scuttle or, at least, disrupt one of Obama's central foreign policy initiatives.

Netanyahu was more than happy to oblige. His diplomatic identification with one political party had earned him the nickname "the Republican Senator from the State of Israel," and the shared patronage of donors like Sheldon Adelson brought the two even closer. More importantly perhaps were the ways Netanyahu aligned the stars in his favor. He scheduled the speech during the week of the Zionist lobby AIPAC's (the American Israel Public Affairs Committee) annual meeting in Washington, DC, and just two weeks before that year's Israeli election. At the time, Netanyahu trailed in the polls. He wagered correctly that his bravado in defying President Obama would impress Israelis at home exactly as his campaign "phone banks reminded voters that Netanyahu's opponents had the support of 'Hussein Obama.'"[1] As Netanyahu did his part to affirm the Republican raison d'être, so Speaker Boehner accommodated Netanyahu's political linking of the Holocaust and Iranian threats to Israel by inviting Holocaust survivor and Nobel Laureate Elie Wiesel to attend Netanyahu's congressional address.

Along with its significance in the Israeli electoral calendar, the March 3 date landed Netanyahu in the halls of American power on the eve of the Jewish holiday of Purim, which celebrates how the intrepid Queen Esther saved the Jewish people from certain annihilation at the hands of a Persian political advisor by risking everything to approach the tempestuous king for protection. Implying his role as a modern-day, male Esther, the prime minister did not hesitate to equate the story of ancient Persian threat with the contemporary Iranian scenario or to see the story as factual precedent for "the Jewish people's right to defend themselves against their enemies."[2] The speech's most pointed moment of biblical interpretation, however, did not concern Esther, but rather was a passing reference to the leader of conquest, Joshua.

Toward the end of the speech, Netanyahu had most of the audience on its feet applauding the right of the Jewish people—understood as Israel—to defend itself.[3] With a dramatic glance above as if to God on Sinai but actually to the walls of the House Chamber, he said, "Overlooking all of us in this august chamber is the image of Moses. Moses led our people from slavery to the gates of the Promised Land. And before the people of Israel entered the land of Israel, Moses gave us a message that has steeled our resolve for thousands of years. I leave you with this message today." Breaking into Hebrew for the first and only time, Netanyahu quoted, "Be strong and resolute, be not in fear or in dread of them" (Deuteronomy 31:6).[4]

1. David Remnick, "Base Appeals," *New Yorker*, March 22, 2015, http://www.newyorker.com/magazine/2015/03/30/base-appeals.

2. Benjamin Netanyahu, "The Complete Transcript of Netanyahu's Address to Congress," ed. Washington Post Staff, *Washington Post*, March 3, 2015, https://www.washingtonpost.com/news/post-politics/wp/2015/03/03/full-text-netanyahus-address-to-congress/?noredirect=on&utm_term=.fa375ffd612b.

3. Many prominent Democrats did not attend in protest of the affront to President Obama.

4. The exhortation to "be strong and bold" echoes the salute of the secular, socialist Hashomer Hatzair movement, as well as the 1977 charter of West Bank settlements; see Michael

In the immediate context of the speech, the "them" who should neither be feared nor dreaded are the Iranians, with the implication that the United States should not fear Iran's nuclear capacity to the point of signing an agreement to curb that capacity. But the reference is slippery because fear of Iran constitutes the basis for Netanyahu's argument why members of Congress should reject the agreement. Fear is the very emotion stoked by his evocation of "a dark, genocidal regime" and his conclusion that "Iran can't be trusted." Another level of meaning in the exhortation to "be strong and resolute" likely reverberated among the Republican audience. Were they not heeding Moses by being "strong and resolute" as they flouted President Obama's authority and brought Netanyahu to Congress? As he affirmed Republican righteousness, Netanyahu endowed unwavering support of Israel with biblical import; his use of biblical citation pointed to a two-sided "them" who should neither be feared nor dreaded that included both Iran and the Democratic Party.

The citation carries yet a third meaning relating to Israel's domestic policy. Here the biblical context matters quite a bit, as does the history of Israeli biblical interpretation in which the phrase "be strong and resolute" cues the Zionist program broadly and Israeli military action specifically. The strength and resolve at issue involves a lack of "fear or dread" of Arab opponents. The very point of this book is to show the trajectory of biblical interpretation that leads to Democrats, Iranians, and Palestinians alike figuring as a dreaded and fearful "them" to be opposed at all turns. Let us now observe the operation in brief.

In the book of Deuteronomy, Moses urges the People of Israel to "be strong and resolute" as he initiates Joshua as his successor. The occasion is momentous because the book dramatizes Moses's struggle with his divinely ordained death outside of the Promised Land, which means that his appointment of Joshua marks a certain reconciliation with his fate. Furthermore, Moses will be spared the wars "to wipe out and dispossess" the peoples of Canaan, since this job falls to Joshua (Deut 31:3). Joshua has served as Moses's loyal apprentice throughout the wilderness journey, showing his military prowess when necessary. Joshua figures as the ideal type of military man—fearless, strong, and resolute—and God promises to fight beside Joshua on Israel's behalf. Still, Moses enjoins the quarrelsome people to act like an army and maintain fearlessness and resolve during the impending battles to conquer the Promised

---

Feige, *Settling in the Hearts: Jewish Fundamentalism in the Occupied Territories* (Detroit: Wayne State University Press, 2009), 48.

Land. "Be strong and resolute, neither fear nor dread them" becomes the mantra of the conquest that celebrates the annihilation of the peoples of Canaan.

In his speech, Netanyahu introduced the quotation with assurance that the message "has steeled our resolve for thousands of years," by which he meant the Jewish people during thousands of years of oppression. In fact, the militaristic mantra of conquest was largely neglected by Jews and Jewish interpreters because Judaism developed in the Diaspora, where notions of conquest and homeland held little relevance and posed a danger to social stability in Christian and Muslim lands. Moses, of course, remained central as a figure of liberation and law giving, but Joshua held little appeal, particularly after Christian interpreters claimed him as a forerunner of Christ. Joshua assumed new importance in early Zionism as a self-sufficient leader who brought the People of Israel into an era of national independence and waged a prolonged war with the natives. As I will show, the book of Joshua became a foundational text in modern Israel in contrast to its marginal status in Diaspora Judaism. In the meantime, I would correct Prime Minister Netanyahu's timeline and point out that the biblical directive, "be strong and resolute, neither fear nor dread them," has steeled *Israeli* resolve in the context of ongoing war with Palestinians.

This point becomes clearer by reflecting on Netanyahu's words before he raised his eyes to the image of Moses:

> We are no longer scattered among the nations, powerless to defend ourselves. We restored our sovereignty in our ancient home. And the soldiers who defend our home have boundless courage. For the first time in 100 generations, we, the Jewish people, can defend ourselves.[5]

Not surprisingly, Netanyahu employs all of the central tropes of Zionism: discounting of the long history of Diaspora Judaism as a time of sheer Jewish powerlessness, total claim over occupied territories as part of an ancient homeland that can accommodate Jewish sovereignty alone, and justification of militarism and occupation as defense. He drives home the notion of defense by repeating it three times and having soldiers stand for the entire Jewish people. The defense that involves systematic aggression does not stand in contrast to ideas of a nonmilitarized state but rather to the Holocaust. According to this reasoning, the annihilation of Jewish Europe justifies military occupation, and the "them" whom Israelis cannot afford to fear or dread are Palestinians.

5. Netanyahu, "Complete Transcript."

After his biblical turn, Netanyahu brought America back into the equation. "My friends, may Israel and America always stand together, strong and resolute. May we neither fear nor dread the challenges ahead. May we face the future with confidence, strength, and hope."[6] America's continued standing with Israel certainly entails continued American funding for Israel's extensive military at the same time that Netanyahu hammers the point that his Republican allies should remain resolute in opposing the Iran deal, a wish fulfilled when Donald Trump withdrew the United States from the agreement negotiated under Obama. His invitation to a brilliant shared future suggests that as Israel continues its Occupation, America should reject the agreement with Iran and Republicans should remain steadfast in opposition to Palestinians, Iranians, and Democrats alike. The final note of "hope" works with the Joshua reference to ironically subvert Obama's authority—"hope" having served as one of the main slogans of the 2008 Obama campaign during which Civil Rights leaders dubbed Barack Obama the harbinger of "the Joshua Generation" ushering Dr. Martin Luther King Jr.'s vision into a new era.[7] As he assumed the rhetoric and reference, Netanyahu sought to unseat the hopes of this American Joshua.

The Jewish War

This book tells the story of how the biblical figure of Joshua entered modern political life. I tell it as a Bible scholar who studies the political interpretation and use of biblical images, as well as the political rhetoric of the Bible itself. So, in order to understand moments like Netanyahu's address to Congress or the contrasting notion that Barack Obama's election indicated the onset of the Joshua Generation, we will move through the book of Joshua itself, an

6. Netanyahu, "Complete Transcript."

7. The Rev. Otis Moss Jr. dubbed Obama Joshua, explaining, "You're part of the *Joshua generation*." See William Safire, *New York Times Magazine*, November 30, 2008, https://www.nytimes.com/2008/11/30/magazine/30wwln-safire-t.html; David Remnick, "The Joshua Generation: Obama and the Politics of Race," *New Yorker*, November 17, 2008, https://www.newyorker.com/magazine/2008/11/17/the-joshua-generation; and Jonathan Alter, "With a Little Help from Our Kids," *Newsweek*, November 17, 2008, p. 28. Analysis of the book of Exodus in African-American traditions is also relevant; see Allen Dwight Callahan, *The Talking Book: African Americans and the Bible* (New Haven, CT: Yale University Press, 2006); Cheryl A. Kirk-Duggan, "Let My People Go! Threads of Exodus in African American Narratives," in *Voices from the Margin: Interpreting the Bible in the Third World*, 3rd ed., ed. R. S. Sugirtharajah (Maryknoll, NY: Orbis Books, 2006), 309–333.

alternate reading of the biblical text, and the history of its Israeli interpretation. At each stage, I analyze the political currency of the idea of a Promised Land. As I provide a cultural genealogy of the term "occupation" in Hebrew, I analyze the rhetoric of war and its relationship to social reality.

Political and economic factors certainly set conflict in motion, but here I pursue the internal cultural logics that sustain a group of people in a state of endless war. Foremost, I find that nationalism, with its insistence on territorial integrity and unified citizenry, cannot exist without war stories constantly deployed to send citizens off to battle. By marking certain people as nationals and others as opponents, I argue, war rhetoric plays a dominant role in national formation. Importantly, within this formation, the army represents a cohesive entity not evident in civilian life. Because society—which is always heterogeneous in nature—does not support nationalist claims, the army becomes a key icon of the nation. An integral part of such national formation—and militaristic formation more generally—involves denial of the social realities that do not support national cohesion or ethno-linguistic unity. Just as military incursions seek to overpower opposition, so war rhetoric wages a battle against a social landscape that does not conform to its desires. And, because social reality remains out of step with nationalist conceptions, war stories become the primary place where the nation actually exists. Bearing the burden of sustaining the existence of the nation, war stories become publicly ritualized and reiterated with passion at moments and places where national bonds begin to dissipate. For many states, as well as disenfranchised groups, a founding war story operates to enforce the collective and to stir the kind of emotions that can lead residents to counterproductively turn against those sharing the same space.

As much as war stories bring the nation into being, they also end up preserving the very social realities that they set out to deny. This occurs in a few different ways. First of all, the representation of enduring opponents records the presence of neighbors in some way resistant to the national formation. Acknowledgment of these neighbors points to the fragile, incomplete nature of national projections. Secondly, the insistence that an army signifies the nation shows that civilian society cannot alone support the image of a unified collective. The stark oppositions of conflict play a vital role in bringing the national unit into relief. Finally, the fervent nature and ritual repetition of militaristic narration reveals the insecurity of the narrators facing social settings that do not match the political entity dramatized in their stories. War stories then not only rally troops and citizens with gripping accounts of heroism and sacrifice, but they also impose a nationalist framework on a heterogeneous society. At the same time that battle tales mobilize against existing social structures, they unwittingly record the failures of nationalism. The failures become apparent not only in shrill tones and genocidal allusions, but also in admissions of persistent localized forms of governance.

I support these arguments about war and the nation-state with two interconnected instances of war rhetoric. The first comes from the biblical book of Joshua and the second from the significantly later 1958 book of Joshua study group held at the home of David Ben-Gurion, the first prime minister of Israel.[8] The two are not only linked as a biblical text and its political interpretation, but also as the primary consolidations of Jewish war rhetoric. Through the work of Ben-Gurion's study group, the terms of Joshua's conquest came to resonate with modern Israeli militarism. In modern Hebrew, the word for the Israeli Occupation (כיבוש/*kibbush*) derives from the biblical Joshua's systematic wars against Canaanite peoples.[9] The word for settlement in the book of Joshua (נחלה/*nahalah*) similarly forms the root of the word for Jewish settlements in the West Bank (התנחלות/*hitnahalut*). Through use of the word, settlers (מתנחלים/*mitnahalim*) present their "fortified cities" as avatars of the sanctified parcels of land bestowed on biblical tribes (Joshua 19:35).[10] The inseparable valences of conquest/Occupation (כיבוש/*kibbush*) and tribal allotments and militarized settlement (נחלה/*nahalah*), in combination with the selfsame word for a border (גבול/*gevul*), attest to how Joshua's vocabulary informed the lexicon of Jewish nationalism.

While we can, and usually do, think of Israel's wars as discrete events with separate intents—1948, the Suez Canal War, 1967, the War of Attrition, 1973, the Lebanon War, the First Intifada, the Second Intifada, and the wars on Gaza—we could also adapt Toby Jones's framework for thinking about the US-Iraq relationship as one continuous war.[11] The idea of war as a permanent state proves helpful not only as a means of rethinking history, but also as a way of examining the relationship of culture and discourse to war. If a state remains permanently at war, then its rhetoric and culture will forever be bound up with

8. David Ben-Gurion was Israel's longest-serving prime minister until July 2019, when Netanyahu surpassed him, albeit with an uncertain future and inconclusive elections to follow.

9. The use of the word in Joshua 18:1 suggests a completion of the conquest.

10. Feige, *Settling in the Hearts*, 48, 73–76.

11. Toby C. Jones, "America, Oil, and War in the Middle East," *Journal of American History* 99, no. 1 (2012): 208–218.

militarization. This book examines the kind of speech, public rhetoric, and stories that support a situation of ongoing war and persuade a group and its opponents to participate in an unrelenting conflict. In 2020, as Israel's formal occupation of territory spills over its fiftieth year, I consider its founding stories and an alternative politics of place.

Joshua

Joshua, the biblical nationalist text par excellence, turns out to be divided between twelve chapters that narrate the gruesome conquest of Canaan and another twelve that reflect local, tribal traditions of coexistence. This bifurcated structure points to a dialectic that runs through the book and its representation of an ancient state. In addition, a hidden drama rests in the more static second half of the book, in which the very peoples earlier reported as liquidated reappear as long-standing neighbors. Joshua's war does remake the nation, but it does so by displacing (or trying to displace) social categories, not by exterminating indigenous peoples. Although hardly the first to offer a critique of the book of Joshua, I am the first to locate a corrective within the book itself. On my way to doing so, there are many compelling nationalist, Marxist, and postcolonial readings of Joshua that inform my own.

Marxist biblical critics have recognized in the book of Joshua an egalitarian tribal era of "primitive communism" that precedes the era of capital accumulation by landlords supporting the monarchy.[12] Thus a golden age comes to an abrupt end after kings establish a capital in Jerusalem.[13] I share the Marxist appreciation for tribalism and its collective ownership of resources, but resist the idea that the tribes disappeared as their members dissolved into the ranks

12. See Roland Boer on how life was ordered through the extended-family household commune, village-commune, or *musha'* farming: *The Sacred Economy of Ancient Israel* (Louisville: Westminster John Knox Press, 2014). See also Boer, *Political Myth: On the Use and Abuse of Biblical Themes* (Durham, NC: Duke University Press, 2009), 9–115.

13. "David Jobling, following Norman Gottwald, has argued that under the monarchy we find what may be termed a 'tributary' mode of production, a revised form of Marx's Asiatic mode of production. Prior to this, under the ideal of judgeship that appears in Judges and 1 Samuel, he prefers, following Marshall Sahlins, the notion of a 'household' or 'familial' mode of production, one that is somewhat more egalitarian in terms of sexual difference than what follows under the monarchy, to Gottwald's 'communitarian' mode of production." Roland Boer, *Marxist Criticism of the Bible* (London: T & T Clark International, 2003), 100.

of workers serving an owner class authorized by the monarchy.[14] The book of Joshua actually reveals a blended system in which the household economies of a tribal order persist during the monarchy and outlast its destruction. In the double voice of Joshua, I see an ongoing relationship between institutions that involves tension and negotiation alike. But whether or not we see centralization as a negative consolidation of resources or a positive integration of disparate groups, it is vital to take the process of state formation in ancient Israel out of a historical plot of either progress or failure. By seizing upon one representation of the ancient state as its epitome, historical plotlines miss the coexistence of multiple political forms. I suggest that a spatial, rather than historical, reading best accounts for the multiple scales of governance in ancient Israel and their different political fates. So, in the name of eschewing a teleological plotline, I endeavor to loosen Canaan—the Promised Land—from the plot of exodus, where it marks the fulfillment of sovereignty following slavery and wandering. Taken outside of the plot of exodus, the space of the land appears as a dynamic site of contest and shared inhabitation.

As various tribes, clans, and households formed alliances and federated under the umbrella term of "Israel," they did not relinquish their autonomy. Tribes and their subgroupings moved in and out of the alliance, making "Israel" both a comprehensive and a fluid term. Amidst the fluctuations, different groups likely experienced localized moments of liberation, wandering, and struggle for territorial control. In this sense, we should consider the civil wars narrated in the Bible not as indicating the breakdown of national unity, but rather as struggles to force a particular group to affiliate or for that group to defect from the alliance.[15]

Postcolonial scholars correctly denounce Joshua's radical premise that God commands Israel to annihilate the inhabitants of Canaan and destroy all of their property. To them, Joshua is a figure fulfilled in the many violent arrivals

14. James W. Flanagan argues, for example, "For our purposes we may assume that the end of the segmental state is symbolized in the Bible by the loss of the ark reported in 1 Samuel 4." "Chiefs in Israel," *Journal for the Study of the Old Testament* 6, no. 20 (1981): 152. My goal is to step outside the social evolutionary model and look at the simultaneity of institutions.

15. Civil wars may even, as Nasser Mufti contends, determine the bonds and bounds of the nation by establishing certain wars as family affairs and others as outside its conceivable scope. See *Civilizing War: Imperial Politics and the Poetics of National Rupture* (Evanston, IL: Northwestern University Press, 2017).

of settlers to indigenous lands.[16] In a most material way, the crusaders, the explorers, the Boers, and the American settlers framed their enterprises as quests for the Promised Land and understood the book of Joshua as explaining their times and justifying their wars.[17] This book joins in the postcolonial critique of Joshua, as it offers a different mode of reading the Hebrew Bible's most violent book. Parallel to my argument for separating the space of Canaan from the plot of exodus, I propose a nonethnic interpretation of the difference between Canaanites and Israelites. Read against the grain of the exodus plot, these labels and their subcategories do not denote distinct ethnic groups as nationalist and postcolonial scholars have suggested. The many dexterous studies of the dichotomy between "Israel" and "Other" in the Bible ultimately convince me not that the terms are empty, but that they are political.[18]

Rather than descendants of twelve sons of Jacob, I understand the twelve tribes of Israel as groups that at some point pledged allegiance to a centralized state or protostate.[19] As noted by the twentieth-century German Biblicist Martin Noth, whose theories influence my own, twelve represents a kind of

16. See Naim S. Ateek, "A Palestinian Perspective: Biblical Perspectives on the Land," in Sugirtharajah, *Voices from the Margin*, 227–234; Michael Prior, *The Bible and Colonialism: A Moral Critique* (Sheffield: Sheffield Academic Press, 1997); R. S. Sugirtharajah, *The Bible and Empire* (New York: Cambridge University Press, 2005), 77–79, 88–91; Robert Allen Warrior, "A Native American Perspective: Canaanites, Cowboys and Indians," in Sugirtharajah, *Voices from the Margin*, 235–241.

17. On the pilgrims: Cotton Mather, *Magnalia Christi Americana: or, the ecclesiastical history of New-England, from its first planting in the year 1620. Unto the year of our Lord, 1698* (London, 1702), 55–56; L. Daniel Hawk, "Indigenous Helpers and Invader Homelands," in *Joshua and Judges*, ed. Athalya Brenner and Gale A. Yee (Minneapolis: Fortress Press, 2013), 109–121. Jonathan Boyarin observes both "the ethnic-moral analogy, in which Israelites were to Egyptians and to Canaanites as Puritans were to Papists and to Indians" and "the geographical analogy, in which Egypt was to England as Canaan was to America." *Palestine and Jewish History: Criticism at the Borders of Ethnography* (Minneapolis: University of Minnesota Press, 1996), 56. On the Boers: Prior, *Bible and Colonialism.*

18. For example: Robert L. Cohn, *The Other in Jewish Thought and History: Constructions of Jewish Culture and Identity* (New York: New York University Press, 1994); Robert Polzin, *Moses and the Deuteronomist: A Literary Study of the Deuteronomistic History, Part One: Deuteronomy, Joshua, Judges* (New York: The Seabury Press), 145.

19. Because tribes and clans circled in and out of the federation, maintaining the number twelve required some elaborate arithmetic. For example, the tribe of Joseph has two component groups—Ephraim and Manasseh—that are further bifurcated into the eastern and western halves of Manasseh. The tribe of Levi owns no land and therefore isn't counted as one of the twelve, and groups like the Clans of Yair become folded into other tribes. In other words, I don't think that there were ever twelve tribes or only twelve tribes, but rather that this symbolic

ideal number also used to indicate the ancient Greek city-states participating in the amphictyony at Delphi.[20] The groups that did not affiliate with state centralization, I propose, appear in biblical texts as interloping peoples of the land ineligible for marriage with Israelites. As with most political binaries, there are plenty of mediating cases.[21] By analyzing Joshua outside of the exodus plot of liberation, transition, and establishment of a state, I conclude, along with archaeologists, that the nation of Israel did not emerge during the escape from Egypt and migration to a lost homeland, but instead was consolidated when regional groups supported a national army intended to resist imperial military threats.[22]

The rise of local empires, particularly the Assyrian Empire, motivated the amalgamation of tribes and influenced the content of Joshua.[23] Small tribal groups had no chance of standing up to imperial forces and so, in a process likely resembling 1 Samuel 8:4, the tribes appealed for a king. Biblical texts portray the consolidation as less than ideal and perpetually plagued by divisions between north and south, east and west.[24] Furthermore, kingship is

---

rendering accounted for a process of state formation in which a range of local groups pledged varying degrees of alliance to a federation and central power.

20. Martin Noth, *Das System der zwölf Stämme Israels* (Stuttgart: Wissenschaftliche Buchgesellschaft, 1930).

21. Such as the tribe of Benjamin, which may have submitted only after military defeat (Judges 19–21) or the Hivite peoples of the region of Gibeon, whose inclusion entailed a lower-class position.

22. Along with Israel Finkelstein and Nadav Na'aman, I see the groups that eventually constitute Israel as largely indigenous while involved in migrations common to settlement in the era. In addition, I lean on the theories of Mendenhall and Gottwald that Israel consolidated during an anti-imperial revolt, although I imagine the revolution as primarily discursive. The succession of empires faced by Israel, I propose, produced an acute anxiety regarding survival that motivated processes of centralization in the north and south and, it seems, alliance between them. Whether an army resulting from these alliances actually fought imperial or local opponents or is simply imagined as doing so, I recognize the trope of a unified army as evidence of consolidation and nationalization.

23. Thomas B. Dozeman notes "the influence of the Neo-Assyrian royal conquest accounts in the composition of Josh 9–12" and suggests that "the polemical perspective of the author against kings and city-states would represent a critique of the Neo-Assyrian Empire, using the royal conquest accounts as a story of revolt against the empire." *Joshua 1–12: A New Translation with Introduction and Commentary*, The Anchor Yale Bible Commentaries (New Haven, CT: Yale University Press, 2015), 27.

24. The book of Judges, for example, tells of a war between eastern and western tribes (12) and a vicious campaign of multiple tribes against Benjamin (19–21).

rarely portrayed as suitable or desirable to the tribes and their confederated structure, appearing as something forced upon them by external geopolitical realities. Only out of necessity did these regions seem to have sustained periods of alliance. Rather than from the people, the real push for centralization seems to have come from the monarchy based in Jerusalem, which simultaneously enlisted scribes in the project of writing national history.

This history, known to (and disputed by) biblical scholars as the Deuteronomistic History, contains the books of Deuteronomy, Joshua, Judges, Samuel, and Kings. Along lines first proposed by Martin Noth, I see the project of creating this history as reflecting the very process of nationalization.[25] Reading strongly along narrative lines, one could even say that the Deuteronomistic History produces the People of Israel. As the Jerusalem monarchy absorbed and enlisted tribes from different geographic regions in a process of state centralization, its scribes adapted local tribal traditions into a national story.[26] The consolidation of this collective history played a key role in the process of political consolidation. Thus I identify, like Noth, pre-Deuteronomistic tribal traditions that Deuteronomistic scribes compile and incorporate into their plot of conquest. Departing from Noth, however, I perceive agency behind these sources—a demand for legitimacy on the part of smaller sociopolitical groups prior to acceding to centralization. Analyzing the relationship between the literature of Joshua and social institutions results in a picture of ongoing, tenuous political negotiation. The tenuousness of such negotiation, ironically enough, produces brutal, absolutist rhetoric of holy war.

The centrality of the army contributes to the formulation of the nation as male and renders masculinity a stipulation for its soldier-citizens. Exceeding the national depictions of other biblical sources, the book of Joshua repeatedly emphasizes that fighting men comprise "all of Israel." However, this national portrait dissipates when the war story ends. The second half of Joshua depicts a tribal system characterized by subdivisions of clan and household. Female

25. Martin Noth, *The Deuteronomistic History*, trans. Jane Doull and rev. by John Barton, Michael D. Rutter, D. R. Ap-Thomas, and David J. A. Clines (Sheffield: JSOT, 1981).

26. My analysis is indebted to early twentieth-century biblical scholarship that saw war as key to the confederation of Israelite tribes and suspected that unity only existed during times of war. However, where scholars such as Albrecht Alt, Martin Noth, and Rudolph Smend believed that unity resulted from actual war, I see it as a product of war stories. Albrecht Alt, *Kleine Schriften zur Geschicte des Volkes Israel* (Munich: Beck, 1953), 2:187; Martin Noth, *Das Buch Josua* (Tübingen: Mohr Siebeck, 1953), 61; Rudolph Smend, *Yahweh War & Tribal Confederation: Reflections upon Israel's Earliest History*, trans. Max Gray Rogers (Nashville: Abingdon Press, 1970).

figures appear as vital members of the household, often in charge of its sustenance and survival. I am not suggesting that women in ancient Israel were relegated to the household, nor am I proposing that women's lives transpired in a private, domestic space. Rather, I build on Carol Meyers's work about the household as the dominant site of economic production in order to argue that it was also a political institution.[27] It appears that households leveraged their economic potential in order to gain protection from the larger entities of tribe and state. As the primary site of production, the economic leverage of the household translated into political terms. Deuteronomistic sources in general, as well as the book of Joshua in particular, show women in public, political roles related to the household. In this way, the book of Joshua attests to a political sphere separate from the nation and the army. As it eclipses tribal autonomy, Joshua's war story downplays the constitutive role of the household and the necessary involvement of its female leaders. But just as allegedly decimated peoples reappear in Joshua, so its female characters ensure the survival of their households in full view. Exactly as Joshua strives to tell the most nationalist story possible, nonnational institutions like the household become apparent.

The question of authorship—for the most part *the* question in mainstream biblical scholarship—often hijacks scholarly arguments to the point where literary texts are transformed into mathematic equations regarding the combination of sources and academic panelists duel in the name of their imagined author. This trend carries a share of irony insofar as the authors in question are inferred from the texts themselves. Still, every interpretation requires a context, and suppositions or fictions about ancient authors may be as valid a context as any other. Bemusement and all, I participate in the project by recognizing distinct terms and grammars employed by different biblical sources, identifying certain passages in Joshua as nationalist and others as tribal, and relying on the interpretive horizon set by Noth's theory of a Deuteronomistic History. The need to infer authorial intention is intensified by the questions of who might

27. Through the prisms of anthropology and archaeology, Carol Meyers shows that Israelite women worked to harvest and convert grains into edible form. "The role of women in performing this vital subsistence task (and many others—such as producing other foodstuffs, household textiles, and various utilitarian objects and installations) would have been highly valued. It was also the source of considerable household power in a society that lacked a market economy, except perhaps in several urban centers in the late monarchic period." "Foregrounding Ordinary Israelite Women," *AJS Perspectives: The Magazine of the Association for Jewish Studies*, Fall 2014, http://perspectives.ajsnet.org/the-peoples-issue/foregrounding-ordinary-israelite-women/.

have formulated a particular line of political rhetoric to further what ends. At the same time, I find the obsession with authorship unduly constraining, particularly in light of the hypothetical nature of our assumed authors. And so, as I propose that scribes supporting centralization and monarchy folded long-standing local and regional traditions into their story of a conquest sometime during the eighth to seventh centuries BCE, I perceive dynamics at work in the book of Joshua that could relate to other periods. Taking seriously Noth's theory of an exilic revision of the Deuteronomistic History, for example, I can see how the story of "all Israel" marching in line behind Joshua could promote social cohesion during the crisis of dislocation and loss of sovereignty. I can also accept Thomas Dozeman's assessment of the late, blended Deuteronomistic and Priestly language throughout the book of Joshua.[28] Although they differ on the nature of central authority, both of these biblical sources, in my estimation, promote centralization as a political strategy. Later editors could well have continued a process of combining traditions begun at an earlier point in time.

My argument hinges on the premise that the book of Joshua relates to the consolidation of an ancient nation-state or, at least, the strong desire to consolidate; the dynamics of consolidation are of more interest than fixing a particular period in which this must have occurred. Although I place this in a relatively early time period, there is plenty of evidence in later biblical texts of smaller-scale, regional social groups that required unification or consolidation in order to survive the onslaughts of empire. The model I propose about the absorptive function of state formation would be relevant in both pre- and postexilic eras.[29] Therefore, I hope that even those readers who take issue with my dating might recognize the applicability of the reading I advance.

Joshua in Judaism

The book of Joshua has been transformed through interpretation almost as much as it has been tragically implemented in real time. Jewish thinkers of the Second Temple Period lionized Joshua as a hero worthy of Hellenistic

28. Dozeman, *Joshua 1–12*.

29. For example, the model could work even in Dozeman's exilic or postexilic timeframe for Joshua: "The all-Israel focus indicates that the author of Joshua is not sectarian but is writing a myth of origin that is intended to include both the northern Israelites in Samaria and the southern Israelites in Judea during the Persian period." Dozeman, *Joshua 1–12*, 29.

acclaim.[30] Yet in the wake of Jewish military defeat at the hands of the Romans, rabbinic interpreters largely neglected Joshua and turned their interest to Moses as a man of the book.[31] In both their cycle of public scriptural recitation and their more exclusive academic dialogues, the Rabbis skipped over most of Joshua.[32] Early Christian interpreters read Joshua as a prefiguration of Jesus whose crossing of the Jordan River and conquering of the land predicts the redemption of baptism and the defeat of sin. However, this figuration never stopped Christian warriors or colonists from justifying their conquests as holy wars sanctified by verses from Joshua.[33]

The archetype of biblical warrior did not play much of a role in diasporic Jewish consciousness. Many people might see this as a good thing or even wish that its pages had been excised from the *Tanakh* (Hebrew Bible), but the book was always present and sometimes associated in Jewish and Christian traditions with apocalyptic aspirations. When some Jews began to desire collective sovereignty and territory, the book of Joshua became a newly relevant

30. For the nuances and differences among Second Temple and Hellenistic conceptions, see Zev Farber. Farber points out, for example, how Ben-Sira celebrates Joshua as the best of warriors, a sentiment echoed in 1 Maccabees. Philo, in a later and diasporic setting, sees Joshua as a "pupil and imitator of Moses, as well as a philosopher." *Images of Joshua in the Bible and Their Reception* (Berlin: Walter De Gruyter, 2016), 154.

31. Farber details the different rabbinic iterations of Joshua. In some part influenced by the early Christian favoring of Joshua as a prefiguration of Jesus, who surpasses the old era of Mosaic law, the Rabbis not only celebrate the unsurpassed Moses, but also attribute some of Joshua's miracles to Moses. The rabbinic Joshua is an ideal disciple of Moses, who never ceases to study Torah (an interpretation of Joshua 1:8) and transmits laws (b. Baba Qama 80b–81a); *Images of Joshua*, 464.

32. However, in rabbinic war taxonomy, Joshua's conquest of Canaan figures as a "commanded war," in which all must fight, in contrast to "discretionary war," from which individuals can easily defer. Mishnah Sotah 8; Reuven Firestone, *Holy War in Judaism: The Fall and Rise of a Controversial Idea* (Oxford: Oxford University Press, 2012), 74, 89. By limiting commanded war to Joshua's conquest alone, Firestone argues that the Rabbis "essentially eliminated the dangerous wild card of holy war because Commanded War was associated with a historical occasion that had long passed" (74); BT Sotah 44b and PT Sotah 8:1.

33. See L. Daniel Hawk, *Joshua in 3-D: A Commentary on Biblical Conquest and Manifest Destiny* (Eugene, OR: Cascade Books, 2010), xxv–xxvi. As Jonathan Boyarin points out, this trajectory is more complex than simple influence, "The crucial innovation in Christian legal thought that paved the way for the rationalization of Renaissance-era conquests occurred during the Crusades, in a mid-thirteenth-century commentary written by Pope Innocent IV. True, the fact that the Crusades, as a model for European colonization, focused on the land once promised and now holy reminds us that the culture of colonialism has biblical grounds as well." *Palestine and Jewish History*, 44.

text. Insofar as it describes the People of Israel emerging from a long exile to settle a dimly remembered homeland, the book of Joshua suddenly seemed to speak directly to modern Jewish nationalists. As Israeli historian Anita Shapira has argued, Zionist pioneers (חלוצים/*Halutzim*, the name for the infantry in Joshua 4:13) turned to the Bible as artifact, mythos, and mediator of their strange homeland.[34] Developed under British imperial rule, which related to Palestine and its people (present or aspiring) through the prism of the Bible, the Zionist movement found it expedient to weave biblical allusion through requests for territory and autonomy submitted to the Colonial and Foreign Offices.[35] At the same time, Zionist writing painted British Mandate Palestine as the twentieth-century manifestation of the biblical Promised Land.[36] Performing the role of Hebrews returning to their ancient homeland for Christian audiences left an imprint on the national culture and psyche. But the role was not merely self-serving or cynical; it was one that had always been on hand, at least in imaginative terms, for Jews who saw themselves and were accused of being the hereditary descendants of Abraham meant to return to the land of his sojourning. Within the nationalist framework, the *Tanakh* seemed to possess the power to teach Jews how to dwell in the land of the Bible and restore them to the farmers, soldiers, and sovereigns that they had been in the ancestral past.[37] Further influenced by the militarism of European nationalist thought, Zionist exegetes pulled the image of the Jewish warrior from the pages of Joshua and animated it during modern Israeli wars.[38] In this way, the fighting of actual wars became entwined with biblical interpretation.

34. Anita Shapira, "Ben-Gurion and the Bible: The Forging of an Historical Narrative," *Middle Eastern Studies* 33, no. 4 (1997): 647.

35. Rachel Havrelock, *River Jordan: The Mythology of a Dividing Line* (Chicago: University of Chicago Press, 2011), 218–241.

36. The urtext in this case is Abraham Mapu's 1853 novel, *Ahavat Tsiyon* [Love of Zion] (repr., New York: Asap, 1918), which expressed nineteenth-century enthusiasm for the Holy Land with a particular Jewish spin. See also Shai Ginsburg, *Rhetoric and Nation: The Formation of Hebrew National Culture, 1880–1990* (Syracuse: Syracuse University Press, 2014).

37. Referencing Israel Bartal, Boaz Neumann notes, "By 'ascending' to and settling in the Land of Israel, the *halutzim* [Zionist pioneers, named after the infantry in Joshua] sought to negate the exile, its way of life, and its existential presence. In this regard, the pioneer act was revolutionary. It brought about a fundamental transformation." *Land and Desire in Early Zionism* (Lebanon, NH: Brandeis University Press, 2011), 18.

38. On the making of masculinity and the soldier in modern Israel, see Daniel Boyarin, *Unheroic Conduct: The Rise of Heterosexuality and the Invention of the Jewish Man* (Berkeley: University of California Press, 1997).

Joshua in Israel

Of the Jewish national interpretations of the book of Joshua, none had more impact than the Joshua study group sponsored by Prime Minister David Ben-Gurion in 1958. Not only was the prime minister's Joshua study group well publicized, but it was also an endeavor of elite group interpretation emulating the model of the rabbinic academy while seeking to subvert the centrality of the religiously oriented Yeshiva.[39] Ben-Gurion invited politicians, justices, generals, archaeologists, and biblical scholars into his home twice a month for biblical study. Several of the participants positioned themselves as both public figures and experts on the Bible, so there was little distinction between political and academic interpretation. Although the members of the group insisted on the scholarly precision of their arguments—a central tenet of the project was that Zionism enabled a correct historical reading of the Bible—their commentaries reveal the degree to which present political frameworks inflect biblical interpretation. Through the study group, Ben-Gurion hoped to promote Israeli national unity and to foster a collective identity based on biblical images.[40] He chose Joshua, the book concerning the conquest and settlement of the Promised Land, to inaugurate the prime minister's study group.[41] Ben-Gurion, who developed the army as an institution to absorb and naturalize immigrant Jews, became the foremost modern interpreter of Joshua.

Ben-Gurion saw the biblical war story as constituting an ideal basis for a unifying narrative of national identity. Not only could modern Israelis relate to the processes of conquest and settlement, but through the prism of Joshua they could also understand them as reenactments of the biblical past. This

39. In her book about novelist S. Y. Agnon's position within a culture of Ben-Gurion inspired "Bible-Mania" (a term coined by Anita Shapira), Ilana Pardes notes Agnon's ironic view of Zionist exegetes: "While they aspire to break with the culture of the yeshiva and ignore the exegetical traditions of their predecessors, in their obsessive immersion in the Bible, in their insistence on devoting their lives to this ancient text and to its study *ad olam*, they turn out to be—if antithetically and heretically—part of the chain." *Agnon's Moonstruck Lovers: The Song of Songs in Israeli Culture* (Seattle: University of Washington Press, 2013), 123.

40. An initial condition of participation in the study group was a biannual public presentation on the Bible to the public by each of the members, but Ben-Gurion later dropped this stipulation. Haim M. Y. Gevaryahu, "Recollections from the Bible Study Circle at D. Ben-Gurion's Home," in *Ben-Gurion and the Bible: The People and Its Land*, ed. Mordechai Cogan (Beer-Sheva: Ben-Gurion University of the Negev Press, 1989), 71 (Hebrew).

41. The group followed the Joshua discussions by studying the books of Judges and Kings.

would enable the strengthening of Israeli resolve to undertake battles and development and the dissolution of diasporic and nonnational affiliations. Ben-Gurion also hoped that the analogy with Joshua would promote international support for Zionism as the revival movement of the People of Israel and recognition that the revival could only transpire on the soil of the ancient homeland.[42] For Ben-Gurion, Joshua stood as the veritable symbol of "actualized Zionism."[43]

Ben-Gurion succeeded in forging a national myth, and his study group's interpretation impacted Israeli culture. It certainly raised the profile of a long-disregarded book in Jewish tradition and animated its lexicon. Thereafter, it became hard to think of Joshua differently. Through interpretation, ancient tropes of war merged with modern national militarism. However, the narrative that Ben-Gurion and his study partners created reflects their struggle to make a nation out of a nascent society comprised of immigrant Jews from different countries and a range of socioeconomic backgrounds. As they sought to include and refashion these Jews as Israelis, Ben-Gurion and his associates looked to distance Israelis from their neighboring Arabs.

In this sense, Ben-Gurion's commentary mirrors the book of Joshua itself. Both represent compensatory strategies intended to assert unity and cohesion in a shifting and varied social setting. Joshua's conquest and Israel's founding narrative generate a war story attesting to national unity in order to obscure the presence of nonnationals and overcome the patchwork nature of a society comprised of different ethnic, religious, ideological, and linguistic groups.[44] The war narrative produces the collective by acknowledging its soldiers as representatives of a social and political unity and marking its enemies as those beyond the political and geographic limits that define the nation. Yet the nonnationals, however excluded from the political unit, do not disappear from the national space. Their persistence motivates ritualized retellings of their military defeat, as if the story of people's disappearance could actually render them invisible. The intensity of the story arises from the desire to dispel present

42. Adam Ackerman, "The Biblical Nationalist Thinking of David Ben-Gurion," *Kivunim* 2 (1979): 101 (Hebrew). See also Shalom Goldman, *Zeal for Zion: Christians, Jews & the Idea of the Promised Land* (Chapel Hill: The University of North Carolina Press, 2009), 293.

43. Shimon Peres, "Joshua Son of Nun—the Symbol of Actualized Zionism in the Eyes of David Ben-Gurion," *Yediot Ahronot, Saturday Supplement*, April 4, 1980.

44. This is, admittedly, a circular process, since the myth also marks the people it seeks to obscure as nonnationals.

enemies. Yet the narrative of unity works better during war than it does during peace, when disparate factions among the nationals prevail. Working double-duty to impose itself on a social reality that doesn't match, national myth in such cases becomes all the more fervent.

The argument and its instantiating examples unfold in four chapters. The first chapter, "The Conquest of Land and Language," appraises the conquest as described in the first half of the book of Joshua and shows how the war story forges the collective of Israel. The book of Joshua tries to balance a unifying national narrative that enlists disparate groups in a project of centralization and the recognition of the relative independence and legitimacy of the constitutive groups. At the same time that the conquest appears to be successful as a mobilizing story, it also points to underlying disunity. I propose that a competition between a movement of centralized nationalism and a decentralized social order best explains the two distinct sections of Joshua. As the nation takes form through the image of the army, groups opposed to centralization acquire the label of "foreign," and tribal institutions run by women become suspect. The chapter follows the conquest and analyzes the dynamics of its representation, ultimately assessing how the account of total war models the confederation of distinct local groups.

The second chapter, "'So Very Much Left to Conquer' and the Persistence of the Local," speculates on the nature of the ancient Israelite confederation through a close reading of the geographic traditions and boundary lists in the second half of Joshua. I argue that this record of "the land that remains" attests to the decentralized, ethnically and politically varied social landscape that the conquest narrative seeks to obscure. It shows that the tribes of Israel live alongside a host of others, Jerusalem is divided "until today" (Josh 15:63), no national army repels local opponents, and a tribal system of negotiations and marriages maintain a social balance. The social balance rests on the household as maintained by women. As well as marking the persistence of decentralized political institutions, the second half of Joshua attests to the incorporation of local traditions as a component of the very project of state-building. In analyzing the relationship of spatial language to social forms, I discover local systems that cut across the territorial integrity of the represented nation.

The third chapter, "The Joshua Study Group at the Home of David Ben-Gurion," invites the reader into Prime Minister David Ben-Gurion's home, where in 1958 some of the leading minds in Israel together pondered the book of Joshua. As it analyzes the interpretations and discussions of the group, the chapter highlights the degree to which the participants reflected on the 1948 war through passages in Joshua. In many ways, they made explicit a connection already evident in the name of Operation Bin-Nun, the 1948 battle at Latrun to open the road to a besieged Jerusalem, after the biblical Joshua Bin-Nun. Ben-Gurion, who declared that no one had better interpreted Joshua than the Israeli Defense Forces in 1948, saw the enactment of biblical archetypes as the most fitting form of biblical commentary.[45] He invited colleagues over in order to sketch the outlines of such archetypes. Similar to the book of Joshua, the official Israeli interpretation sought to unify the disparate Jewish immigrant communities through a war story. And, like the writers and editors of Joshua, the Israeli interpreters wanted their audience to put aside competing affiliations to align with a national culture. However, as in Joshua, the military myth of nation becomes an unwitting record of nationalism's failure. Despite defeat and dispossession, Palestinians remained present within the new borders and just beyond them. Israeli settlement had to confront this exactly as it established facts on the ground to deny it.

Conquest rhetoric echoed in Israeli politics, institutions, and statistics attempting to erase the presence of Palestinian people jointly inhabiting the land. Chapter 4, "The Tribes of Joshua Land," shows the post-1958 legacy of Joshua and its elaboration in Ben-Gurion's study group in Israel. The sociologist Baruch Kimmerling described Israeli society as characterized by a strong central government and unified national culture until 1967, at which time differing responses to holding occupied territories fractured the culture into distinct, and often oppositional, camps.[46] Following his thesis, the fourth chapter considers Moshe Dayan's appropriation of Joshua to describe the occupation of the West Bank as the fulfillment of the Bible and political Zionism alike and how educators, settlers, leftists, and neoconservatives responded to the formulation. After Dayan, Joshua became increasingly important to religious settlers citing the biblical grant of the land as their charter. Like the early Zionists, these fundamentalist settlers proclaim the Bible as their mandate, yet unlike their secular predecessors, they favor righteous zeal over attainment of practical goals. For them, Joshua offers precedent for militarized settlement and continued displacement of Palestinians. A Joshua doctrine governs the expansion of the settlement project, which often relies on the Israeli army to enforce its claims.

45. For the IDF as interpreters of Joshua, see Shapira, "Ben-Gurion and the Bible," 651.

46. Baruch Kimmerling, *The Invention and Decline of Israeliness: State, Society, and the Military* (Berkeley: University of California Press, 2005).

I conclude the book with an appeal to "End This War" and its shrinking cadre of oligarchic beneficiaries. I follow the impacts of both by visiting the southern coastline, where constant siege causes Gaza's wastewater to stream into the sea where it is then sucked up by desalination pipes to become Israeli drinking water. This drinking water flows through pipes designed by Ben-Gurion as he pored over the book of Joshua, yet it subverts his vision of nationalized water by falling under privatized ownership. Alongside a restrictive, violent Occupation that suppresses Palestinian sovereignty, Israelis experience eroding jurisdiction as they lose public assets and benefits to private equity. It thus seems the perfect moment to explore other sociopolitical configurations and to move past the era of conquest to that of adaptive cohabitation. I conclude by taking the decentralized politics of the second half of Joshua as seriously as Ben-Gurion's cohort took the first half and thinking about localized and confederated forms of governance as a template for a politics of place that offers a range of inhabitants jurisdiction over their resources and labor. Faced with accelerated global trends of extraction and privatization, as well as the mounting violence necessary to enforce the boundaries of the nation-state, the Middle East may be the ideal place for an emergent local, bioregional politics. If the bloodiest book of the Bible offers such an alternative, then perhaps a modern site of conquest can likewise manifest it.

1

The Conquest of Land and Language

> Joshua is, I venture, the least attractive text in the canon. It records tribal arrogance and cruelty with undoubted relish. It is brimful of malediction and triumphalism.
>
> GEORGE STEINER, "A PREFACE TO THE HEBREW BIBLE," 68–69

MOST MODERN READERS would agree with George Steiner's position on the book of Joshua, even associate the narrated massacre of the Canaanites with later acts of genocide, expulsion, and colonization. Why, then, am I asking you to consider the book of Joshua? To begin, because the theme of glorious conquest has played such an instrumental role in the territorial dominance of empires and the nation-states that succeeded them. Where once I considered writing a book about the many such usages of Joshua, I ultimately decided to focus on its reception in the modern State of Israel, which proved to be the most prominent of the twentieth century and to have lasting implications for twenty-first-century Judaism and Christianity.[1] My focus on Israel is not meant to single out the country or to excuse other egregious occasions of military conquest.

Beyond its political applications, we should also read the book of Joshua as a premier example of how a war story tries to forge unity when no such accord

1. For a survey of global uses of Joshua, see Mark G. Brett, "Settler Mandates: Reading Joshua Ethically," in *The Cambridge Companion to the Hebrew Bible and Ethics*, ed. Carly Crouch (Cambridge: Cambridge University Press, forthcoming). For a focus on early Jewish reception, see Zev Farber, *Images of Joshua in the Bible and Their Reception* (Berlin: Walter De Gruyter, 2016).

exists on the ground. As an ancient prototype, this most violent of biblical books exhibits the nationalist impulse to conceal social heterogeneity beneath the rousing story of an army marching in lockstep to definitive victory. After the battles are declared won, the text pivots to reveal political fissures and component parts. In the hope that these reasons for reading Joshua persuade, let us turn to the ancient tale of conquest and explore how it preserves what it wants to deny—the plurality of constituent groups and presence of neighbors resistant to the national formation.

What Is the Book of Joshua?

The compact book of Joshua is a composite text in many regards. Significantly, it is a book that scholars easily separate into two parts: an initial twelve chapters that narrate an action-packed, miraculous campaign by twelve tribes of Israel to reclaim their homeland and another twelve chapters that mostly enumerate a monotonous roster of the towns and borders claimed by specific tribes following victory on the battlefield. Put differently, the first half of Joshua narrates a scorched earth conquest while the second half provides descriptions of regions wherein the tribes of Israel blend with the very peoples they were just said to have exterminated. Concentrated attention on the boundary lists quickly undoes the image of an integrated army settling on emptied land. Why would a founding story about the indelible link between a people and a territory so quickly betray itself?

Joshua's conquest is first and foremost a story intended to produce national cohesion through the representation of a collective war effort. Military representations, we can observe, endeavor to impose collectivity on a complex social reality in the name of producing the nation. Because social life never quite exhibits nationalist traits, military rituals and acts of war serve as essential evidence that a unified collective exists.[2] The representation of a "whole nation" that does battle against apparent enemies polemicizes against local and regional governance systems, what Stephen Russell refers to as "structures of

2. In ancient Israel, this reliance on a war story may have its roots in actual contact of dispersed people on the battlefield. Daniel E. Fleming notes that military muster, more than religious festivals, "may have been one occasion for contacts across greater distances." *The Legacy of Israel in Judah's Bible: History, Politics, and the Reinscribing of Tradition* (Cambridge: Cambridge University Press, 2012), 314.

distributed power."[3] Tribal leaders, regional practices, and local land claims all pose problems for nationalist writers and therefore assume an ambivalent position in their texts. Yet the writers face a problem of their own. They must make a nation out of something, and geography requires that this something be the people already present in the desired territory. Some degree of imposition and projection of identity is possible, but motivating people to join a political entity requires persuasion along with reciprocity, at least at the onset. I propose that the book of Joshua reveals the negotiations among smaller social units necessary for a state in the making and that attention to its seams and overlaps offers insight into the components of the successful confederation of discrete groups.

The book of Joshua, albeit reluctantly, also records the agency of autonomous groups and localized forms of sovereignty. Certainly, the dominant narrative voice advocates for a centralized state represented by a unified military and a capital city. However, because the state in question emerges through the absorption of smaller constitutive groups, the narrative reflects negotiation with representatives of kingdoms, tribes, clans, households, and sacred centers. In the name of confederating, such groups must lend adherence to some level of statist ideology and, more importantly, pledge their militias and monies to the cause. To my eyes, the book of Joshua, as well as its larger context of the Deuteronomistic History, reflects these tradeoffs. Its authors advance ideas about the monarchy, collective accountability to the law, and the homeland as they adapt local traditions to their historical chronology. Their dream of authoritative centralization is checked by the demands for autonomy and recognition by diverse parties. Whereas the book of Joshua has been implemented and analyzed as a charter for both imperial control and settler-colonialism, our approach allows us to see other forms of political configuration unwittingly depicted in the text.

These processes become particularly legible in the book of Joshua in two ways. First, by the fact that the very conquest fought by "all of Israel" for "all of the land" contains battles that reflect local traditions, and, second, by the book's central paradox that allegedly national territory gains description through nonnational frames. The second half of the book points to smaller-scale politics involving households, towns, and tribes, supporting Carl Schmitt's sense that "the sovereign State is actually an expression of

3. Stephen C. Russell, *The King and the Land: A Geography of Royal Power in the Biblical World* (New York: Oxford University Press, 2016), 20.

heteronomous society."[4] The sovereign state as depicted in Joshua appears largely as the stitching that would bind together component groups. The alleged bond already starts to fray in the battle stories, composed as they are through the adaptation of tales pertaining to particular places. With an agenda of suppressing local jurisdiction working in tandem with a project of incorporating and placating provincial leaders, the book of Joshua anxiously pushes military unity before conceding to decentralized sites and networks of power. In sum, the bifurcated structure of Joshua provides an exemplary case of a nation figured as an army at the same time that it admits to a social scenario diffuse enough to require a bloody and protracted war story intended to rouse a sense of unifying sacrifice.

The composite text of Joshua further reflects the emergence of a composite polity. Several levels of social organization become evident in the text, suggesting the fluid and overlapping affiliations of a segmented society. As much as I depend on the language of nation and state to account for the motivations of Joshua's editors, the terms help us to identify political aspiration as much as reality in the ancient Near East. The first half of Joshua expresses the will for unity among distributed groups along with administrative centralization approximating the forms of nation and state.[5] At the same time, smaller scales of social organization, including kingdoms, tribes, clans, cities, and households, can be glimpsed in the text. My analysis dispenses with the social evolutionary sense that localized forms of governance gave way to monarchy and state, instead relying on Daniel Fleming's conclusion that "the collaborative political

4. This gloss on Schmitt's theory of sovereignty comes from Stathis Gourgouris, *Dream Nation: Enlightenment, Colonization and the Institution of Modern Greece* (Stanford: Stanford University Press, 1996), 21.

5. I recognize the anachronism of these terms as I use them to make the point about Joshua's will to centralization. One can also employ Bruce Routledge's term for Moab in the period, "the 'Un-state.'" He notes, "In the Iron II period (1000–550 B.C.E.), across the Levant, a variety of small-scale polities (Israel, Aram-Damascus, Moab) emerge that slip between the interstices of traditional social evolutionary categories. At once integrative and decentralized, these polities are neither strictly kin-based, nor marked (especially in their early phases) by significant administrative specialization or class stratification." "The Politics of Mesha: Segmented Identities and State Formation in Iron Age Moab," *Journal of Economic and Social History of the Orient* 43, no. 3 (2000): 225. I recognize a similar dynamic in Joshua, which Routledge identifies in the Mesha Inscription, "attempts to transform a pre-existing model of political identity based on social segmentation and local affinity" (227).

structure of Israel probably remained active under kings."[6] The authors of the Deuteronomistic History promoted the vision that early unity under the banner of Joshua's army gave way to tribal fragmentation until a stable dynasty arose in Jerusalem and centuries of biblical exegetes extended it as a vision of progress. More contemporary scholarship, in which this book plays a part, advocates for the simultaneity of different, sometimes competing, political configurations.

A clear political division into two distinct kingdoms parallels the bifurcated nature of the book of Joshua, although the two splits do not neatly map onto one another. The kingdoms are the northern kingdom of Israel and the southern kingdom of Judah. Daniel Fleming, a scholar of the ancient Near East who has authored the most sustained study of how Israelite and Judahite traditions mix and meld in the Hebrew Bible, rejects the popular designation of Northern and Southern Kingdoms because it suggests equivalence when, in fact, the two were significantly different. For one, the wealthier, cosmopolitan Kingdom of Israel had access to more copious sources of water, a fact that is perhaps reflected in its capital city of Samaria once decked in ivory.[7] Along with an understanding that political boundaries are porous, there is evidence that the Kingdom of Israel had an open, rather than restrictive, sense of identity as its royalty forged alliances with neighboring peoples.[8] The Kingdom of Israel developed and seems to have reached its apex earlier than the Kingdom of Judah.[9] Judah's outsized influence results from its weathering the storm of Assyrian invasion, which scattered the subjects of Israel as the famous ten lost tribes, as well as its restoration of a temple city in Jerusalem during the Persian

6. Fleming, *Legacy of Israel*, 153. Fleming elaborates upon "the interplay of political influence between kings and an Israelite tradition of noncentralized power" that lacked "a single moment of transition from one type to the other" (298).

7. Israel Finkelstein, "Patriarchs, Exodus, Conquest: Fact or Fiction?," in *The Quest for the Historical Israel: Debating Archaeology and the History of Early Israel*, ed. Brian B. Schmidt (Atlanta: Society of Biblical Literature Press, 2007), 49.

8. Fleming speaks of Israel in terms of "collaborative politics," which we can imprecisely cast as a tribal system: "The tradition of constituent peoples within Israel, defined tribally or otherwise, would have coexisted with the rule of kings." *Legacy of Israel*, 68. On boundaries in the Kingdom of Israel, see Rachel Havrelock, *River Jordan: The Mythology of a Dividing Line* (Chicago: University of Chicago Press, 2011), 64–84.

9. Fleming posits that the narrative arc of the books of Genesis through Judges came from the Kingdom of Israel in the ninth to eighth centuries BCE, a time of state consolidation throughout the ancient Near East. *Legacy of Israel*, 12.

Period and ultimately the Kingdom of Judea in Hellenistic times. It is possible that the more restricted view of ethno-political identity familiar from the Bible developed in Judah in response to Israel's wealth and capaciousness or that it is a product of exilic and postexilic editors who refashioned the stories to reflect the kind of clannishness necessary to maintain group identity in the absence of state sovereignty. In hindsight, it appears that Judah's political power depended upon the talents of its scribes. Their kingdom may have paled in comparison to the larger, more fertile Israel and met its end at the hands of the Babylonians, but the narrative form that they pioneered outlasted the poetic epics of their neighbors.

If the scribes of Judah were such good writers, then why did they bother absorbing the stories of other groups? This question, which is key to my argument, relates to the larger politics of self-representation. I submit that the process in which scribes in Judah forged their grand historical narrative mirrors political movements of alliance and confederation. In short, the scribes collated traditions because it was necessary to bring the bearers of the traditions into the fold. As Fleming shows, central traditions—including the Jacob and Joseph stories, memories of Moses and Exodus, and the bulk of the book of Judges—all derived from Israel.[10] Such traditions curve the narrative arc of the Hebrew Bible because emergent Judah's affiliation with the Kingdom of Israel was vital for economic and military reasons. We will attend to places where Israelite traditions come into view in a book that skews toward Judah while accounting for the other evident scales of social organization.

Considering Israel and Judah as emergent polities, rather than administrative states, brings their composite nature into view. Although weighted with the heavy baggage of a misused analytic category, the tribe indicates a key social unit whose power is both recorded and contested in biblical narrative. It appears that the tribe, comprised of a group that traced its origin to a remembered ancestor, organized local self-defense as it weighed and enacted mergers and alliances with other tribes and clans.[11] Rather than twelve tribes

10. Also relevant is Nadav Na'aman, "Out of Egypt or Out of Canaan? The Exodus Story between Memory and Historical Reality," in *Israel's Exodus in Transdisciplinary Perspective—Text, Archaeology, Culture, and Geoscience*, ed. T. E. Levy, T. Schneider, and W. H. C. Propp (Cham, Switzerland: Springer, 2015), 527–536.

11. Fleming adapts Anne Porter's distinction that where the state is "intrinsically a political category, the tribe is a social category that may be adapted to a variety of political settings and forms." *Legacy of Israel*, 183.

of Israel that grew from a family to a nation, it seems that as tribes migrated and expanded, some became incorporated into a federation called Israel and some rejected or abandoned the alliance, thereby acquiring the label of offending Canaanites or another, allegedly repugnant, group. Such aspersions, in other words, convey political opposition rather than ethnic enmity. Clans seem to have been a unit smaller than the tribe that could operate autonomously or under a tribal umbrella. Vitally, the household—בית אב/*beit av*—formed the backbone of larger social units as the site of economic production and occasional surplus. The household was comprised of a family that traced its origins to a living ancestor, and, as Cynthia Chapman's groundbreaking work shows, was itself made up of constitutive nested units.[12] Because the word "father"—אב/*av*—constitutes the name for the household—בית אב/*beit av*—the clear association between women and this essential site of production has often been missed. Chapman's and Carol Meyers's studies go a long way toward correcting the omission, and this book attends to how women's political engagement is both recorded and contested at this scale. Along with the kingdom, the tribe, the clan, and the household, the city with its rural "daughter settlements" forms an operative political category with Canaanite corollaries and thus an ambivalent status in the text. The book of Joshua brings these social units into view, allowing for a sense of their plausible interrelationship.

In pursuing the relationship of these social forms to literary texts, my interest veers from mainstream biblical studies primarily concerned with approximating when the various strata of the text were written. My aim is to show how textual composition reflects political practices and to produce a model with relevance to a range of possible periods, yet the question of dating the text cannot be bypassed. It is in vogue to see the book of Joshua—along with most of the Hebrew Bible—as the product of Persian period scribes inventing a precedent for their desired temple and a state. However much I recognize that

12. Cynthia Chapman aligns the categories as such: "The Israelite *bayit* was a nested entity such that an individual's house was understood to be part of a larger extended family household complex, which was, in turn, understood as an entity within a larger village and ultimately national house. We see this in the oft-cited hierarchy of terms whereby several houses of the father (*bêt 'āb*) or an especially large, extended-family *bêt 'āb* could become a *mispacha* or 'clan.' Several clans comprised a *shevet* or *matteh*; both terms are usually translated as 'tribe,' and several tribes made up an *'am*, a 'nation' or 'people.'" *The House of the Mother: The Social Roles of Maternal Kin in Biblical Hebrew Narrative and Poetry* (New Haven, CT: Yale University Press, 2016), 25.

scribes mobilized and reshaped older traditions in an expedient manner, I hold that there is a pre-exilic core to the book of Joshua that precedes the Assyrian defeat of the Kingdom of Israel in 720 BCE. Reflected in the book of Joshua, I recognize a process of political consolidation that likely transpired during the ninth to eighth centuries BCE.[13] Several scholars explain the absorption of northern traditions as part of a salvage project following the fall of Israel when refugees streamed into Judah and the Judahite kingdoms aspired to expand northward.[14] While such a scenario is not implausible, the very nature of composing historical narratives suggests that oppositional viewpoints do not tend to be included in the name of preservation or hope for the future. Writers—and those representing political parties all the more—tend to draw from rival traditions only when it is necessary to do so. I propose that the disparate traditions in Joshua were first collated when it became necessary to muster smaller militias in order to answer the growing threats of Assyrian invasion. The very tangible fear of defeat by a sophisticated imperial army hastened processes of political consolidation already underway in the ninth century BCE. Israel and Judah, which were themselves emerging polities formed through alliance and absorption, experimented with unity in the run-up to the Assyrian invasion, a fact reflected in the pre-exilic layer of biblical texts.

The political investments of the book of Joshua come into view in its structure, as well as in its place in what scholars name (and dispute as) the Deuteronomistic History, a sequence of biblical books expressing a pro-Judah position—although not blindly so—that seems to have been penned by writers based in Jerusalem who were either the ideological proponents of the

13. The thematic parallels between the Moabite Mesha Inscription and the book of Joshua advance a ninth-century dating. Bruce Routledge's analysis of the Mesha Inscription brings many of these parallels to the fore, including a triumphant battle report as a means of "legitimizing and reproducing kingship," the evocation of *ḥērem*, and the textual copresence of Moab as "a well-established collective identity" and many "hierarchically linked geopolitical units." "Politics of Mesha," 225, 231.

14. Israel Finkelstein sees the cultural reconciliation of north and south as reflected in Deuteronomistic texts—the "pan-Israelite idea" as the result of the fall of the Northern Kingdom to Assyria and "the migration of a large number of Israelites into Judah and the transformation of Judah from a sparsely settled, homogenous, clan-based marginal kingdom to a densely settled, demographically mixed vassal of the Assyrian empire." "Saul, Benjamin and the Emergence of Biblical Israel: An Alternative View," *Zeitschrift für die Alttestamentliche Wissenschaft* 123, no. 3 (2011): 366. I attribute the project of absorbing different regional groups into a federated unit to an earlier moment, but acknowledge what Finkelstein describes as a key juncture when the process accelerated and intensified.

monarchy or scribes on the king's payroll. Among the compelling aspects of the Deuteronomistic History is its tendency to voice antithetical positions in a persuasive manner.[15] While recognizing the literary skill of the scribes,[16] I perceive the voicing of oppositional positions as reflecting the political imperative of scaling up the polity of Judah.

Multiple lines of political wagering run through biblical texts: Deuteronomistic editors promote a program of state centralization, subsidiary groups try to safeguard their autonomy, and the flux of regional divisions and consolidations are captured in passing references. Representing, pacifying, combining, and chastising constituent groups shape the stories of the Hebrew Bible and help to account for their contradiction and overlap. We will focus on the rhetorical strategy of Deuteronomistic writers who pen the conquest story and adapt local traditions from cities, as well as tribal hinterlands, where decentralized groups sustained themselves through multigenerational households. The very nation for which the Deuteronomistic writers advocate requires the incorporation of various smaller social units. Therefore, the national narrative must accommodate local and regional forms of power as it enlists them in the project of a centralized state. Centrist, royalist Deuteronomistic scribes advocating for political, territorial, and ritual unity may have composed a war story to support consolidation, but the continued autonomy of consolidating groups becomes evident in the preservation of their distinct traditions.

Where the will of the constituents forced the nationalist, royalist party to acknowledge at least a bare minimum of local autonomy, it expresses no such restraint when it comes to groups that refuse to affiliate with the state. The vitriolic, murderous stance against the peoples of Canaan, as I understand it, begins as a rhetorical attack on groups resistant to nationalization and crystallizes in their demonization as a corrupting presence deserving extermination. Foremost among the points that I want to make here is that Canaanites, Jebusites, and the various peoples of the land were likely not ethnically or racially different from the tribes of Israel. It seems rather that the mark of their difference arises from the unwillingness of these groups to participate in a

15. This comes to the fore in the oppositional positions on the monarchy expressed in Deuteronomy 17:14 and 1 Samuel 8. See Moshe Halbertal and Stephen Holmes, *The Beginning of Politics: Power in the Biblical Book of Samuel* (Princeton, NJ: Princeton University Press, 2017).

16. Among their skills are pioneering aspects of narrative history and interior dialogue familiar from modernist fiction; see Robert Alter, *The Art of Biblical Narrative* (New York: Basic Books, 1980).

movement toward state centralization.[17] The so-called peoples of Canaan did not confederate with the tribes of Israel or Judah, but rather pursued alternate political forms such as the city-state. This means that although the conquest of Joshua reads like a genocidal attack on indigenous people by a colonizing group, its origins lie in a political movement seeking to reinforce the integrity of the state and dissuade its member groups from dropping out. Among the paradoxes that make the book of Joshua a compelling read is that the fundamental opposition between the nation and the Canaanites holds only for the duration of the conquest story.[18] After the din of war quiets, smaller internal rifts become amplified. The tense relationship among various scales of governance ultimately explains and elucidates the contradictions in the text of Joshua.

Who Is Joshua?

The transition from the visionary, often-enraged Moses to the obedient warrior is jarring, but it successfully links northern traditions about Moses to the political aspirations of southerners.[19] The blending of traditions is apparent in the character of Joshua bin Nun who, according to his burial tradition, hails from the northern tribe of Ephraim. However, he perfectly enacts Judahite ideals of loyalty to covenant and centralization of the state, embodying the command to "be strong and very bold in faithfully observing all of the Torah . . . do not deviate from it to the right or left" (Josh 1:7).[20] Like the theoretical king

17. See also Lori Rowlett, "Inclusion, Exclusion, and Marginality in the Book of Joshua," in *The Historical Books: A Sheffield Reader*, ed. J. Cheryl Exum (Sheffield: Sheffield Academic Press, 1997), 71.

18. Robert Polzin, *Moses and the Deuteronomist: A Literary Study of the Deuteronomistic History, Part One: Deuteronomy, Joshua, Judges* (New York: The Seabury Press), 131–134; Gordon Mitchell, *Together in the Land* (Sheffield: Sheffield Academic Press, 1993), 96; L. Daniel Hawk, *Every Promise Fulfilled: Contesting Plots in Joshua* (Eugene, OR: Wipf and Stock Publishers, 2009), 98–100. Hawk presents the dualism as "two opposing voices in Joshua": "a dominant voice (that) trumpets claims of ethnic superiority, military triumphalism, national idealism, divine destiny" and "a subtle voice" that "speaks of a larger vision of Israelite identity, one that dismantles Israel's 'us/them' ethnic consciousness." *Joshua in 3-D: A Commentary on Biblical Conquest and Manifest Destiny* (Eugene, OR: Cascade Books, 2010), xxii–xxiii.

19. Ron Hendel, "Remembering the Exodus in the Wake of Catastrophe," in *The Fall of Jerusalem and the Rise of the Torah*, ed. Peter Dubovský, Dominik Markl, and Jean-Pierre Sonnet (Tübingen: Mohr Siebeck, 2016), 330.

20. Significantly later traditions that link Joshua with Jesus and Rabbi Joshua in the Galilee support a northern provenance; see Elchanan Reiner, "The Transformation of a Biblical Story

of Deuteronomy 17:14–20, Joshua possesses a Torah scroll to guide him (Josh 1:8),[21] organizes warriors into battalions (Josh 4:12–13), and negotiates treaties (Josh 9:15). Some scholars have proposed that Joshua models the ideal Deuteronomistic king emplaced in an early golden age,[22] where others imagine him the hero of a "North Israelite conquest story" later adapted to southern geography.[23] The royal aspects of Joshua's character cannot be denied, but I would nuance the proposal to suggest that he represents the process of centralization more than the figure of the monarch. The Deuteronomistic writers fashion the warrior Joshua as a symbol of the unification of tribes and territory; his leadership transcends tribal divisions, and his battles produce a landscape that gestures toward a continuous whole. Joshua further strikes a balance between charismatic and dynastic leadership, the two forms that the Deuteronomists weigh through their characters. Where the book of Judges exposes the instability of charismatic leadership and the books of Samuel and Kings run up against the problem of bad monarchs elevated by dynastic succession, Joshua represents an ideal that has no title.

What office does Joshua hold? Biblical texts bestow only the titles of "apprentice" to Moses (Exod 24:13, 33:11) and "servant of God" (Josh 24:29). Never named a judge, Joshua becomes animated by a divine force that enables military victory similar to the charismatic leaders in the book of Judges (Numbers 27:18).[24] Yet, insofar as God actually intervenes in his battles, Joshua

---

to a Local Myth: A Chapter in the Religious Life of the Galilean Jew," in *Sharing the Sacred: Religious Contacts and Conflicts in the Holy Land, First Fifteen Centuries CE*, ed. Arieh Kofsky and Guy G. Stroumsa (Jerusalem: Yad Itzhak Ben-Zvi, 1998), 223–271.

21. Physical copies of the Torah intended as a guide appear only in Deuteronomy 17:18 and Joshua 8:32, where Joshua imprints a copy of Moses's Torah on the rocks of Mount Ebal; see Richard D. Nelson, "Josiah in the Book of Joshua," *Journal of Biblical Literature* 100, no. 4 (1981): 533; and Roy Porter, "The Succession of Joshua," in *Proclamation and Presence: Old Testament Essays in Honour of Gwynne Henton Davis*, ed. John I. Durham and J. R. Porter (Macon, GA: Mercer University Press, 1983), 116.

22. Mark Smith, *The Memoirs of God* (Minneapolis: Augsburg Fortress, 2004), 61; William M. Schniedewind, *How the Bible Became a Book* (Cambridge: Cambridge University Press, 2004), 80; Marvin Sweeney, *King Josiah of Judah: The Lost Messiah of Israel* (New York: Oxford University Press, 2001), 135.

23. Nadav Na'aman, "Rediscovering a Lost North Israelite Conquest Story," in *Rethinking Israel: Studies in the History and Archaeology of Ancient Israel in Honor of Israel Finkelstein*, ed. Oded Lipschits, Yuval Gadot, and Matthew J. Adams (Winona Lake, IN: Eisenbrauns, 2017), 296.

24. Albrecht Alt, "Josua," in *Werden und Wesen des Alten Testaments*, ed. Paul Volz, Friedrich Stummer, and Johannes Hempel, BZAW 66 (Berlin: Töpelmann, 1936), 13–19. The resonance

surpasses the Judges. Joshua succeeds the greatest of prophets and is elevated to his status (Josh 4:14), but has no revelation and is never called a seer. By rallying the tribes and leading the conquest, Joshua behaves most like a general whose battles found a state. Even the most gruesome battles do not upset his equilibrium, making Joshua nothing like Moses, Saul, or David with flaws, gnawing doubt, and challenges to God. Furthermore, the image of Israel as a disciplined army does not resonate beyond the immediate military contexts. Why is the book so flat?

Who Are the People of Israel?

In presenting a cohesive (and largely silent) national collective locked in mortal combat with utterly depraved opponents, the book of Joshua lacks the depth and ambivalence characteristic of biblical narrative, offering instead certainty and rigidity. Joshua's voiceless army has the difficult task of representing an idealized collective marching in lockstep and ameliorating the image of the cantankerous, contrary People of Israel.[25] Joshua and his people are drawn in the name of pure function—to motivate national unity and impress upon local leaders the need to fold their militias into a centralized army and their assets into a treasury. What the book lacks in character, it tries to compensate with plot.

Local war stories are stitched together with nationalist ideology as the twelve tribes of Israel cross the Jordan River, face groups of allied kings, and seize "all of the land" (Josh 10:40, 11:23). The image of "all of the warring nation" stands to represent the collective of Israel (Josh 10:7), as vanquished kings and ruined cities attest to their difference from other peoples of the land. That a polity of "all the people" emerges from a tale of conquest proves theorist Etienne Balibar's suggestion that heterogeneous populations unify "under the imaginary signifier 'the people' not by suppressing all differences, but by relativizing them and subordinating them to itself [the nation] in such a way that it is the symbolic difference between 'ourselves' and 'foreigners' which wins

between Joshua's name and the "victory" promised Israel when God fights on their behalf (Deut 20:4) suggests that Joshua may be more of a type than a character. Of further note is that the spirit Joshua receives comes from Moses, not technically from God (Num 27:12–23; Deut 34:9); see Havrelock, *River Jordan*, 148.

25. See Ilana Pardes, *The Biography of Ancient Israel: National Narratives in the Bible* (Berkeley: University of California Press, 2000).

out and which is lived as irreducible."[26] Applying this to Joshua illustrates the symbolic burden of the army in signifying "the people" and expressing distance from foreigners as its organization into twelve tribes relativizes and subordinates smaller social units in the service of the nation. The theme of eradicating Canaanites from the land creates the irreducible difference of "ourselves" and "foreigners."

The horror of Joshua's plot is somewhat mitigated by cracks and breaches in this image of Israel and undercut in the second half of the book. Consistent with Balibar's point, this section expresses considerably less hostility toward the peoples of Canaan—read nonaffiliates of the nation. Beneath the national rendering, we glimpse a "segmentary state" in which a "centralised government exists, but occurs in conjunction with numerous peripheral administrative units over which it exercises limited control."[27] In social terms, the People of Israel appear to have been a fluid amalgamation of tribes, clans, households, and geographically based confederations; it is from such groups that biblical stories and motifs derive. By crafting a narrative in which many of these traditions figure as part of the chronological development of a nation, the scribes create the collective character of Israel.

Holy War

The writers of Joshua so wish to differentiate their Israel from Canaan that they figure Canaanites as indigenous and the tribes of Israel as immigrants. The myth of conquest, we might say, counters a myth of autochthony. Because the distinction is so vital to the book, questions of purity and distinction repeatedly arise. It opens with a collective crossing of the Jordan River meant to signify the washing away of exile and the transition to national independence. Migrations and water crossings no doubt played a role in localized tribal histories, but the mass crossing of the Jordan by a unitary nation is a beautifully epic invention. There are numerous cosmological, ritual, and political reasons for the invention, which I have treated elsewhere, so let us now focus on centralizing effects of the story.[28]

On the banks of the Jordan, the Ark of the Covenant exerts a power strong enough to halt the flow of the river and open a dry path into Canaan. This

26. Etienne Balibar, "The Nation Form: History and Ideology," *Review: Fernand Braudel Center* 13, no. 3 (1999): 347.

27. Routledge, "Politics of Mesha," 239–240.

28. Havrelock, *River Jordan*, 85–105.

attests to "the living God" who directs Israel and His intent to "dispossess the Canaanites, Hittites, Hivites, Perizzites, Girgashites, Amorites, and Jebusites" (Josh 3:10). The ritual scene enacts the difference between the tribes and these peoples as well as unity among the twelve tribes each represented by a ceremonial stone placed on the riverbed and shore (Josh 4:1–9, 19–24). The recalcitrant eastern tribes even stand at the head of the troops armed as infantry (Josh 4:12–13), and the priests obey Joshua's order (Josh 4:15–17). The story enlists all allies in the homecoming, which provides a common point of origin intended to override local tales of arrival.[29] In case their traversal of the Jordan as a disciplined army insufficiently expresses the masculine character of the nation, the collective circumcision performed just west of the Jordan at Gilgal confirms it (Josh 5:2).

Before he lifts his own sword in combat, Joshua encounters a heavenly soldier on the outskirts of Jericho. The angel draws a sword, suggesting an imminent struggle like those faced by Jacob and Moses at a threshold. When his opponent fails to attack him, Joshua poses the definitional question: "are you on our side or that of our enemies?" (Josh 5:13). Joshua perceives all relationships in terms of a war binary—two sides, two political options, and his encounter with the angel confirms the binary in celestial terms. "No," the angel begins, correcting Joshua's perception. "I am the captain of God's army and now I have come" (Josh 5:14), which implies that God's general has come to fight alongside his terrestrial counterpart as a sign of authorized holy war. In a gesture of submission, Joshua falls to the ground to receive his marching order, which turns out to be simply recognition of the sacred: "Remove your shoes from your feet because the ground on which you stand is holy" (Josh 5:15). The order stipulates simply how a human is to confront the divine and echoes the instructions to Moses as he faced the burning bush on Mount Sinai. This time, however, God is manifest not in the fire, but in the sword.

29. There is even evidence that the account in Joshua is comprised of different versions of the Jordan crossing story; see Havrelock, "The Book of Joshua and the Ideology of Homeland," in *River Jordan*, 85–105. American readers might relate to this national story of arrival in terms of Thanksgiving. Thanksgiving resembles the feast of local produce enjoyed by Joshua and his men (Josh 5:11–12) with similar implications for indigenous peoples, but most Americans celebrate a national immigration at Thanksgiving whether or not they are descended from the Puritans. Thanksgiving celebrations do not impinge on the acknowledgment and memorialization of familial and ethnic immigration stories. In parallel, we can imagine the tribes remembering the crossing of the Jordan, as well as their own accounts of arrival.

Scholars like to be careful about terminology, and the term "holy war" demands particular caution. Classifying wars matters not only because of taxonomy, but also because particular motivations for war and their justification can then be identified across history. While acknowledging the nuanced avoidance of the term "holy war" in relation to Joshua's conquest—no one in the book, for example, ever refers to it as such—I classify the conquest, with some anachronism, as a holy war nonetheless.[30] The conquest qualifies as a holy war for the simple reason that God commands Israel to attack, having punished the previous generation for refusing to do so, and supports Israel by fighting on its behalf.[31] The very theory of war in the Hebrew Bible maintains that Israel only wins its battles when reconciled with God and in compliance with covenant, but the conquest distills the theory into a stark choice: Israel can either face punitive death in the wilderness or stand with God in combating the peoples of Canaan.

The holy nature of the war intensifies the demand on the soldiers. Along with fidelity to the basic tenets of the law, the army must maintain radical separation from all other social units. Here we begin to see the social effects of holy war in creating a hermetic group bound to a code that elevates killing to the level of mission. A shared sense of heightened righteousness separates such warriors from apparent enemies, as well as nonenlisted peers. In the case of the conquest, heightened righteousness results from a unique degree of purity.[32] Although not spelled out in terms of biblical purity codes, the operative precept maintains that as long as God fights with Israel, Israel must fight for God alone. This gets to the heart of the horror of Joshua, insofar as fighting for God requires complete extermination of populations and dedication of all spoils.[33]

Why must warriors fighting for God annihilate women and children along with their opponents? In keeping with the heightened stakes of holy war, such a command articulates a radical dualism not actually evident in daily life. Social groups, particularly when in proximity, tend to share many customs and practices. Producing difference thus requires either pressure on seemingly

30. Reuven Firestone notes that in the Hebrew Bible "no consistently recurring term . . . distinguish[es] between divinely authorized fighting—what we identify here as holy war—and fighting that is independent of divine concern." *Holy War in Judaism: The Fall and Rise of a Controversial Idea* (Oxford: Oxford University Press, 2012), 18.

31. The image of God fighting for Israel recurs in the book of Nehemiah 4:14.

32. Lauren Monroe, "Israelite, Moabite and Sabaean War-ḥērem Traditions and the Forging of National Identity: Reconsidering the Sabaean Text RES 3945 in Light of Biblical and Moabite Evidence," *Vetus Testamentum* 57, no. 3 (2007): 318–341.

33. Monroe, "Israelite, Moabite and Sabaean War-ḥērem," 319.

visible distinctions like gender or ethnicity or ascribing distinction through definitions of normativity and deviance. Both trends are operative in Joshua. For example, women and Canaanites alike are linked with heterodox practices abhorrent to God.[34]

Behind the conquest stands the idea that the practices of the Canaanites contaminate the very soil of Canaan to the point that God cannot reside therein, so if Israel wants to establish a sanctified country, then the offending residents must be annihilated. In place of local covenants of peace (Deut 7:2), Israel is to abide by *the* covenant with God (Deut 7:9).[35] Such absolute opposition, however, creates a thematic problem: when Canaanites remain in the land, does it mean that there is no longer a living God amidst Israel? Since the proposition of God's failure is too radical, the nations that remain can only attest to Israel's shortcomings. In this way, the inability to completely nationalize territory figures as sin. We can see such declarations of holy war as indicators of social landscapes that do not reflect the purported homogeneity or desired purity. In other words, when holy warriors violently rage or grimly execute their task, I recognize the varied political field that does not support them. Often tragically, their recognition of the same inspires mass violence.

The specific tactic of Joshua's holy war is the *ḥērem*, the ban on goods confiscated from the enemy that also implies total destruction of life (Josh 6:17–19).[36]

34. Saul Olyan, *Asherah and the Cult of Yahweh in Israel* (Atlanta: Society of Biblical Literature, 1988).

35. Freidrich Schwally's 1901 theory of Israel connected the ideas of federation and holy war; *Das heiligen Krieg im alten Israel*, vol. 1 of *Semitische Kriegsaltertümer* (Leipzig: Deiterich, 1901). Gerhard von Rad elaborates: "Schwally used the German term *Bund*, 'covenant,' to refer properly to Israel as a federation, and only in a derivative sense to Israel's theological conception of its relation to Yahweh. He claimed that 'covenant' referred first to a federation between Israel and Midian and was then expanded to refer to Israel itself—a covenant or federation of the people. This understanding of covenant as a federation, Schwally said, provided the basis for a theology of covenant in which God was worshipped as a warrior. And this official, corporate worship—the Israelite sacrificial cult—itself constituted the context in which war was conducted. That can only mean that war, as Israel conducted it, was holy war: it was an activity undertaken by Israel as the army of Yahweh in defense of the federation (covenant), over which Yahweh was sovereign." *Holy War in Ancient Israel*, trans. John H. Yoder (Grand Rapids, MI: Wm. B. Eerdmans Publishing, 1996), 27–28.

36. "The term for *ḥērem* (cognate with Arabic *ḥaram* '(religiously) forbidden; sanctuary' source of the modern 'harem') . . . is often translated with the somewhat wooden and neutral-sounding term 'ban,' but it goes a good deal further than 'bans' on, say, unpasteurized cheese." Seth L. Sanders, "On the Reality of Ritual Genocide (ḥērem) in Biblical Conquest Accounts and Israel's Origins in Denied Resemblance," *sethlsanders* (blog), July 9, 2019,

Along with murder and the confiscation of goods, the ban on enrichment through booty promotes an image of classless equality among the soldiers, whose rigorous discipline maintains purity and ensures success.[37] All spoils of war must be sanctified through dedication to God (Josh 6:18–19). The premise extends to all land captured—first the soldiers must control it, then transfer it to God, and finally receive portions according to tribal divisions. In this way, the book of Joshua insists upon total national unity and then admits to tribal divisions by accounting for the unity as an effect of battle and the division as an outcome of settled life. The sacred land won in a concerted war effort later appears as a set of component parts.

Ironically, *ḥērem*, the ban on foreign objects that defines Joshua's army, appears to be a tactic derived from the practices of neighboring groups.[38] Scholars differently understand the adaptation and application. Philip Stern argues that the proscription on war spoils aims to order social chaos by establishing identitarian boundaries around native and foreign.[39] Susan Niditch advances the idea that the ban's value rests "in preserving the idea of the nation,"[40] but notes how its sacrificial dimension clarifies internal politics, as well as external distinctions. Niditch interprets the ban's exacting degree of conformity as enabling the exclusion of resistant groups from the collective.[41] Lauren Monroe's

---

https://sethlsanders.wordpress.com/2019/07/09/fake-massacres-and-the-authenticity-of-the-israelite-conquest-of-canaan/.

37. Rabbinic interpreters saw the battles of the conquest as equalizing insofar as they "were obligatory for every individual Israelite." Firestone, *Holy War in Judaism*, 89. See BT Sotah 44b and PY Sotah 8:1. Maimonides, as Firestone explains, also identified a desire for equalized cohesion in Joshua's actions: "This is why Joshua and his court divided all of the Land of Israel into tribal divisions even though it was not yet conquered—in order that there would be no individual conquest through the acts of each tribe to conquer its own territory (Hilkhot Terumot 1:2)" (118–119).

38. See Monroe, "Israelite, Moabite and Sabaean War-ḥērem." For Assyrian parallels, see Moshe Weinfeld, *Deuteronomy and the Deuteronomistic School* (Oxford: Clarendon, 1982); John Van Seeters, "Joshua's Campaign of Canaan and Near Eastern Historiography," *Scandinavian Journal of the Old Testament* 4, no. 2 (1990): 1–12; and K. L. Younger, *Ancient Conquest Accounts: A Study in Ancient Near Eastern and Biblical History Writing* (Sheffield: JSOT Press, 1990), 226–228.

39. Philip D. Stern, *The Biblical Herem: A Window on Israel's Religious Experience* (Providence: Brown Judaic Studies, 1991), 179.

40. Susan Niditch, *War in the Hebrew Bible: A Study in the Ethics of Violence* (New York: Oxford University Press, 1993), 70.

41. In this sense, the ban assists emerging states in gaining "control over personal 'ethnic hostilities, the military independence of kin-based groups, and the freedom of individual groups to undertake revenge mission.'" Niditch, *War in the Hebrew Bible*, 15.

seminal study shows that *ḥērem* was a common Near Eastern device of statecraft deployed as "tribal confederacies" morphed "as viable political state[s]."[42] Considering Joshua in light of Monroe's study reveals both its parallel political aim and the particular ways in which its writers adapt the proscription of their neighbors and their movable property to the narrative of arrival. Concerned with *ḥērem* in the Mesha Inscription, Bruce Routledge notes its emergence in a text that celebrates the military occupation of territory as a means of advancing a statist agenda. Like the book of Joshua, the Mesha Inscription declares a total ban as it attests to constitutive units including northern and southern regions, zones marked by their major cities, and "daughter settlements" themselves comprised of smaller social groups. Ultimately, Routledge avers, the ban allows for an opposition to groups like the "Men of Gad" who affiliate with Israel and thus enables the discursive emergence of Moab "as a workable, and independent national identity."[43]

We observe how the book of Joshua similarly mobilizes the *ḥērem* to suppress various scales of local affiliation in the name of a cohesive polity and to create "equivalency [with other emergent states] through differentiation."[44] This orients our reading of Joshua such that we no longer see a national army annihilating a series of highland towns and no longer recognize a unified state emerging through the claim of its military prowess. Instead, repetition of the command to ban absorption of "enemy" property attests to recurrent attempts to block regional networks in the name of promoting a centralized state and monarchy. Its emphatic tone bespeaks a kind of desperate will to existence.

Creation

Creation imagery resonates in descriptions of the conquest that dramatize displacement and extermination as a divine reordering of the world.[45] This illustrates how nationalist myth appeals to world-making moments of beginning as if, more than a coincidence of historical contingencies, the rise of a

42. Monroe, "Israelite, Moabite and Sabaean War-ḥērem," 336, 318. A parallel example from Sabaean inscriptions points toward social structures similar to those suggested by Joshua: "ancient South Arabia was comprised of independent territorial communities known as *sha'bs*, and that at some point in the early first millennium BCE, the political leaders (*mlk*) of the tribal community of Sabā created a huge 'commonwealth' of *sha'bs* that occupied most of the South Arabian territory."

43. Routledge, "Politics of Mesha," 238.

44. Routledge, "Politics of Mesha," 237.

45. See Stern, *Biblical Herem*, 141.

nation represents a fulfillment of destiny that purifies and renews the world. These types of stories further show the realignment of ideas about creation to support the political form of the nation. This merger of creation and political aspiration corresponds with Mircea Eliade's theory of how myth operates in public life.[46] Eliade saw myth as preserving certain primal forms tied to the emergence of polities or religious collectives. This meant that power and purity were located in the original state of things preserved in myth. Following their emergence, "the terror of history" took over by degrading such pure forms and compromising their initial integrity. Something similar occurs in the daily lives of humans worn down by mundane tasks, social humiliations, and personal failures. Myth's link to ritual—particularly rituals of the new year—signaled to Eliade the reparative possibility of reconnecting with original forms. Celebrations of the new year allow participants to reconnect with the unsullied primordial forms described in myth and, as a result, to experience purgation of exhaustion and indignity that results in a sense of restoration and renewal. In this way, Eliade understood that beyond recording a primal beginning, stories of creation offered a way out of history and a return to ideal forms.

Scholars have explored the links between the theory of eternal return and fascist ideology, as well as Eliade's own fascistic leanings. More than nostalgia, the very idea of return in political discourse often coincides with dangerous notions of "pure" blood and authoritarian purges. In this way, motifs of creation can be mobilized to advance absolute social divisions in the pursuit of alleged political purity. I suggest a similar dynamic at work in the cosmic descriptions of Joshua's battles and their attendant ethnic cleansing in which the conquerors become identified with a transcendent force ushering the proper order back to a holy land corrupted by chaotic mixtures and historical practices. Let us note, however, how myth constructs—rather than restores—the categories and social units in question, defining itself as more authoritative than historical record.

Israel's first battle commences at Jericho. The image of its impenetrable walls recalls the lost Eden similarly enclosed and guarded by cherubs armed with flaming swords (Genesis 3:24; Josh 6:13). In this case, Joshua has the help of an angel in breaching the walls and gaining entrance to a terrestrial paradise that flows with milk and honey. His strategy begins with a ritual encirclement that references creation as it initiates total destruction. As in the seven days of

46. Mircea Eliade, *The Myth of Eternal Return: Or, Cosmos and History* (Princeton, NJ: Princeton University Press, 1971).

creation, God launches the battle with promissory speech enacted by Israel (Josh 6:2–3).[47] For six days, Israel circumambulates Jericho a single time with seven priests carrying seven ram's horns marching before the Ark of the Covenant. On the seventh day, the People encircle Jericho seven times as the priests blow vigorously on their shofars (Josh 6:4, 15). The shofars initiate the cry of the People that shakes the foundations and brings down the walls (Josh 6:5).

Along with the reanimation of creation motifs, the mythic opposition between silence and noise characterizes the defeat of Jericho.[48] Joshua instructs the priests and People alike to move in total silence as they leave camp and encircle Jericho (Josh 6:10). The control exerted over sound in myth—what Lévi-Strauss called continence—plays an important role in securing life or losing immortality.[49] At Jericho, silence displays the discipline of the army and the degree to which the people have seemingly overcome the subversive tendencies of the previous generation. With contesting voices muffled, the modulation of sound attests to unified purpose and reconstitution as a nation. Silence holds until the specified moment on the seventh day when "all the nation" hears the shofar blasts and raises its collective war cry (Josh 6:5). The breaking of silence functions as a sign as Joshua tells the People, "God has given you the city" (Josh 6:16).

The narrator maintains the classifications of shofar-blowing priests and shouting soldiers, but the People coalesce in noisy opposition as the wall of Jericho tumbles down (Josh 6:5, 20). Their defenses shattered, the population of Jericho—with the exception of one woman and her household—falls to the sword. Israel's ritual acts that recall creation result in the fiery annihilation of Jericho (Josh 6:24) and Joshua's curse on whoever endeavors to recreate it (Josh 6:26). Like the story of creation, the battle ends with a curse, but the

47. The symbolic numbers of six and seven operate here: this is the "sixth occurrence of the identical formula (1:1; 3:7; 4:1,15; and 5:9). A similar formula occurs in 5:2 . . . making a total of seven times that Yahweh addresses his field commander, in preparation for the capture and destruction of Jericho." Robert G. Boling and G. Ernest Wright, *Joshua. Anchor Bible* (New York: Doubleday, 1982), 6:205.

48. These motifs, along with the emphasis on *kohanim* and the Ark, attest to elements familiar from the Priestly source. A structure of opposition is perfectly priestly as well, although silence vs. noise is not common in priestly narratives. For the importance of silence to the priests, see Israel Knohl, *The Sanctuary of Silence: The Priestly Torah and the Holiness School* (Winona Lake, IN: Eisenbrauns, 2007).

49. Claude Lévi-Strauss, *The Raw and the Cooked,* trans. John Weightman and Doreen Weightman, vol. 1, *Mythologiques* (Chicago: University of Chicago Press, 1983), 134.

concluding verse emphasizes sound as "hearings," or tales, of Joshua, spread across the land.

Ruin

The din of war turns out to have concealed individual action. When the people's voice sounded in accordance with God's dictates and the nation acquired form through collective battle, one person found cover for his defiance. Rather than a pat example of corporate responsibility, the story of Achan's transgression exposes the fissures in the national construction and briefly aligns the book of Joshua with the biblical narratives famous for being "fraught with background" and marked by indeterminacy.[50] The scenario problematized here, I argue, is the persistence of local affiliations during a push toward state centralization.

The narrator opens the episode by exposing the violation of the ban on plunder by Achan of the tribe of Judah, consistently identified in terms of "house, clan, tribe," "the three concentric circles within which the individual identified himself."[51] Construing oneself in this manner, the text suggests, leads to transgression and imperils the national unit. According to Lori Rowlett, identifying and rooting out antinationalists from the imagined community serves as the central purpose of the holy war ban on foreign persons and objects, with the story of Achan sounding a warning to all who would persist in pursuing alternate political goals during a period of national formation.[52] The disruption becomes apparent to Joshua through a tactical error and stinging defeat at the battle of Ai (Ruin) following Jericho.

Prior to that battle, Joshua conducts due reconnaissance by sending spies to Ai. Underwhelmed by the opposition, they recommend a limited offensive

50. Erich Auerbach famously identified the layers of background in biblical characterization as requiring continuous interpretive work. "Odysseus' Scar," in *Mimesis: The Representation of Reality in Western Literature*, trans. Willard R. Trask (Princeton, NJ: Princeton University Press, 1953), 12; Robert Alter noted the intention of biblical writers "to produce a certain indeterminacy of meaning, especially with regard to motive, moral character and psychology." *Art of Biblical Narrative*, 12.

51. Boling and Wright, *Joshua*, 6:225. Reading Joshua 7 as a literary bridge constructed to connect the Jericho and Ai stories, Fleming suggests that "the hierarchical system of tribe, clan, and family is therefore idealized and cannot be taken as evidence for such a tiered scheme in early Israel." Fleming, *Legacy of Israel*, 137. Whether these units existed at the same time or in different periods, the story is clearly invested in scrutinizing and demonizing the institutions.

52. Rowlett, "Inclusion, Exclusion," 71.

of two or three thousand men. Their recommendation of a limited force already signals erosion of the vaunted collective: "Don't send all the nation . . . why exhaust the whole nation there where they are so few?" (Josh 7:3). In other words, the spies undermine the cooperative basis of their recent victory. Significantly, the text records three thousand warriors departing "from the nation" to do battle in Ai, as if fragmentation is both cause and result. The reduced army is quickly trounced, fleeing in humiliation from Ai's city gates.

A confused Joshua, no longer certain of his purpose, speaks to God in the questioning tones of Moses.

> Why did you bring this nation across the Jordan only to deliver us into the hands of the Amorites in order to destroy us? Would it not have been better for us to remain east of the Jordan? Oh, Lord, what can I say now that Israel has turned in defeat from its enemies? The Canaanites and all inhabitants of the land will hear, surround us, and erase our name from the land. What then will happen to Your great name? (Josh 7:7–9)

Joshua probes the very nature of the national project, expressing the thought that perhaps Israel was better off not crossing the Jordan. Such a thought is usually expressed by the politically suspect two and a half tribes from east of the Jordan, whose loyalty Joshua himself interrogates.[53] But since there is likely no going back across the Jordan, Joshua employs the rhetoric of Moses, who often asked God to consider the effects on His reputation should Israel be destroyed. Since victory over Jericho advanced the reputation of Joshua and his God, will not defeat have the inverse effect? What will it mean if those who have come to exterminate are exterminated? What effects will the erasure of Israel's name on the landscape engender? In Joshua's view, the negation of a people and their God alike.

God responds with an order that Joshua rise from the ground where he mourns and conduct another ritual to purify Israel. Enumerating Israel's many missteps—"Israel sinned, violated my covenant which I commanded them, took from the banned items, stole, practiced deception, and placed the items in their vessels" (Josh 7:11)—God explains that Israel now falls under its own ban of sorts and will score no military victories until the wrongs are righted. The purification rite requires the location and extraction of any proscribed item, with the implication that harboring foreign objects or nonconformist members will ruin the collective. The conquest is frozen until internal cohesion can be reestablished.

53. See Havrelock, *River Jordan*, 106–127.

The institutions under suspicion come to light during the ritual lineup: "in the morning present yourselves according to your tribes, the tribe that God seizes upon will present itself by clans, the clan that God seizes upon will come forward as households, and the household that God seizes upon will come forward as individual men" (Josh 7:14). Israel crossed the Jordan and conquered Jericho as a whole (with priests, at times, differentiated), yet under scrutiny its members appear as affiliates of intersecting groups. As blame is directed at the constituent units, the text betrays their existence as the very basis of the social order. The narrowing movement from tribe to clan to household to individual places each unit under surveillance as if to institute a manner of self-policing among them, as well as among later audiences. Along with the shock at Achan's transgression and punishment comes the question, where do my alliances lie? The ritual of purification promises to salvage the entire social order by locating an individual transgressor and casting him into the fire as a sacrifice to redeem the nation as a whole (Josh 7:15).

"The elders of Israel" cover their heads with dust and bewail the defeat in harmony with Joshua (Josh 7:6). Recurrent characters in Deuteronomistic literature, the elders are associated with tribal leadership and, consistent with the editorial agenda, depicted in vague terms. Such treatment encapsulates the Deuteronomistic program of reducing tribal authority while acknowledging its existence when necessary, yet makes it particularly challenging to discern the role of the elders.[54] They appear as tribal representatives at collective gatherings, suggesting that they could steer a tribe's involvement or resistance. At the very least, their mention implies an insistence that their authority gain recognition in the annals of the nation. The book of Deuteronomy domesticates the elders within the system of national law by imagining their authority over the family in a scaled-down version of the king's authority over the state.[55] Rather than representing their actual duties, this seems to be a fictive structure in which overlapping jurisdiction is refashioned as a component part of a centralized state system. In this context, the elders' involvement in Joshua's

54. Michael Walzer notes that the role of the elders "is not established by covenant, like the monarchy and the priesthood; its members are not called, like the prophets; nor is there a divine command that they be appointed, as with judges." *God's Shadow: Politics in the Hebrew Bible* (New Haven, CT: Yale University Press, 2012), 195.

55. Joshua Berman notices that elders "adjudicate matters that are naturally within their jurisdiction as senior members of the clan: clan and family law." "Constitution, Class, and the Book of Deuteronomy," *Hebraic Political Studies* 1, no. 5 (2006): 546.

rituals of mourning indicates that the dynamics of tribal and national authority are being worked out in the scene of violation and punishment.

The tribe of Judah harbors the guilty party, a surprising fact when considering the Judahite affiliation of the editors.[56] Martin Noth here drew evidence for his theory that the book of Joshua began as a collection of tales associated with the tribe of Benjamin, which was eager to denigrate its ascendant neighbor to the south.[57] This, or a related variation, seems altogether plausible. The stories of Jericho, Ai, and Gibeon might even be coded stories about how the proud people of Benjamin were folded into an alliance. In this case, the story of a bad Judahite who almost ruined everything could sound a warning to southerners to uphold the connection with Benjamin no matter their personal interests. In keeping with my argument, the story might also voice caution that moments of tribal synthesis create a larger whole that under no circumstances should be subverted.

Whatever the story's original intent, Judah here stands accused of working at cross-purposes with the nation. Perhaps the implication is that the tribe in general, rather than the specific tribe of Judah, fosters problems for national unity. The investigation narrows its scope until Achan son of Carmi son of Zabdi son of Zerah of the tribe of Judah is identified. Given the opportunity to confess, Achan admits to his sin and enumerates the items in his buried treasure. In their commentary, Boling and Wright point out that when confessing guilt, Achan uses the word for legitimate spoils of war rather than contraband, as if rejecting the very premise of the ban on foreign objects.[58] Rendered all the more exotic as the cause of Israel's calamity, Achan reveals what he took from Jericho: a cloak woven of local fabrics, two hundred shekels of silver, and a block of gold weighing fifty shekels.[59]

The gruesome act of purification that follows exposes the coercive violence at the root of the collective. With "all Israel" following, Joshua leads Achan, his

56. The existence of the story in the final form of Joshua is further surprising when considering Fleming's conclusion that the book incorporates different material into a "Judahite perspective." At the same time, Fleming identifies Joshua 8 as the most "plausibly Israelite material." *Legacy of Israel*, 133.

57. Martin Noth, *Das Buch Josua* (Tübingen: Mohr Siebeck, 1953), 12–15. We likely see the countertrend in which Judah skewers Benjamin in the final episodes of the book of Judges.

58. Boling and Wright, *Joshua*, 6:218.

59. Although difficult to assert with certainty, the local cloak and wealth could also indicate that such riches are best directed toward the capital and its tax collectors rather than being harbored in the localities.

banned items, children, cattle, tent, and belongings out of the camp to the Valley of Achor (Josh 7:24). The name "Achor"—or "trouble"—gains explanation as Joshua declares, "For the trouble you have brought upon us, now God will trouble you today" (Josh 7:25). After "all Israel" stones and burns Achan's family, coordinated, collective action again becomes possible. The nation, it appears, can be mobilized through struggle with opponents both internal and external.[60] The people pile a large mound of stones over Achan as a lasting memorial to the fate of transgressors, and the landscape commemorates the grim event through the name, Valley of Trouble. The violence quells or, rather, redirects God's rage to external enemies.

The rubble multiplies as a reinvigorated Israel reengages Ai with new determination. Joshua turns the prior defeat into an advantage by playing off the perception of his army as weak. Just as extricating transgression reinforced the collective, so defeat made Joshua into a better strategist. Even the rules of engagement change as a result. Following the stoning of Achan, certain items can be seized as booty from destroyed cities. God stills limits the acquisitions, but designates that only human beings need be killed; the livestock can now be incorporated into Israel. Along with the severity of punishment, the rules of *ḥērem* have eased.[61] With the social structure and the laws of war altered, Joshua marches "all the warring nation" out to crush Ai (Josh 8:1).

Rather than by ritual procession, God instructs Joshua to attack Ai by ambush. The ambush requires that the troops break into units, but the narrator emphasizes how "all the warring nation" works in tandem (Josh 8:3, 11). Thirty thousand warriors lie in waiting as Joshua sleeps with the other troops. At dawn, Joshua and "the elders of Israel" lead the people forward (Josh 8:10). The emphasis on unity presses the point that Joshua does not err in separating troops for the purpose of ambush. When the king of Ai detects Joshua's battalion, he rallies every last soldier to repel the returning force. Playing on the perception of their weakness, Joshua's troops run as if in fear so that, in hot pursuit, the men of Ai leave their city abandoned and undefended.

60. Hawk notes that the Hebrew term describing Achan's act—*nebalah* (outrageous thing)—"denotes an act that sunders the bonds that hold the kinship network together." *Joshua in 3-D*, 86.

61. Fleming contends that the story of Ai's defeat is the clearest example of an Israelite tale incorporated into a book with a Judahite slant. "Ai's *ḥērem* in Josh. 8:2, 26–7, directly contradicts the Deuteronomy law (Deut. 20:16–18) and corresponds exactly with what is done to the towns of Sihon and Og in Deuteronomy 2–3." *Legacy of Israel*, 139.

Joshua then raises his javelin toward Ai as a signal to commence the siege. The hidden soldiers rise to action, capture the city, and set it aflame. In an illustrative moment of perspectival shift, the men of Ai see smoke rising from their city and surely know where there is fire. "Joshua and all Israel" then suspend the ruse to go on the attack against their exposed opponents (Josh 8:21). Joined by the ambush squad, the Israelites slaughter their enemy, leaving only the king alive to face Joshua. Those who somehow survived the burning of the city are killed once the troops return from the battlefield. Joshua (in what is likely a repetitive doublet) himself incinerates Ai so that it becomes an eternal ruin. After a public impaling, the king of Ai's body is laid at the gate from which Israel once fled. As Israel piles a mound of stones on the corpse, the Ruin, as well as the Valley of Trouble, signals the imminent destruction of those who would oppose Joshua's army. The story of the second round at Ai salvages the collective and shows its resilience to internal sabotage.

The Second Torah

After piling stones on the corpses of Achan and the King of Ai, Joshua undertakes construction of a monument to unity. As he builds an altar to Yahweh, God of Israel on Mount Ebal, law follows war in shaping the landscape. The book of Deuteronomy explicitly outlines that the People of Israel are to replace the peoples of the land and that the law of Israel is meant to reconstitute the territory of Canaan. Without enactment of the law—the Torah of Moses—Canaan cannot be a homeland. Therefore, the law stipulating how the Torah must be copied on native stone is cited before Joshua builds the altar to fulfill the proper execution of divine commands (Josh 8:31–32; Deut 27:1–8). The altar on Mount Ebal is made of whole stones never cut by metal tools, an image of geologic wholeness. Upon the stone altar, the people offer sacrifices and experience a ritual connection with God.

On the uncut surface, Joshua writes "a second Torah of Moses" (Josh 8:32) before the eyes of the people. This second Torah etched onto immobile stones illustrates a motif found across sources of the Hebrew Bible in which an original finds more enduring form in a copy. The first set of commands brought down from Sinai, for example, are shattered then replaced by a second set painstakingly carved by Moses. Aaron's sons Nadav and Abihu, first successors to the high priesthood, are annihilated instantly when they approach God with offerings of "strange fire" (Leviticus 10:1). Their brothers, Eleazar and Itamar, so completely assume their place that the first brothers are never mentioned again. In both cases, the lost original is not mourned, perhaps because the immediate copy signifies the very possibility of replacement. Biblical narrative thus provides a non-Platonic theory of the copy in which a secondary form is not derivative but rather commands particular authority.

Moses's Torah—itself a second—is not lost but held in the Ark carried before Joshua's army into battle. Rather than loss, the doubling suggests the need for the Torah to be part of the land as much as it is part of the wandering people. The law here gains its double valence—both national and extraterritorial. The national meaning becomes manifest in an inscription anticipated during an extraterritorial moment of revelation, yet the mountains of Ebal and Gerizim where the people stand to hear the recitation of Torah are no Sinai.[62] No fire burns, no shofar blasts, no revelation occurs. Joshua, the nonprophetic successor of Moses, simply reads what has already been revealed. His talent rests in faithful delivery: Joshua reads "every word of the Torah, the blessings and the curses exactly as written in the book of Torah. There was not a word of all that Moses commanded that Joshua did not read before the whole community of Israel" (Josh 8:34–35).

The law achieves enactment in the land at the same time that it exceeds its boundaries. During the recitation of Torah, Israel is configured as "all of the community of Israel" (כל קהל ישראל/*kol kehal Israel*) (Josh 8:35) rather than "all of the nation" (כל העם). This is significant because it suggests that Israel forms the nation when it engages in the conquest, but constitutes the community when hearing the words of Torah. The difference becomes all the more palpable when the community is qualified as including "the women, the children, and the stranger who walks in their midst" (Josh 8:35). War may indeed bring the nation into being, but the collective created by law transcends the army. The agenda of the book of Joshua—representing a cohesive nation at war in the name of creating such a polity on the ground—gains nuance in this ritual scene. "All Israel" encompasses multiple forms of leadership including "elders, officers, judges, and Levite-Priests" (Josh 8:33).[63] The text depicts these leaders from different sectors of society along with "stranger and citizen" lining up on either side of the Ark, half facing Mount Gerizim and half facing Mount Ebal in order to receive "the original" blessing for "the nation of Israel" anticipated by Moses (Josh 8:33). As the passage fulfills its role of reconciling

62. Or, as the Deuteronomists like to call Sinai, Mount Horeb.

63. For the tribal provenance of Levite-Priests, see Mark Leuchter, *Samuel and the Shaping of Tradition* (New York: Oxford University Press, 2013).

Israel's past and present, decentralized leaders and national aspirations, it admits that the conception of Israel unified through war against others is itself secondary. The "original" Israel encompasses women and members who are not ethnic affiliates in a community defined by adherence to a shared code of law (Josh 8:33, 35). Such a community and those empowered to administer it stand before the mountains as a testament to the Israel that is not an army.

The Allies

The depiction of a civilian Israel that includes members outside of ethnonational definitions leads to a story about a treaty rather than a battle.[64] The story of how local Hivites use costumes and props to trick Israel into alliance shows Joshua as lacking diplomatic instincts, but more significantly reveals the composite nature of Israel. The book of Joshua both denies and admits to a social reality in which various local and regional groups affiliate with a political unit called Israel and sometimes defect from it. Chapters 1–12 of the book of Joshua include a maximal number of such groups—registered largely as tribes or their constitutive clans—in the ranks of Joshua's army. The disaffection of some groups registers later as apostasy or civil war (see, for example, Joshua 22 or Judges 20–21). Joshua 9, which reveals the kind of treaty making through which a unit called Israel likely comes into being, deals with a parallel problematic: how to account for neighbors who should be, according to the conquest narrative, enemies? To drop the designation of "enemy" altogether would be to abandon the national construction of Israel, so instead the story of how the Gibeonites stealthily become allies accounts for neighbors who are not enemies in terms of class and ethnicity.

The motif word (*Leitwort*) "heard," along with associated lexemes, points to how stories make the nation of Israel manifest. The *Leitwort* further reminds us of the oral underpinnings of the written text and how stories circulated among different groups.[65] The story begins when all of the kings west of the Jordan "hear" an undefined tale of Israel and resolve to oppose them with "one mouth" (Josh 9:1–2). The Gibeonites, who "hear" the tales of Joshua at Jericho and Ai, decide to approach the Israelite warrior in disguise. Dressed in worn clothing

64. One notes how the last phrase in the prior covenant scene is "the stranger that walks in their midst" (Josh 8:35), and then the question of included "strangers" is taken up in Joshua 9.

65. See Dan Ben-Amos, "Folklore in the Ancient Near East," in *The Anchor Bible Dictionary*, ed. David Noel Freedman (New York: Doubleday, 1992), 818–828.

and carrying stale bread alongside leaky water skins, the Gibeonites present themselves as travelers from a distant land pursuing peace. The men of Israel voice suspicion, yet Joshua—seemingly naïve for a star general—accepts their terms. By outsmarting the People of Israel, the Gibeonites join their ranks.

The Gibeonites further distinguish themselves as expert tellers of Israel's story. They sway Joshua with their dramatization of how they "heard the hearing" of God's work in their distant land. They elaborate upon "all that He did in Egypt; all that he did to the two Amorite kings east of the Jordan, Sihon the king of Hesbon and Og king of Bashan who lived in Astarot" (Josh 9:9–10). They conceal their motivation in Abrahamic garb: when they heard tell of God, they journeyed from afar to find His people. Either Joshua is taken in, or their offer of civil submission appeals to his strategic sensibilities. His only precondition is to test the staleness of their bread as a measure of how far they traveled. Satisfied, Joshua and his men enter into a peace treaty with the visitors without seeking advice from "the mouth of God" (Josh 9:14). After Joshua establishes a covenant of peace and the tribal leaders swear to an oath, the alliance can never be broken.

The ruse falls apart when the people of Israel "hear" that their sworn allies are proximate neighbors (Josh 9:16). The people take issue with the decisions of their leaders, yet God says nothing. The treaty has no popular support within Israel—the people express nothing but regret and anger—yet becomes validated by God's silence. God raises no objections to the alliance, and it is never categorized as a violation of any sort. Israel upholds its promise, marching to protect the Gibeonite towns of Gibeon, Chephirah, Beeroth, and Kiriath-jearim when they are attacked.

To answer the frustrations of fighting men, Israel's leaders impose servitude on their new allies. Joshua enforces the ruling that the Hivites will forever serve as "hewers of wood and carriers of water" (Josh 9:21, 23). Faced with their new reality, the Gibeonites explain the cause of their deception: "Your servants were told how Yahweh your God promised Moses his servant to give you all of the land and to destroy all of the land's inhabitants from before you" (Josh 9:24). Joshua's deceivers echo the driving point of the conquest narrative: "all of the land" falls to "all Israel" as they vanquish "all the inhabitants." The vanquished who survive voice the book's central themes of totality and unity. And so the Gibeonites become incorporated in Israel as subordinates serving the community and the altar "until today" (Josh 9:27).[66]

66. Joshua 21:17 lists Gibeon as a sanctuary city in the region of Benjamin. The cities of sanctuary are associated with the priesthood.

An unexposed seam holds together the stories of the second Torah and the Gibeonites (Josh 8:30–35 and 9) or at least explains the editorial logic behind their juxtaposition. The seam—based on verses about the assembly of Israel in the book of Deuteronomy—joins the idea of the people to that of the outsider. Deuteronomy 29:9–10 addresses "all of you" who constitute Israel; after the requisite list of leaders and acknowledgment that "every man of Israel" is present comes a supplementary recognition of "your children, wives, and the stranger in the midst of your camp, from the hewer of wood to the carrier of water" (Deut 29:10). "Women, children, and the stranger in your midst" are likewise recognized as present at Joshua's covenant ceremony beside the mountains of Ebal and Gerizim. The story of the Gibeonites offers explanation for how such strangers might find themselves chopping trees and conveying water. It also encodes the ways in which variant political positions figure as ethnic and class differences.

The story betrays that the people of Israel are comprised of groups with different backgrounds and histories loosely bound by alliances. In many cases, the backgrounds and histories become incorporated, like the groups themselves, into Israel's narrative. In exceptional cases—like the sacred servitude of the Gibeonites—difference demands markers of otherness.[67] The Gibeonites present an exceptional case of a group within the network of alliance still marked as outside of the nation proper. I maintain that the ethnic label of "Hivite" does not itself indicate that the Gibeonites are substantively different from groups like Reubenites or Benjaminites. Another factor requires accentuation of their ethnic difference, possibly the fact that they constituted a competing form of priesthood, relegated in the text to subservience at the temple.[68] They may also have held a distinct relationship to alliance or centralization or refused to fight in the army, which demanded that they be singled out in both class and ethnic terms. At the same time, the story of their absorption speaks to how a centralizing movement incorporates groups even when it holds them up for special consideration. Had the Gibeonites been more assimilated, then the story of their founders would likely have found a place within sanctioned genealogy (thirteen tribes?). However, because their

67. 2 Samuel 21:2 describes the Gibeonites as "not part of the People of Israel, but a remnant of the Amorites."

68. A similar trend characterizes the treatment of Levites in Priestly texts; see Adrienne Leveen, *Memory and Tradition in the Book of Numbers* (Cambridge: Cambridge University Press, 2008), 22.

absorption was partial, we read instead about their stratagem of inclusion that, in fact, dramatizes the entire process of consolidation among regional groups.

In his book about the Gibeonites, Joseph Blenkinsopp reads Joshua 9 in light of the Amarna letters, which "reveal the rapid formation and equally rapid disintegration of coalitions. . . . States were bound together by treaties, implying the taking of oaths and acceptance of responsibilities, such as we find described in Joshua 9."[69] This historical evaluation brings us to the paradox at the heart of Joshua—the book uses tales of ethnic warfare in order to obscure Israel's development through a series of alliances and treaties, yet at the same time unwittingly attests to it. The writers may simply understand audiences: historical treaties stir few, whereas many feel called to affiliate by gripping stories of war. Just such a story follows the inadvertent treaty with the natives.

The Southern Wars

Joshua and his army next face leagues of kings from the south and north. These grand battles heighten the sense of conquest as social transformation and embed the portrait of a unified people with distinct southern and northern flanks. Characterized by miraculous reversals, these tales from the battlefront depict God rendering the impossible possible, likely a nod to the inherent difficulty of the coalition politics proposed by the book. As holy war blends with cosmogony in Joshua 10, God recreates His people as a nation of heroes and battles the forces of chaos in the form of Canaanite kings.

The battle begins when the king of Jerusalem contemplates with terror the implications of what he has "heard" of Joshua's capture and proscription of Jericho and Ai (Josh 10:1). The recent alliance between Gibeon, "the great city filled with warriors," and Israel extends the implications to a point intolerable to the King of Jerusalem (Josh 10:2).[70] The King of Jerusalem first speaks of the Gibeonites, rather than Israel, as heroes. This would seem counterintuitive in a formative national story, yet it conveys something important about the

69. Joseph Blenkinsopp, *Gibeon and Israel: The Role of Gibeon and the Gibeonites in the Political and Religious History of Early Israel* (Cambridge: Cambridge University Press, 1972), 33.

70. L. Daniel Hawk observes that Joshua presents "kings of the land, rather than its peoples as the enemy that threatens Israel." As a city without a king, Gibeon is a legitimate ally of Israel. Hawk also imagines that the story of Gibeon is a local tradition ultimately assimilated to "the party line." "Conquest Reconfigured: Recasting Warfare in the Redaction of Joshua," in *Writing and Reading War: Rhetoric, Gender, and Ethics in Biblical and Modern Contexts*, ed. Brad E. Kelle and Frank Ritchel Ames (Atlanta: Society of Biblical Literature, 2008), 145–147.

nature of Israel. Although the Gibeonites tricked Israel into this alliance and bear the mark of unbelonging and subservience, they hold a treaty with Israel. The battle at hand substantiates that such a treaty can be neither dissolved nor disregarded. The urgency of this point, pressed in reference to the Gibeonites, speaks to the nature of Israel as a conglomeration of clans, tribes, migrants, and local signatories to a treaty. "Israel" serves as the umbrella term for these groups, and each act of joining Israel, in turn, requires reinforcement of the idea of Israel and the treaties that constitute it. That Gibeonites, not ethnic Israelites, are protected dramatizes the strength of the treaty. "Making peace with Israel" is no light matter (Josh 10:1).[71]

Adonai-zedek, King of Jerusalem, builds his own alliance of five southern kings to besiege Gibeon. The Gibeonites immediately call upon Joshua to leverage the terms of their treaty: "Do not fail your servants, come to us quickly, deliver us, help us, for all the Amorite kings of the hill country have gathered against us" (Josh 10:6).[72] As direct as it is, the Gibeonite plea also contains a pun on Joshua's name. In asking Joshua "to deliver" them, the Gibeonites, in effect, ask Joshua—whose name means "deliverer"—to fulfill his narrative function. Joshua does what he is meant to do by going to Gibeon with "all" the nation and "all the heroes of war" (Josh 10:7). Where the king of Jerusalem spoke of Gibeonite warriors, Joshua manifests the warriors of Israel. God promises victory and Joshua goes out for a surprise ambush. By leaving Gilgal to protect an ally, the warriors of Israel become a "whole nation." The emergence of a unified Israel is nothing less than a cosmic event: "neither before nor since has there been such a day" (Josh 10:14). Giant stones fall from the sky as the sun and moon halt their circuits in order to witness the war. The victory is decisive: Israel "crushes the necks of the kings beneath their feet," and Joshua becomes canonized as the only man to call God into war (Josh 10:14).

A mound of stones geographically marks the shift of regimes. Israel's victory belongs to God, who halts the very cycles of creation as He dispenses with Israel's enemies. In the only poetic interruption of the narrative, Joshua voices divine language to commemorate the cosmic import of the day on which Israel

71. The peace between Gibeon and Israel represented here, I suggest, reflects a "political form" in which regions, groups, and tribes formed treaties of nonaggression and mutual defense. This "was referred to eventually by its adherents with the name Israel." Robert B. Coote and Keith W. Whitelam, *The Emergence of Early Israel in Historical Perspective* (Sheffield: Sheffield Academic Press, 1987), 131.

72. Just as the Gibeonites are accused of being Amorites, so they charge their attackers.

slayed the five kings of the south (Josh 10:12–13). The military ritual is as elaborate as the divine orchestration in establishing the new era of Israel's supremacy. The five kings flee God's hailstorm, as did Lot, to a cave. Joshua orders terrestrial stones as big as those that fell from the sky to be set at the entrance to the cave where he stations his men. Meanwhile, the army pursues the fugitives to prevent them from returning to their cities. By the time Joshua and his troops have finished cutting down men in the open field, only a few survivors make their way into other fortified cities. As the warriors return to camp triumphant, not a soul dares to taunt the soldiers of Israel. The stones in front of the cave are removed, the kings are taken out from within the cave to parade before Joshua, where his officers break their necks with their feet. As he commemorated God's role in the battle, Joshua marks this moment with formulaic language characteristic of Deuteronomistic literature: "do not be afraid and do not be discouraged, be strong and be bold, for thus will God do to all the enemies you engage" (Josh 10:25). With that, Joshua impales the kings and leaves them hanging until evening, after which he has their corpses thrown back in the cave and piles up the stones as a sign of mastery.

Subsequent battles ensue, all victorious. Each announcement of triumph emphasizes the total annihilation of inhabitants and their kings. The ban on assimilating spoils and foreign bodies finds its execution (Josh 10:28, 35, 37, 39), and a summary of conquered territories concludes the miraculous victory of Joshua over the cities of the south:

> Joshua conquered all of the land, the mountains, the Negev, the coastal plain, and the watersheds. Not a survivor remained from all the kings and every soul was proscribed as the Lord, God of Israel, had commanded. Joshua conquered them from Kadesh Barnea to Gaza and from all the land of Goshen to Gibeon. Joshua captured all these kings and all their land in one fell swoop because the Lord, God of Israel, fought on Israel's behalf. Joshua and all Israel returned to the camp in Gilgal (Josh 10:40–43).

These descriptions support and spectacularize the central claim that Joshua conquered "all of the land."[73] Initially, geographic features—"the mountains . . .

73. Moshe Weinfeld analyzes this passage as evidence that "the editor of the book of Joshua, who depends on Deuteronomy, tried to render an image of the conquest as proceeding according to commandments of the book of Deuteronomy." *The Promise of the Land: The Inheritance of the Land of Canaan by the Israelites*, Taubman Lectures in Jewish Studies 3 (Berkeley: University of California Press, 1993), 90–91.

the watersheds"—characterize the extent of the conquest. The accomplishment is then reiterated in terms of slaughtered kings and decimated populations. Finally, a set of southern border points specifies the location of Israel's new patrimony.[74]

However, "Kadesh Barnea to Gaza and from all the land of Goshen to Gibeon" is not the area conquered in the preceding battles. Robert Boling finds it strange that a purported summary "covers both more and less than is reported."[75] I identify it as one of the many collated regional traditions that show how locals, as much as nationalists, can be invested in their boundary systems. As we will see, this also characterizes the double voice of the second half of Joshua—traditions that contest the national paradigm appear constitutive. Oriented toward southern deserts and Egypt, the coordinates do not correspond with the picture of the homeland presented at the beginning of the book: "your borders will be from the desert to the Lebanon and from the Great River—the River Euphrates—all the land of the Hittites to the Great Sea where the sun cycles" (Josh 1:4).

Not only do the alleged boundaries of Joshua's southern victory—"from Kadesh Barnea to Gaza and from all the land of Goshen to Gibeon"—fail to realize God's initial promise to Joshua, but they also contradict other records of the selfsame places. "All the land of Goshen" is, in anachronistic terms, the "ghetto" where the People of Israel dwelled in Egypt. A boast following Joshua's defeat of the northern alliance lists Gibeon as the one city that made peace with Joshua, leaving "the Hivites dwelling in Gibeon" (Josh 11:19). The proud assurance that Joshua destroyed everything "from Kadesh Barnea to Gaza" destabilizes the very claims of the conquest. Kadesh Barnea, as recorded in Numbers and Deuteronomy, serves as the People of Israel's primary desert home. There, the spies contest God's story of the Promised Land and persuade

74. The borders that attest to national triumph themselves imply the hand of scribes from Judah: "The Judean provenance of Josh 1–12 is deduced not from the stories, which are of mainly Benjaminite origin, but from the concluding summaries after the two final battles (Josh 10:40–42, 11:16–20). The language of the résumé following the battle against the southern coalition describes the conquest of the future territory of the kingdom of Judah in the most hyperbolic terms: Joshua subdues the whole country (i.e., the territory of the kingdom of Judah) at a single stroke, 'for the LORD, the God of Israel, fought for Israel.'" Nili Wazana, "'Everything Was Fulfilled' versus 'The Land That Yet Remains': Contrasting Conceptions of the Fulfillment of the Promise in the Book of Joshua," in *The Gift of the Land and the Fate of the Canaanites in Jewish Thought*, ed. Katell Berthalot, Joseph E. David, and Marc Hirshman (New York: Oxford University Press, 2014), 33.

75. Boling, *Joshua*, 6:287.

their cohorts to resist a life of endless war, and there, in retaliation, God condemns a generation to death in exile.

Conflicting traditions confer an ambivalent status on Gaza. One text recounts that Joshua's heroic slaying of giants stopped short "only in Gaza, Gath, and Ashdod," where giant Anakites remain (Josh 11:22). God later reminds Joshua of his failure: "you are old, past your prime and much of the land remains to be seized. . . . Namely, that of the five Philistine lords of Gaza, Ashdod, Askelon, Gath, and Ekron" (Josh 13:3). If Kadesh Barnea recalls the failings of his fellow spies, then Gaza points to Joshua's most egregious failure. An alternate tradition emplaces Gaza, its satellites, and villages within the territory of Judah (Josh 15:47). The book of Judges ascribes an active victory over Gaza to the tribe of Judah: "Judah captured Gaza and its borderlands, Askelon and its borderlands, and Ekron and its borderlands" (Judg 1:18).[76]

The claims accrue and assume a simultaneous nature in biblical texts. As they suggest competing sites of power articulated in terms of biblical traditions, the unstable nature of borders and the overlapping claims of sovereignty result in a contested land within the text of the Bible. Multiple claimants and various inhabitants appear in the space conquered by Israel and chosen by God. The nation of Israel and the God who fights on its behalf are concepts projected onto the space of the land in the name of fixing a political form unsupported, it seems, by the social setting. Ultimately, these concepts share the space of the land with other interests, and the banished peoples reappear as neighbors. The second half of Joshua portrays the copresence of different groups who seem to move in and out of alliance and affiliation with Israel. Periods of peace and war fluctuate according to external military threats, as well as how local resources are shared. With such shaky support from allegedly constitutive traditions, the conquest seems to be the tradition most out of step with settlement patterns.

The Northern Wars

As word of Joshua's army travels north, Yavin king of Hazor forges alliances with his neighbors similar to the bloc in the south. Geographic and ethnic descriptions emphasize the total opposition and, therefore, the difficult odds. "All the kings of the north, in the mountains, in the Aravah south of Lake Kinneret, in the lowlands, and towards Dor by the sea," including "Canaanites

76. Yet another tradition preserved in the Septuagint amends the verse to "But Judah did not capture Gaza."

FIGURE 1.1. Map of Kingdoms and Regions in Ancient Israel, Roni Blushtein-Livnon.

from the east and west, Amorites, Hittites, Perizzites, Jebusites in the hills, and Hivites beneath Mount Hermon in the region of Mizpah," rise as rivals to Israel (Josh 11:2–3). In short, this battle pits Israel against everyone living in the land. The massive number of northern troops arrayed with battle chariots emphasizes the miraculous dimension of the impending victory,[77] and the unity of the allied northerners—"all of these kings joined forces, came out to battle, and camped together at the Waters of Merom in order to fight Israel" (Josh 11:5)—attests to the responsive cohesion of Israel. The words stressing opposition and collectivity reveal the intention of the conquest story to redraw the boundaries in the north where literary and archaeological evidence attests to a decentralized polity where interaction and intermixing among different groups was the norm.[78]

God promises Joshua, "By tomorrow at this time I will lay them out slain before Israel and you will hamstring their horses and burn their chariots" (Josh 11:6). Joshua mobilizes "all of the warring nation" in an ambush that wipes out the allied forces; God's promise comes into being. The destruction of the city of Hazor symbolizes Israel's sweeping northern victory. Joshua doubles back to capture Hazor and slay its king as punishment for leading the coalition. The soldiers of Israel enact the ban, putting every person to death and reducing Hazor to ashes. Other northern cities, the narrator reports, meet the same fate in Joshua's perfect fulfillment of divine promises made to Moses (Josh 11:12, 15).

Amidst the record of total annihilation comes an explanation for all the other peoples still in Israel's midst: "however, all of the towns standing on mounds were not burned down by Israel, only Hazor alone was burned down by Joshua" (Josh 11:13). Furthermore, Israel appropriates the material goods not subject to the ban, suggesting the existence of a material culture that, like the landscape, fell out of step with the tale of total ethnic opposition in the north. The insistence upon Joshua's complete fidelity to the law further seeks to downplay the cultural patchwork of the north. In a familiar compensatory tone, the episode concludes with a final note of totality: Joshua "left nothing undone of all that the Lord had commanded Moses" (Josh 11:15).

77. The northerners are described as being "as numerous as the sand on the seashore," an inverted echo of the promise to Abraham about his descendants. Nili Wazana rightly notes that the northern battle "is devoid of spectacular supernatural elements," but it seems that the battle odds suggest the wonder of divine intervention. "Joshua," in *The Oxford Encyclopedia of the Books of the Bible*, ed. Michael D. Coogan (Oxford: Oxford University Press, 2011), 491.

78. Fleming, *Legacy of Israel*, 34.

The Land

Just as the southern campaign ended with a narrative mapping, so the northern campaign provides a boundary list intended to support the claim that "Joshua captured all of the land" (Josh 11:16).

> The mountain and all the Negev, all the land of Goshen, the Shefelah and the Arabah, and the mountain of Israel and its plains, from Mount Halak that goes up to Seir until Baal Gad in the Lebanon valley beneath Mount Hermon. Joshua captured all their kings, struck them down and killed them. . . . There was not a single city that made peace with the People of Israel apart from the Hivites who dwell in Gibeon. They took everything through war (Josh 11:16–19).

Along with the usual report that the peoples of the land united in opposition against Israel who, in turn, slaughtered all enemies and captured all necessary territory comes mention of the treaty with the Gibeonites. Because this exception already begins to unravel the totalizing claims of the conquest, it is couched between two proclamations that everyone was killed and all seized.[79]

God seemingly stoked the fierce opposition for the same reason He hardened Pharaoh's heart: "it was God's plan to harden their hearts to cause them to wage war with Israel so that, in turn, they [Israel] would subject them to a ban without sanctuary and wipe them out as God had commanded Moses" (Josh 11:20). According to the circular principle, fulfillment of the law required annihilation of the land's inhabitants, which itself depended upon their unwavering opposition, which, with the exception of the Gibeonites, God secured. According to the reasoning in Joshua 1–12, no opponent can be left standing. Such a grim equation, I submit, was born of the political need to foster an indissoluble bond among groups that took form as a story of absolute ethno-religious antagonism.

The conquest concludes with Joshua felling the Anakites, the giant, primordial opponents who stalked Canaan back when Joshua was a young spy (Num 13:28). As Joshua brings down giants with his own hands, Israel predominates even over semidivine creatures. However, a concession to the fact that Anakites remain in "Gaza, Gath, and Ashdod" precedes the triumphal conclusion that

79. Weinfeld notes that "such a portrayal stands in complete contradiction to the core accounts of the tribal conquest in Judges 1 and their parallels in the book of Joshua, according to which the Canaanite inhabitants persisted in the coastal cities and in the lowlands." *Promise of the Land*, 91.

"Joshua took all of the land exactly as God commanded Moses. As Joshua gave Israel their territory according to their tribal divisions, the land was quiet from war" (Josh 11:23).[80]

Joshua's conquest calibrates the landscape according to an emerging national map, which is itself a composite of regional geographic traditions. Cities associated with a previous order are annihilated (Josh 8:22, 28) as their property is barred from inclusion in the nation's wealth (Josh 6:17). The world destroyed by Israel remains perceptible only in mounds of rubble beneath which lie former kings (Josh 8:29). Just as a place name like Gilgal records the onset of normative memory, so a name like the Valley of Acor, where Achan the defiant Judean was stoned, embeds deviance in the landscape. However, admission of the component units—both absorbed and resistant to a centralized Israel—stands alongside the proclamation of heroic feats accomplished by "all of Israel" and "all the land" vanquished by Joshua.[81]

Incongruously, the battles in the south and north conclude with different geographical claims about "all the land." As analyzed above, the conclusion of the southern campaign defines this as "from Kadesh-barnea to Gaza, all the land of Goshen, and up to Gibeon" (Josh 10:41), and that of the northern campaign as "from Mount Halak, which ascends to Seir, all the way to Baal-gad in the Valley of the Lebanon at the foot of Mount Hermon" (Josh 11:17). The two traditions were likely brought together during a period of alliance or unification between the southern and northern kingdoms. One of the Hebrew Bible's greatest literary accomplishments rests in the fusion of northern and southern traditions at the same time that each set maintains its integrity. Rather than perceiving these differences as merely exposing the absence of a unified conquest, I see them as demonstrating a successful example of confederation—unification on necessary issues such as threats posed by imperial armies in conjunction with maintenance of local governing bodies and land stewardship.

If Joshua 10 indicates a southern tradition and Joshua 11 a northern tradition or redaction thereof, then why are reports of battles at the named cities of Jericho and Ai included? In his adaptation of Albrecht Alt's thesis, Martin Noth

80. Wazana notes that this "final appended summary reinforces the picture of the separation of the two processes, conquest and settlement." "'Everything Was Fulfilled,'" 17.

81. Weinfeld describes this in terms of an editorial process: "In order to describe an all-inclusive and one-time conquest of the land of Canaan, the editor of the material in Josh. 1–12 used several separate conquest traditions that were available to him, as well as a schematic list of Canaanite cities and their kings (Josh. 12)." *Promise of the Land*, 150.

maintained that Joshua 2–8 derives from the war chronicle of the tribe of Benjamin that was ritually commemorated at Gilgal, Israel's first campground west of the Jordan.[82] As Benjamin became incorporated into the war alliance, this tradition was adapted to the story of conquest and expanded into Joshua 2–12. There are at least two ways to think about the coincidence between the early battles of Joshua and the significant Benjaminite sites. The first accepts the chronology of the Saul story—through military prowess, a Benjaminite judge allied various tribes before he lost power to a Judahite usurper.[83] In this scenario, accounts of victories at Jericho and Ai and compromises with Gibeon would have been incorporated both during times of Benjaminite ascendancy (let's say, the era of Saul) and Judean predominance (the Davidic dynasty) in order to satisfy Benjaminite pride. The second mode of appraisal looks at the biblical chronology more skeptically and reasons that bringing the formidable Ben-Yamini, *People of the Right Hand,* into a centralized alliance required prominent placement of their battle stories.[84] The civil war between Benjamin and the other tribes with which the book of Judges concludes would then indicate either the breakdown of the alliance or its prehistory. If the near annihilation of Benjamin preceded their entry into the federation, then highlighting Benjaminite war stories in the conquest and honoring the tribe's leadership by recognizing Saul as the first king of Israel may have been necessary concessions for their compliance.

Daniel Fleming reads the Benjaminite stories in Joshua in terms of this second possibility, viewing Joshua 8 and the civil war story in Judges 20 as reflecting "Israel's conflict with Benjaminite peoples in the early days, when Benjamin could have been no different from other 'Amorites' who were associated with the western highlands."[85] In other words, when Israel conquers Ai in Judges 8, they are conquering Benjamin. What comprises Israel at such a moment is, of course, open to question. Fleming appraises Benjamin as autonomous even as they joined forces with Israel and Judah. Residing in the

82. Albrecht Alt, *Kleine Schriften zur Geschichte des Volkes Israel* (Munich: Beck, 1953), 1:176–192; and Noth, *Das Buch Josua,* 12–16.

83. "The abiding reverence for this hero among the people of Benjamin would have provided the setting for the preservation of Saul stories and composition of Saul texts through the generations after his royal house ceased to compete for rule over Israel." Fleming, *Legacy of Israel,* 154.

84. "The most striking linguistic match between an Israelite people and a group known from other Near Eastern evidence has always been between Benjamin (Bin-yamin) and Mari's Binu Yamina." Fleming, *Legacy of Israel,* 145.

85. Fleming, *Legacy of Israel,* 141.

band of territory between Israel and Judah, Benjamin's presence could not be denied. Any alliance between north and south would have to include Benjamin for reasons of strategy and contiguity. Ultimately, the book of Joshua does concern "all of the land" in the sense of contiguous terrain defined by interlinking stories. As we have seen, the terrain is also characterized by resistance to the alliance, which yields the categories of rebels and other "peoples in the land."

To summarize, the people of Israel cross the Jordan River from the east, confront enemies in the border zone between north and south, fight for Jerusalem and its neighboring cities, and finally capture Hazor and the north. The opening encampment east of the Jordan—however problematic—represents a nod to including the eastern tribes in Israel.[86] Battles at Jericho and Ai, along with the treaty with the Gibeonites, enlist Benjamin in the confederation. The larger scale of the northern and southern campaigns points to the magnitude of the kingdoms of Israel and Judah. The book of Joshua employs a geographic premise to model an ideal of centralization. In other words, the conquest narrative is conquest by narrative. Its stories absorb a maximum number of allies and set them against the groups resistant to incorporation. All the while, the autonomy of the allies remains apparent in a narrative claiming absolute unity.

The first half of Joshua concludes with a geographic summary that reiterates the territorial gains east of the Jordan (Josh 12:1–6), in the north (Josh 12:7), and in the south (Josh 12:8). It then shifts to a substantial list of defeated kings with the refrain of the number one—"the king of Jericho one, the king of Ai, near Bethel one" (Josh 12:9)—which calls to mind the credo of Deuteronomy 6: "Hear, O Israel, The Lord is our God, the Lord is one" (Deut 6:4). Aspirations for political unity thus mirror conceptions of the Godhead as the enumeration of thirty-one defeated kings echoes the book of Joshua's themes of cohesion and totality.

86. On the Transjordanian tribes, see Havrelock, "Crossing Over" and "The Other Side," in *River Jordan*.

2

"So Very Much Left to Conquer" and the Persistence of the Local

Autonomous egalitarian "tribal" existence.

—NORMAN GOTTWALD, *TRIBES OF YAHWEH*, 38

THE SECOND HALF of the book of Joshua shifts the theme from conquest to settlement. Despite the triumphal declarations that all of the land now falls under Israel's control, the conquest remains resolutely incomplete and positions settlement as war by other means. However, the Canaan we encounter here is entirely different from, even antithetical to, the place depicted in the war stories. Pitched enmity dissolves into neighborly resentments, control of the land vacillates with uncertainty, and regional centers command distinct authority. Modes of social organization that have nothing to do with the army emerge to suggest that the very movement toward political centralization or a protostate required constant negotiation with localized sites of power. Why has no one before so appraised the second half of Joshua? Likely because there is no getting around the fact that, after the high action of conquest, the sequel seems boring. Its exhaustive lists of boundary lines and major cities relate to the necessary, often tedious, bureaucracy of governance, particularly on the local level. The contradictory, controversial material of Joshua lies buried among litanies of geographic features tucked into the denouement of a high-stakes war of establishment.[1] Yet, the key to the political tensions that

1. The formulaic language of the boundary lists has led some to suggest a Priestly hand; see Moshe Weinfeld, *The Promise of the Land: The Inheritance of the Land of Canaan by the Israelites*, Taubman Lectures in Jewish Studies 3 (Berkeley: University of California Press, 1993); Robert

generated the book of Joshua in the first place rests in this roster of borderlines. One can imagine that some early audiences recognized prized stakes of ownership in these lists and that those without skin in the game, like their modern counterparts, may have been happy to gloss over large sections.

The shift from tales of war to frontier settlement occurs abruptly. Following a triumphal listing of the slain—"all kings, thirty-one in total"—the scene shifts to God chiding an aged Joshua, "Your days are numbered and so very much of the land remains to be conquered" (Josh 12:24, 13:1). As God elaborates on the land that remains, the reader becomes acclimated to, or at least lulled by, the recurrent enumeration of topographical names. Still, it is worth paying attention because the record of "the land that remains" attests to the decentralized, religiously and politically diverse social landscape that the conquest narrative seeks to obscure. If one can slog through the boundary lists, then some remarkable admissions become apparent. The clans of Israel live alongside a host of others, Jerusalem is divided "until today," no national army repels local opponents, and a tribal system of exchanges and marriages maintains a social balance.

The editors of Joshua stage the contradictory images of Israel as a national army and Israel as a conglomeration of households as phases of nationalization—first a unified army conquers the land, then the tribes settle it. Biblical scholar Nili Wazana observes, "The second half of the book of Joshua presents a tribal, at times even individual, point of view, versus the national outlook of the first half."[2] Like many scholars before, I seek to disrupt the narrative sequence. Going beyond the usual confines of biblical discourse, however, I do not proffer a variant timeline of social evolution but rather stress the continuous, shifting relationship among political forms and their representation. The boundary lists, I argue, attest to a varied social order comprised of several different units that the centralizing party sponsoring the book of Joshua would like to overcome. Why include the geographic traditions then? Because incorporating the land, wealth, and fighting men of constitutive

---

Boling and G. Ernest Wright, *Joshua*, The Anchor Yale Bible (New Haven, CT: Yale University Press, 1995), 66–67; and Shmuel Ahituv and Moshe Greenberg, eds., *Joshua: A Biblical Commentary for Israel* (Jerusalem: Magnes Press, 1995). Others perceive the work of the later priestly writers labeled H.

2. Nili Wazana, "'Everything Was Fulfilled' versus 'The Land that Yet Remains': Contrasting Conceptions of the Fulfillment of the Promise in the Book of Joshua," in *The Gift of the Land and the Fate of the Canaanites in Jewish Thought*, ed. Katell Berthelot, Joseph E. David, and Marc Hirshman (New York: Oxford University Press, 2014), 14.

groups required recognition and record of their defining boundaries and related lore. Furthermore, beyond the grandiose visions of "all the land," these were the territorial traditions available to the editors.[3]

Employing the terminology of the Bible, I suggest that families, clans, and tribes inhabited and migrated through the regions described in the book of Joshua. At various junctures, these groups affiliated with the kingdoms in the north and south, which perhaps, as the books of Samuel and Kings describe, themselves unified at one point. It appears that some groups, like Benjamin, were forced into alliance and that others, like Gilead, dropped out or felt an ambivalent connection. Groups that never joined or overtly opposed centralization, I argue, became labeled as offending, contaminating peoples of the land. In contrast, when a group moved into Israel, they could slide into the structure of twelve tribes as a subgroup or constitutive clan. The split tribe of Manasseh best illustrates this process.[4] The geographic traditions of a range of social groups are collated in the second half of Joshua and bear traces of extensive revision amidst political flux. Where other biblical geographers have puzzled over the possible coordinates of the tribal boundaries and their cities, I analyze how the rhetoric of presence operates alongside the rhetoric of expulsion and thus discover local systems that cut across the territorial integrity of the represented nation.

The social balance in question pivots on the household, the primary site of economic production with occasional surplus. As we attend to the close, sometimes synonymous, link between women and the household, modern conceptions of a nuclear family between four walls must give way to an indoor-outdoor complex where several nested units interacted with animals and plants alike. The relationship of woman and house, then, is not one of pure domesticity or enclosure, but rather a scale of production most tied to survival

3. According to Martin Noth, Joshua 13–19 derives from two sources: a "system of tribal borders" collected around 900 BCE and a list of the twelve districts in Judah from the end of the seventh century; *Das Buch Josua* (Tübingen: Mohr Siebeck, 1953), 11, 13–15. Nili Wazana suggests an implied urtext: "The literary affinities between Joshua 13–21 and Judges 1, alongside the pro-Judahite inclination of Judges 1 versus the Shiloh-oriented motif of Joshua 13–21, point to their mutual reliance on a tribal source, depicting local clashes of families or tribes, such as can be found in other biblical traditions (1 Chronicles 4:39–43, 5:7–17, 7:20–29)." "Joshua," in *The Oxford Encyclopedia of the Books of the Bible*, ed. Michael D. Coogan (Oxford: Oxford University Press, 2011), 494.

4. Rachel Havrelock, *River Jordan: The Mythology of a Dividing Line* (Chicago: University of Chicago Press, 2011), 117–120.

and transmission of culture. The Hebrew Bible, as well as subsequent Hebrew writings, provides ample evidence that women had political recognition at this scale and often served as representatives of the household in larger arenas.[5] In contrast to a society in which the individual is the fundamental social unit, one that relies on the household absorbs interlocking networks of relationship that, in turn, exert their influence on the umbrella institutions.

The materiality of the household has been documented by Carol Meyers, a cultural anthropologist who lives among the ancient Israelites through text and excavation. She avers, "The Israelite household was the immediate and determinative social context for everyone" and served "as the basic unity of both production and consumption." However, its foundational nature should not lead us to view the household as "functionally subordinate to clan, tribe, or monarchy."[6] Instead, with its interlocking spine of networks, the household formed the backbone of the system and supported public political life.[7] The woman-run household contained "a built environment consisting of persons, their *hardware*—that is, their material culture, including the dwelling and all its associated installations and artifacts—and also their activities."[8] More than the builders, Meyers explains, women bore the responsibility of maintaining the household as a socioeconomic unit. This also meant managing the natural and human resources needed to support the household.[9] The economic partnerships required to operate a successful household entailed women's participation in public ritual and political life.

Meyers further demonstrates the correlation between agriculture and the household, as well as industry and the state.[10] Industry, as it narrows the

5. Lori Rowlett, "Inclusion, Exclusion, and Marginality in the Book of Joshua," in *The Historical Books: A Sheffield Reader*, ed. J. Cheryl Exum (Sheffield: Sheffield Academic Press, 1997), 70; Cynthia Chapman, *The House of the Mother: The Social Roles of Maternal Kin in Biblical Hebrew Narrative and Poetry* (New Haven, CT: Yale University Press, 2016); Mieke Bal, *Lethal Love: Feminist Literary Readings of Biblical Love Stories* (Bloomington: Indiana University Press, 1987); Cynthia Baker, *Rebuilding the House: Architectures of Gender in Jewish Antiquity* (Stanford: Stanford University Press, 2002); Charlotte Fonrobert, *Menstrual Purity: Rabbinic and Christian Reconstructions of Biblical Gender* (Stanford: Stanford University Press, 2000).

6. Carol Meyers, *Rediscovering Eve: Ancient Israelite Women in Context* (New York: Oxford University Press, 2013), 103.

7. Meyers, *Rediscovering Eve*, 174.

8. Carol Meyers, *Household and Holiness: The Religious Culture of Israelite Women* (Minneapolis: Fortress Press, 2005), 24.

9. Meyers, *Rediscovering Eve*, 143.

10. Meyers, *Rediscovering Eve*, 122.

beneficiaries of resource extraction and processing, needs the state to maintain its scale and regularize its modes of production. Industry also reclaims the husbands—in the sense of husbandry—as workers, fostering intimate solidarity among men. The state amplifies these affiliations through conscription and iconic representation of the military. In place of singular soldiers who carry the banner of the nation, households sponsored militias that fought decidedly local battles. A militia must defend its territory and may try to expand it, but its violence remains confined within a particular radius. The thrust of Joshua involves transforming the victories of such militias into a story of national conquest. For this reason, its battles are local and its army nearly characterless; it also explains why the later chapters punctiliously record land claims—in order to placate the very families who pledged their militias to the kingdom in the name of defense or expansion. We can then shift our thinking to consider the simultaneity and ongoing interaction of households and the state based on the evidence that the statist narrative of Joshua attests to the persistence of the household, a move likely intended to appease its leaders and maintain their support.[11] As I build on her pathbreaking work, I diverge from Meyers in recognizing the endurance of local systems during the upheavals of nationalization, commercialization, and ancient industrialization.[12] No matter the grandeur of its aspirations, the state must still try to feed its people or empower those who do.

The Household

It is the institution of the household, rather than the term "woman," that seems to signify continued female political engagement with the state. For example, Deuteronomy 12 summons "you and *the households* with which God has blessed you" to "the place God chose from out of all your tribes to put His name" (Deut 12:5–7). Indeed "the households" seem subsidiary to the central male addressee, "you," and the metonymic continuum of house and woman is not without its problems, but the household registers in the national public

11. Chapman's work enables us to see how biblical narrative records the component units of the household. Importantly, she recovers "a noisy, fully peopled house" from "the biblical patriline" with "a series of maternally aligned kin groups with specific kinship labels that delineate maternal sub-houses within the larger house of the father." *House of the Mother*, 2.

12. This remains consistent with Meyers's insistence on "intersecting systems and multiple loci of power." *Rediscovering Eve*, 198.

realm and bears traces of female leadership. As particular households absorb national norms, they also exert influence on the nation. When biblical texts bring us into individual homes, we can see the strategic, political acts of women like Rahab, Achsah, Yael, Delilah, Michal, Abigail, and Bathsheba.

Mieke Bal's work on the book of Judges reveals the lethal dimension of the home for women.[13] Jepthah's daughter (whom Bal names Bath), Samson's wife (Kallah), and the Levite's concubine (Beth) number among the women of marriageable age who are destroyed in and around the household. Because the house represents lineage—for example, the House of David—as well as position in a clan, fathers and husbands compete for their place as well as their future through the bodies of nubile women. In each case, the house cannot stand under the pressure. The young women die instead of giving birth, and Israel splits into opposing armies as a result of the toppled houses (Judg 20). Adding another layer to Bal's analysis, I propose that the repeated attack on the home represents a nationalist attempt to dissolve the authority of a local site of power. That young women repeatedly meet their end at home further proves that female political power constitutes part of the perceived threat to the nation posed by the household.

The homes of Yael and Delilah, Bal shows, display a reverse dynamic in which women with sexual experience bring about the demise of men.[14] As their homes enter the sphere of war, Yael and Delilah take part in national political maneuvering. This is likewise the case in the only home portrayed in the book of Joshua, that of Rahab the Canaanite. Prior to Israel's march into the land, Joshua sends two spies from the encampment across the Jordan. They go directly to "the house of a woman" (Josh 2:1) positioned in the wall of Jericho (Josh 2:15).[15] Rahab, the woman in question, protects the spies and sets events in motion so that the selfsame wall where she makes her home will come tumbling down. Why would this woman of Jericho want to fell her defining wall?

This scene on which the plot of Joshua depends dramatizes the process through which households scattered among the regions of Canaan sacrificed some of their autonomy in order to confederate and thereby hope to weather

13. Mieke Bal, *Death and Dissymmetry: The Politics of Coherence in the Book of Judges* (Chicago: University of Chicago Press, 1988).

14. Bal, *Lethal Love.*

15. This rare domestic scene illustrates Baker's point that "the 'house,' whether in the village, city, or in the form of a rural villa or farmstead, was rarely a place set aside from society." *Rebuilding the House*, 38.

repeated imperial siege. The tumbling walls of Jericho then symbolize the absorption of Canaanite households and cities into the nation and the army of Israel. When Rahab brings down the barrier, it indicates her alliance along with that of other urban and rural families. The miraculous tale of ritual encirclement and holy noise that shakes the walled city to its foundation contains a quieter scene of negotiation in which Rahab stipulates the terms of alliance as requiring the survival of her household and her leadership of it. The wall may crumble, but the independence of the household endures.

Postcolonial interpretations of the story have discovered a typology in which a native woman aids and abets the colonizers of her land. Like Cortés's translator Dona Marina (La Malinche) or Pocahontas with John Smith, Rahab betrays her people in order to be translated into a new political order.[16] The stock character is a woman, many would argue, because the indigenous people whose land is penetrated by settlers figure as natural, passive, and therefore gendered as feminine. In such readings, one woman stands in for all the local people at the same time that only a woman who can be overcome sexually and domesticated through marriage can be absorbed into settler society. Musa Dube reads Rahab as a "patriarchal construction of land possession rhetoric at critical moments of imperial attack."[17] Judith McKinlay takes Rahab as a projection of colonial standards onto a native.[18] As the text assimilates only the native who colludes with invaders, the standards of inclusion necessitate treason at the same time that the story affects a manner of colonial self-congratulation for acceptance.[19] Another turn of postcolonial analysis

16. On the relationship of Cortés and Dona Marina, see Stephen Greenblatt, *Marvelous Possessions: The Wonder of the New World* (Chicago: University of Chicago Press, 1991), 142. On the analogy between Rahab and Pocahontas, see Lori L. Rowlett, "Disney's Pocahontas and Joshua's Rahab in Postcolonial Perspective," in *Culture, Entertainment and the Bible*, ed. George Aichele (Sheffield: Sheffield Academic Press, 2000), 66–75. Despite the implied erotic charge and some boasts in the memoirs of Cortés and John Smith, both Dona Marina and Pocahontas are recorded as marrying other colonial men. The Bible never speaks of Rahab marrying, but the Talmud weds her to none other than Joshua (BT Megillah 14b). Rowlett also notes the fact that Rahab appears in the Matthean genealogy (Matt 1), implying that she "gave [her] body willing to the colonizer for reproduction." "Disney's Pocahontas," 74.

17. Musa W. Dube, "Rahab Says Hello to Judith: A Decolonizing Feminist Reading," in *The Postcolonial Biblical Reader*, ed. R. S. Sugirtharajah (Malden, MA: Blackwell Publishing, 2006), 142–158.

18. Judith E. McKinlay, "Rahab: A Hero/ine?," *Biblical Interpretation* 7, no. 1 (1999): 44–57.

19. Jennifer Wright Knust calls Rahab the "ideal Canaanite collaborator" in *Unprotected Texts: The Bible's Surprising Contradictions about Sex and Desire* (New York: Harper One, 2011), 133.

recognizes how the encounter between the spies and Rahab produces the categories of native and colonizer, Canaanite and Israelite. The contact is necessary in order for Israel to configure a coherent identity so Rahab, the woman of Jericho, becomes Canaanite as a constitutive reflex. But later, the book of Joshua explains, she becomes a part of Israel. Both turns—the definitional and the absorptive—establish structures of domination over people and place. Erin Runions, sensing humor at play, sees the episode in Rahab's house as blocking the reflex of disgust to the representation of Canaanite racialized sexuality: exactly as the text problematizes the Canaanite household (standard translations take Rahab to be a prostitute), it also becomes subject to toleration in terms of a role-reversing site of humor.[20]

These critiques vitally unpack the significance of the native woman among a colonizing army, but are imprecise in the case of Rahab. Attending to the story without its later parallels opens up a power dynamic not limited to domination. Indeed, the status of "native" is problematized through the ambiguous designation of Rahab as a prostitute, but, since all other Canaanites are slated for annihilation, it stands as more likely that gender here poses the main issue for the writers. As they are busy configuring Israel as an army, the writers almost seem to resent having to credit a female head of household with the origin of landed Israel. Yet, because the nation's constitutive needs require it, they foreground the importance of female volition. Their resentment about having to do so, I suggest, comes through the charge of transactional sexuality that they level against her. We might even understand the charge of prostitution in political terms—the household maintained several alliances and was open to multiple partners. As promiscuous as the editors found the household to be, they admit with the story of Rahab that it is the building block—even the birthplace—of the nation. The homeland begins in a woman's home. Rahab's survival marks the continued presence of non-Israelites—likely anticentralizing parties rather than ethnic others—in the land and the continuation of the household as a site of authority. On the level of narrated events, Rahab facilitates the conquest at the same time that she remains present in the space of the land. On the level of political rhetoric, Rahab indicates the persistence of the household—a site of female authority—during a process of

20. "It uses humor to represent the racialized nonheteronormative subject positively, and it undercuts the positive aura surrounding the Israelites' conquest." Erin Runions, "From Disgust to Humor: Rahab's Queer Affect," *Postscripts: A Journal of Sacred Texts and Contemporary Worlds* 4, no. 1 (2008): 43.

nationalization.[21] In the reciprocity through which Rahab shields her life and those of her relatives along with the autonomy of the household, we can discern the force of her authority.

Having set first foot in the land, Joshua's spies fumble as they are detected and identified by the King of Jericho. Rahab's house serves as their refuge, where she hides them like Yocheved, Moses's mother, did when Pharaoh's men came to her door. Used only in the two cases, the verb for this type of protection alludes to Rahab's maternal relationship to the spies.[22] She protects her house from search or seizure by sending the king's men out to the river crossings in pursuit of spies cowering on her roof. When she ascends to address them, her voice shifts to a prophetic idiom.[23]

> I know that God has given you the land because fear of you has fallen upon us and because all the inhabitants of the land melt before you. We have heard how Yahweh dried up the waters of the Red Sea in front of you when you went out of Egypt and what you have done to Sihon and Og, the two Amorite kings on the east side of the Jordan. . . . No one felt the spirit stir within because of you; for Yahweh, your God, is the God of the heavens above and the earth below. (Josh 2:9–11)

Rahab interprets prior events as signs of the future, noticeably speaking of God more than any Israelite to date. Where Joshua has drawn sharp distinctions between the east and west banks of the Jordan (Josh 1:12–18), Rahab connects them in the same political drama that, she predicts, will culminate in the replacement of the status quo by a nation of Israel.

Hardly a pliant inhabitant, Rahab next outlines the terms of such an outcome. "Now vow to me in the name of God that as I have behaved kindly toward you, so shall you behave kindly toward my household [בית אב/*beit av*] and give me a verifying sign" (Josh 2:12). Her expectation of reciprocity is notable: just as she saved the spies from the guards of Jericho, so should her relatives and clan be spared the military onslaught. Such reciprocity resonates

21. Her importance, and that of women more generally within the household, is emphasized when Joshua's spies rescue "Rahab, her father, her mother, her brothers, all that belonged to her, and her whole family [*mishpacha*]" from the burning city (Josh 6:23). This list reverses the order familiar from Deuteronomy in which the male head of household always comes first.

22. ותצפנו appears in Joshua 2:4–5 and Exodus 2:2. See Tikva Frymer-Kensky, "Reading Rahab," in *Tehillah Le-Moshe: Biblical and Judaic Studies in Honor of Moshe Greenberg*, ed. Mordechai Cogan, Barry Eichler, and Jeffrey Tigay (Bloomington: Indiana University Press, 1997), 59.

23. Frymer-Kensky, "Reading Rahab," 62.

beyond the immediate characters to suggest mutual leverage by representatives of the household and the state. Rahab's incorporation in the collective at hand is verified by a scarlet rope tied to her window, a sign made famous through its adaptation as the scarlet letter of Hester Prynne. Couched in the formula of a vow, the terms of Rahab's agreement sound tamely legitimate, yet the plot hinges on its more subversive elements. To begin, Rahab dictates the conditions of Israel's entry into Canaan. She will allow the spies to return to Joshua and initiate the conquest so long as they absorb her household into their nation. Her enabling narrative thus reconfigures the distinction between Israel and the peoples of Canaan such that Israel's presence in the land depends upon entrance of its residents into the community. Vitally, at this formative moment when the agency of tribal leaders and individual Israelites gives way to the command of Joshua, Rahab exerts her autonomy in order to preserve the social unit of utmost importance. In this way, Rahab's household becomes a locus of power in the land, and the nation of Israel begins in the house of Canaan (Josh 6:22–25).

Much more than a domicile, the protected household commands influence in a composite, contingent political system. The term designating the household safeguarded by Rahab—בית אב/*beit av*—marks the very institution that lays claim to a tract of land, its yield, and its workers. Described as a head of the household, Rahab makes provision for the continuation of the social institution that defines her power.[24] The spies agree to her terms, pledging their loyalty so long as Rahab does not betray them. Then Rahab appears to give birth to the nation of Israel as she propels its spies from her window on a scarlet cord. Hanging from the cord, the men hash out the terms of alliance in finite detail as if to prolong the connection. They set limits on their mercy by insisting that every member of the household to survive must gather in her actual house and by releasing themselves from the oath if her behavior changes (Josh 2:18–20). As Ilana Pardes has observed, the entire beginning of Joshua depicts national birth, most dramatically when the waters of the Jordan break open before the People of Israel.[25] This smaller-scale emergence from a

24. Rowlett, "Inclusion, Exclusion," 70. This is similarly the case in Assyria: "From the Neo-Assyrian period, there is also evidence regarding female tribal leaders. Numerous Chaldean, Aramaen, and Arabic tribes wielded considerable influence in Mesopotamia during the first millennium. Some of these tribes had female leaders." Saana Svärd, "Political Leadership: Ancient Near East," in *The Oxford Encyclopedia of the Bible and Gender Studies*, ed. Julia M. O'Brien (Oxford: Oxford University Press, 2014), 1:18–19.

25. Ilana Pardes, "Imagining the Birth of Ancient Israel: National Metaphors in the Bible," in *Cultures of the Jews: Mediterranean Origins*, ed. David Biale (New York: Schocken Books, 2002), 9–42.

woman's home commands its own significance as a metaphor for the support and protection provided by the households of Israel. Rahab's harboring of the spies and narration of Israel's recent past indicate two maneuvers crucial for state centralization: allied households offering their protection, and local leaders inflecting the founding narrative. The story presents a subnational view in which the state in the making depends upon the alliance of component groups that, in turn, preserve their autonomy at a local scale. Rahab indexes their interests in the story of military founding. The image of Rahab giving birth to the spies thus suggests that the people of Israel come into being in a local, Canaanite space and that the alliance of households is what makes the state possible. Rahab is the agent of change from a local city-state to a nation; Israel builds on her story as she subscribes to the new system.

The Spring

Amidst the litany of boundary lines and major cities, the landscape gains texture through the names of mountains, valleys, and other geographic features. Rarely mentioned are water sources so vital to human survival and so valuable in a dry region. A reasonable explanation might hold that archaeological evidence for the use of cisterns to collect rain water in Canaan shows this technology to have been more important than settlement near sources of water, but we should resist this line of thinking and, as with Rahab and the household, look to the story of Achsah for insight into the negotiation of water rights. Not surprisingly, the question of water arises when it comes to rocky lands of Judah in the south. On the level of plot, the characters who determine sites of settlement and access to water include the aging Joshua, his old spy partner Caleb, Caleb's daughter Achsah, and her kinsman husband Othniel. In analyzing the story, we observe how the incomplete nature of the conquest reveals the absence of an ethnically or politically homogeneous Israel and how the book of Joshua balances various territorial and historical traditions in order to satisfy a range of constitutive members.

Among the groups mentioned in the narrative mapping of southern lands appear the People of Judah; the nation of Edom, whose presence sets a border due to its resolute difference; dispossessed giants in the city of Hebron; the Jebusites identified with Jerusalem; a Judahite subgroup named the Kenizzites; and other clans that comprise Judah.[26] Certain locations named in the

26. Noth spoke of a southern six-tribe amphictyony around Hebron consisting of Judah, Simeon, Levi, Calebites, Kenites, and Jerahmeelites.

southern border lists reference episodes in the first half of Joshua. The northern border of Judah, for example, runs from the stone of Bohan the son of Reuben before arriving at Devir, the Valley of Achor (the Valley of Trouble), and Gilgal (Josh 15:5–7). Yohanan Aharoni takes the mention of "the stone of Bohan the son of Reuben" as one of the "clear witnesses to the connections between [the tribes of] Reuben and Judah."[27] Devir is the city formerly known as "Kiriath-Sepher," conquered by Caleb's relative, Othniel (Josh 15:15–17). The first half of Joshua makes the Valley of Achor infamous as the site where Achan, violator of the ban, was stoned to death, and Gilgal is Israel's first camp in the land of Canaan where the shame of enslavement rolled off the bodies of Joshua's army. It appears that local traditions are placed in combination to create the borders of Judah and then expanded to provide the southern borders of the land at large. The mention of such symbolic sites further points to the adaptation of etiological tales into the episodes of the conquest. So, for example, a regional story about a transgressor whose actions characterize a rocky, steep valley—the Valley of Achor (Valley of Trouble)—becomes a decisive event in Israel's foundational war. In its final sweep, the border stretches all the way to the Mediterranean, "the Great Sea" that encompasses "all the clans of the People of Judah" (Josh 15:12).

The dialogues between Caleb and Joshua and then Achsah and Caleb dramatize how a group like the Kenizzites joined the federation of Judah—and, by implication, how one like the Jebusites did not—and how a Kenizzite household found its place in the social structure. As the aged general doles out lands to loyal fighters, the only other surviving member of his generation stands to recall earlier days. Flanked by the people of Judah, Caleb the Kenizzite hearkens back to the time of Moses when only he and Joshua believed in the conquest, an unpopular position among a generation not inclined toward war.[28] With the hindsight of an eighty-five-year-old man, he recalls being a spry forty-year-old walking across the land and returning to Moses with solid

27. "On the boundary between Judah and Benjamin lay the Valley of Achor (Josh. 15.7), where Achan the son of Carmi from the tribe of Judah was stoned (Josh. 7.26), Carmi also being one of the leading clans of Reuben (Gen. 46.9; Num. 26.5–6; 1 Chron. 5.3). . . . The tradition is also interesting that at Migdal-eder, in the vicinity of Jerusalem, Reuben lay with Bilhah, his father's concubine (Gen. 35.21), a deed which brought his father's curse upon his head." Yohanan Aharoni, *The Land of the Bible: A Historical Geography*, rev. ed., trans. A. F. Rainey (Philadelphia: The Westminster Press, 1979), 208.

28. Mention of his Judahite crew suggests an editorial hand that linked traditions about the Kenizzite chieftain with the southern tribe. In Joshua 21, Caleb, along with the Priests, lives in

intelligence. What a spy he made! Unbowed by "my brothers who traveled with me then terrified the people," Caleb held to his martial vision, insisting that Israel march forward into the land no matter the obstacles (Josh 14:8). Caleb's commitment to conquest has served him well, and he now marshals the land grant bestowed on him by Moses: "The land on which you walked will be your territory and that of your descendants forever because you followed Yahweh your God" (Josh 14:9; see Deut 1:36). The specific terrain on which Caleb walked was that of Hebron and its environs. Where his fellow spies perceived primordial monsters, Caleb saw a place that could be vanquished. Ultimately, his attention to material conditions, rather than mythic fears, won him the right to possess it as territory. Lest his old partner in espionage forget as he parcels up the spoils, Caleb had a place well before the conquest began.

If Joshua is the arch-nationalist, then Caleb is every bit the venerable tribal leader with whom the state must contend. Rhetorically, he exerts his power with a great deal of humility and charm. His good fortune depends entirely on God, "who has kept me alive as He said" these additional forty-five years, after which he finds himself "as strong today as I was on the day Moses sent me, my battle strength now is as it was then" (Josh 14:10–11). Caleb gives two reasons why Joshua should "now" give him the mountainous Hebron area: "God promised me on that day" and "you heard that day that the Anakites live there" (Josh 14:12).[29] In line with what Joshua heard, Hebron remains populated by giant native Anakites who live in huge, fortified towns. Caleb reasons that, based on his past luck and current vigor, "maybe God will be with me and I will drive them out as God has commanded" (Josh 14:12). Joshua grants Caleb's request, and Caleb son of Yephuneh the Kenizzite comes to dwell in Hebron, formerly Kiriyat-Arba—"home of the biggest giants"—until today

---

the region of "Mount Judah," suggesting that his encircling cohort in the scene above may be an anthropomorphizing of the mountain range into a tribe (Josh 21:11–12).

29. The astonishing use of the verb "heard" here implies Joshua's audience at the telling of the spies' story of the land rather than participation. Caleb here speaks of "large, fortified cities," a slight reversal of "the fortified cities, very big" recounted by the spies upon their return (Numbers 13:28). This type of reversal, according to Yair Zakovitch, marks a syntactical form indicating quotation. Particularly significant is the status of the Hebron report as narrative rather than experience. See Zakovitch, "Humor and Theology or the Successful Failure of Israelite Intelligence: A Literary-Folkloric Approach to Joshua 2," in *Text and Tradition: The Hebrew Bible and Folklore*, ed. Susan Niditch, SBL Semeia Series (Atlanta: Scholars Press, 1990), 75–98.

(Josh 14:15).[30] Even as Caleb's association with Hebron becomes authorized by a central authority (Josh 14:14), an alternate charter exists that bumps him to peripheral fields and villages alone while conferring the city of Hebron on the direct descendants of Aaron the High Priest among the Kohathite clans of the Levites (Josh 21:10–11). These highly specific claimants gain their rights based on Hebron's status as a city of refuge where accidental murderers can escape vengeance and thus, it seems, live under Priestly oversight (Josh 21:13). Such overlaps point toward simultaneous seats of authority of a local and a ritual-legal nature and, likely, to divergent claims.

When combined with the story of Caleb's scouting mission (Numbers 13:22), his dialogue with Joshua reads as a hero legend of how an ancestor secured territory for his descendants. Mighty at eighty-five, Caleb steps forward to receive his due and then fells the land's biggest giants (Josh 15:14). In place of Joshua bringing down giants to usher in an era of peace (Josh 11:21–23), this tradition ascribes these founding actions to Caleb (Josh 14:12–15; 15:14). On this count, Joshua and Caleb are both contradictory and complementary heroes. Although Joshua is credited with striking down the giants of Hebron (and everywhere else) and Caleb bears the same honor, the text reconciles their claims and presents them as parallel warriors. As joint opponents of the popular movement against conquest, Caleb achieves on a smaller scale what Joshua does for the nation (Josh 15:14–15). By cutting down giants and quieting the din of war, Joshua and Caleb model the figure of warrior-settler. However, even as the text aligns Caleb with a national program and roots him "in the midst of the people of Judah" (Josh 15:13), his position within a local order

30. A tradition or genealogy involving Kiriat-Arba, Anakites, and Hebron appears twice in terms that are difficult to untangle with narrative logic. Joshua 14:15 explains, "The previous name of Hebron was Kiriat-Arbah, he was the biggest man among the Anakites." I have rendered this "home of the biggest giants" above. Joshua 15:13 states, "Kiriat-Araba father of the Anakites [or 'the giant father' or 'father of the giant'] is Hebron." The New Jewish Publication Society translates this, "Arba was the father of Anak." The subsequent verse extols Caleb's dispossession of "Sheshai, Ahiman, and Talmai," called both "people of the Anakites" and "children of Anak" (Josh 15:14). The description of cities assigned to the Priests bumps Caleb out of Hebron proper and emplaces him in the surrounding countryside. Joshua 21:10–13 depicts "the sons of Aaron from the clan of Kehat from the people of Levi" receiving "Kiriat-Arba the giant father, it is Hebron in Mount Judah" from Eleazar the Priest, Joshua son of Nun, and the heads of the ancestral houses (Josh 21:10–11). Caleb's holding is then restricted to "the fields of the city and its satellites" (Josh 21:12). The following verse cites Hebron as a sanctuary city for accidental murderers (Josh 21:13).

becomes apparent. Biblical texts obscure this fact through the reiteration of Caleb's connection to Judah (Josh 15:1–15) and admit to it by repeatedly labeling him the Kenizzite (Josh 14:6, 14).[31] Rather than an exceptional or marginal case, Caleb is best understood as a representative of the kind of local claims that the book of Joshua assembles in order to depict a national narrative.

The story of how Achsah the daughter of Caleb acquires water rights represents the reconciliation of overlapping territorial claims.[32] Married to her relative Othniel as a prize for the conquering of Kiriyat-Sefer (Debir), Achsah returns to her father Caleb in order to renegotiate the borders of her land. She explains the deficiency of her patrimony: "You have given me away as Negev [desert] land, now give me springs of water" (Josh 15:19). Understanding what it takes to survive in the desert, Caleb redistributes a water system with upper and lower springs (Josh 15:16–19; Judg 1:12–15). As one of the few women depicted in the book of Joshua speaks to a collective need, water rights are negotiated within a nonmilitary discourse.[33] This dialogue that pertains to water rather than war stands out in a book focused on battle. The text introduces a female speaker who is, therefore, not a soldier in order to show that no matter the conquering army, access to water concerns everyone present. Water acquisition is a local procedure involving negotiation. After the battles, a young woman faces the necessary fact of residence: everyone has to draw from existing sources of water. This need, more tangible than the national narrative, forms the basis of a regional system. Where Achsah's gender signals the more inclusive nature of regional claims, Caleb's ethnic label points to how the book of Joshua absorbs disparate groups into a national formulation.[34] In

31. "The plural gentilic adjective 'kenizzites' surfaces but once (Gen 15:19), within a promise that Yahweh makes to Abraham in a theophany. Listed in the second position, this is one of ten peoples whose land Yahweh intends to deliver to Abraham's descendants." J. Kenneth Suntz, "Kenaz," in *The Anchor Bible Dictionary*, ed. David Noel Freedman (New York: Doubleday, 1992), 4:17. Numbers 32:12 identifies Caleb in the same way, although Numbers 13:6 presents him as the representative scout of the tribe of Judah.

32. The story is couched between the account of Caleb, Joshua's scout in arms, banishing giants from Kiriath-Arba (Josh 15:13–14) and the confession of an eternally divided Jerusalem (Josh 15:63).

33. This role is consistent with how "women's networks" operate in "traditional societies" to resolve "issues such as water rights, allocation of resources, military action, and leadership positions." Meyers, *Rediscovering Eve*, 143.

34. "The major clans of Judah, according to the genealogical list in Chronicles, Jerahmeel, Ram, and Caleb (1 Chron. 2:1, 8, 25, 27, 43), are foreign and were created by assimilation with

other words, Caleb, Othniel, and Achsah are outsiders who comprise the internal terrain of Israel. They are the figures with which the book of Joshua creates a tribe of Judah and a People of Israel.[35] Their status as Kenizzites/Judahites/People of Israel highlights the local, intersectional nature of their claims, as well as an Israel comprised of multiple, shifting participants.[36]

The archaeologist and biblical geographer Yohanan Aharoni (about whom more in the next chapter) noticed the lack of "internal Judean boundaries even for the tribes that had become attached to Judah, e.g. Simeon, Caleb, Kenaz, etc.," as well as an absence of external borders for the tribe as a whole. "The southern, eastern and western boundaries of Judah are identical with those of the land of Canaan, and that on the north corresponds to the southern boundary of Benjamin."[37] Even the conception of Jerusalem seems more Benjaminite than Judahite. If the push toward nationalization emerges from Judah, then why do its boundaries lack distinctive contours? Differentiating among the territorial lists, boundary inventories, and city lists of Joshua 13–19, Norman Gottwald points out that "the city lists for the southernmost tribes are fullest, while none at all survives for Ephraim."[38] In short, cities appear as more important than tribal borders in the south.[39] The city list is indeed

various peoples in the south and in the Negeb: Edomites, Midianites, Horites, Ishmaelites, and others." Weinfeld, *Promise of the Land*, 115.

35. "The Judahites took possession of the land of Jerusalem south of the city, and Bethlehem became their centre. The more southerly hills of Judah fell to other tribes who eventually became attached to Judah. The hill country from Hebron southward went to the Calebites, including the district of Debir which fell to their relatives the Kenazites. The genealogical tables (I Chron. 2; 4) also show us that the district of Hebron and the hill country south of it were occupied by Calebite families. . . . Still farther to the south were the areas of Jerachmeelites and the Kenites . . . these two tribes [Judah and Simeon] were already connected with the tribal covenant; and therefore, in the final analysis, they are counted with the twelve tribes of Israel while the rest of the southern tribes are joined to them and recorded as their sons in the genealogical tables." Aharoni, *Land of the Bible*, 215.

36. According to Esau's genealogy, the Kenizzites are descendants of Edom, Israel's rival (Genesis 36:11, 15, 42).

37. Aharoni, *Land of the Bible*, 253.

38. Norman K. Gottwald, *The Tribes of Yahweh: A Sociology of the Religion of Liberated Israel, 1250–1050 B.C.E.* (Maryknoll, NY: Orbis Books, 1979), 156.

39. Albrecht Alt argued that the boundary lists are premonarchic and that the city lists are from the reign of Josiah (620 BCE). "Das System der Stammesgrenzen im Buche Josua," in *Beiträge zur Religionsgeschichte und Archäologie Palästinas*, ed. A. Jirku (Leipzig: Festschrift E. Selling, 1927), 13–24.

extensive (Josh 15:21–63). This may imply the importance of city-states or a city-state model in the south or that the officials of southern cities that provided a substantive tax base required acknowledgment as a precondition to their enlistment in a southern federation. Whatever the case, southern space is organized according to an urban paradigm in which areas are defined in terms of a central city with satellite fields ("daughters" of the city). It is within such lands where women like Achsah ensure access to water and the potential for their household production to thrive.

The City

Many biblical texts express an anti-urban, or at least deeply skeptical, view of cities. The chosen configuration of sanctified place throughout the Hebrew Bible is "the land," which perhaps shows how terrain, more than cities, can be conjured to represent a nation. Most famously, the urban Tower of Babel parodies the Babylonian Empire for hubristic claims on the speakers of varied languages and architectural aspirations to reach God. As its builders are scattered from the partially built tower, the editors of Genesis reject empire and turn toward Abraham as representative of a national alternative. His brush with Pharaoh's court, along with his nephew's lamentable choice to live near the city of Sodom, reinforces the favoring of rural outposts, mountains, and villages. Yet Abraham's visits to Jerusalem confer its name: first he gains blessing from the king/priest Melchizedek of Salem, then he appends Jeru/*yireh* when he is seen by an angel and sees the God who both orders and halts the sacrifice of his son. These stories encapsulate the paradox that biblical writers are not fond of cities, but their theology, as it were, takes form through descriptions of Jerusalem. At times, they can step out of the paradox by emphasizing, as with Shechem in the book of Joshua, its mountainous character or by calling it Zion, such that it seems a place apart, but this holy city continues to generate tension.

In the book of Joshua, the trouble with Jerusalem and with cities in general arises from their mixed nature and tendency to draw in different peoples. As sites of contact, exchange, and intermingling, cities don't easily bend to a singular character, which poses a representational challenge. In part, this explains why the book of Joshua, focused as it is on depicting "all the land" and collective unity through the image of the army, doesn't dwell in Jerusalem. When it does, the split nature of the city always leaps to the fore. Ultimately, the Deuteronomistic writers and their literary heirs cope with the divided city of

Jerusalem through their own bifurcations, separating the palace and the bustle around it from the Temple. The book of Joshua knows no Temple, speaking instead of regional shrines like Gilgal, Shiloh, Shechem, and Hebron. With the task of raising a permanent sanctuary left for the era of kings, the writers of Joshua have no recourse to divinity and therefore must deal most directly with the antagonistic urbanity of Jerusalem.

Textual friction arises from the disputed lists of claimants and the discrepant acknowledgments of sovereignty. In Joshua, the Jebusite presence in Jerusalem is the most stable tradition about the city. Where Joshua 10 grants a decisive victory over the king of Jerusalem and his league to the national army, Joshua 15 records the continuous failure of Judah to dominate the city. In this way, a rather static inventory of cities undoes the high action of Joshua's southern campaign. The image of a shared Jerusalem suggests a system of cohabitation that undermines the explicit narrative of conquest. It may further dissipate ethnic interpretations of Joshua insofar as the Jebusite sovereigns appear as a parallel faction that neither allies with nor opposes Judah, remaining outside the state but inside the city. The People of Judah could well have been their fellows who took up the causes of God and monarchy to diverge politically from their neighbors. In this picture, Jebusites, along with Judahites and more recalcitrant Benjaminites who ultimately confederate, dwell in Jerusalem as they affiliate with different political causes. Although Jebusite stakes to the city appear to be older, there is no reason to understand the difference among these groups as primarily ethnic.

One of the tribe of Judah's boundaries skirts "the Jebusites, that is Jerusalem" (Josh 15:8), meaning that Judah's territory comes close, but does not encompass its eventual capital. Joshua 15:63 attests to the Jebusite presence in Jerusalem despite the attempts of the Judahites to expel them, so "the Jebusites dwell with the People of Judah in Jerusalem until today." Joshua 18, which enumerates the overlapping boundaries of Benjamin and Judah, emplaces Jerusalem in Benjamin's domain, but refers to it gentilically as "the Jebusite city, that is Jerusalem" without hesitation or mention of divide (Josh 18:28).[40] These variations record the coextant claims to the Jebusite city by the centralizing party boosted by the writers of Joshua, the leaders of Judah, and the tribe of Benjamin.

The opening story in the book of Judges depicts a praiseworthy Judah prevailing over Gaza and subjecting Jerusalem to annihilation: "the People of Judah fought and captured Jerusalem; they subdued it with the sword and set

40. "The inclusion of Jebus (Jerusalem) in Benjamin suits well the assumption that this boundary is Israelite and not Judean." Aharoni, *Land of the Bible*, 254.

the city aflame" (Judg 1:8). This tribal tradition celebrating Judah's mastery of the capital suggests a lack of awareness or disregard for the tale of Joshua's momentous victory over the King of Jerusalem (Josh 10:22–27, 12:10). Furthermore, in the very chapter of Judges that fixes Judah in Jerusalem, a juxtaposed Benjaminite tradition sounds less sanguine: "The People of Benjamin did not dispossess the Jebusite residents of Jerusalem, so the Jebusites dwell with the People of Benjamin in Jerusalem until today" (Judg 1:21). Even the story that attempts to press Judah's right to Jerusalem lapses and admits to a mixed city of Jebusites and Benjaminites.

The Jerusalem of King David intrigues with its familial dramas and internecine schemes, but before these unfold he too must face the Jebusites. 2 Samuel 5 resolutely declares David king "over all Israel and Judah" before sending him to battle over Jerusalem (2 Sam 5:5). According to popular wisdom about the impenetrability of the city—"even the blind and lame will turn you back" (2 Sam 5:6)—David is not expected to prevail, which adds a miraculous dimension to his victory and subsequent establishment of the City of David. This roots human power in a palace built of cedar from Lebanon, but opens a gap where divine sovereignty should rest. King David, feeling guilty about dwelling in a house of cedar while God wanders homeless, proposes that he initiate temple building, but is answered by Nathan the Prophet that the honor will fall to one of his descendants. In the text that later generates ideas about the messiah, God explains Jerusalem's blueprint to David. It pivots on the word "house," employed to show its multiple, simultaneous connotations: rather than moving to a house—i.e., temple—built by David, God pledges to establish a house—i.e., dynasty—for the king. The parallel houses of palace and temple meant to stand in a future Jerusalem signify the twinning of human and divine power in the Davidic dynasty. Amidst such grandiose promises, it would seem that the Jebusite question reaches a definitive resolution. It does not. Instead, David acquires the site of the future temple in a happenstance manner. Like Abraham, David encounters an angel on the sacred mountain—this time a malevolent one mowing people down in outrage about a census—and seeks to halt the spread of death by offering a sacrifice. Before the king builds the altar that will mark the Temple's place, he must purchase the land from Araunah the Jebusite, who has used it as a floor to thresh grains. Araunah behaves in a uniquely generous manner, offering to give the place and the materials for sacrifice to David with wishes that God grant him favor. Even as the royal founder declines the offer and pays a fair price to Araunah, there is no mention that he or other Jebusites vacate Jerusalem.

Other cities in the book of Joshua resemble Jerusalem in these respects. For example, the cities built by the tribes of Gad and Reuben (Num 32:34–36, 37–38; Josh 13:15–28) are commonly attributed to the Moabites (Isaiah 15–16; Jeremiah 48), and the Moabite witness to the period, the Mesha Inscription, lauds Mesha King of Moab's founding of the selfsame towns.[41] Along with the intermingling of groups, cities thus appear as sites of contest among local rulers. We should take the contradictory attributions not only as evidence for competition, but also for the fact that rule over cities fluctuated and was perceived differently by distinct groups. The importance of cities to tribal and regional claims meant that there was no excising them from the territorial descriptions in the second half of Joshua however much countryside better lends itself to indexing the nation.

Focus on Jerusalem allows us to see the layers of claim and composite nature of cities that prove difficult to efface even in the most nationalist of representations. Moreover, even as the city becomes an icon of a dynasty, a state, a people, and a distinct set of beliefs, its mixed nature and history of cohabitation do not evaporate. Deuteronomistic texts like Joshua can sustain both its iconic nature and the lived reality of perennial contact. Only later texts such as Ezekiel's vision in exile or Ezra's record of homecoming empty Jerusalem or problematize other claimants as genetic hybrids in contrast to "the holy seed" (Ezra 9:2). Certainly the Bible contains moments when the icon of Jerusalem overpowers lived reality, but it is acutely significant that the very book celebrating armed takeover of territory repeats contesting claims. No amount of violence can render Jerusalem homogeneous.

The Tribe

How might individual tribes best interact with a central authority? In many ways, this is the question posed as Joshua doles out portions to individual tribes and, on occasion, castigates their perceived shortcomings. The

41. This is the case with Dibon (Isa 12:2; Jer 48:18, 22) and Aroer (Judg 11:26; Jer 48:19). In Joshua 13:24–25, Aroer belongs to "the land of the Ammonites" at the same time that it is granted by Moses to the tribe of Gad. "While Num 32.34 attributes Aroer to Gad, I Chr 5:8 makes it a possession of a descendant of Reuben." Burton MacDonald, *"East of the Jordan": Territories and Sites of the Hebrew Scriptures* (Boston: American Schools of Oriental Research, 2000), 133. Judges 11:33 reports Jephthah's defeat of the Aroer Ammonites.

impending demise of Israel's founding general necessitates the parceling of tribal lands along with recognition of their autonomy as it correlates his individual fragility with the incomplete national conquest. It further expresses an abiding anxiety about centralization—what will happen to a loose alliance of disparate groups in the absence of a strong leader—as well as admission that many neighbors remain who do not number among Israel. We should take the confessions that the conquest didn't meet its aims and that the allegedly exterminated inhabitants persist as strong evidence that, as narrated in the book's first half, centralization did not occur. The narrative tries to ease the friction of promoting centralization while placating adherents by attributing failure to the tribes rather than the army. Because the breach of divine promise at any scale so undermines the aims of the book of Joshua, the admission of non-Israelite neighbors must be understood as reflecting a social reality that simply could not be denied. Insofar as casting aspersion is hardly the best way to placate constituents, the primary state-building agenda of the book also becomes apparent. How dramatic then that the narrative likewise shows the tribes striking back by preserving "diverse sub-histories" and "local decentralized processes" to counter the wholesale "centralization of politics in a government apparatus, and the resulting stimulus to unify the national traditions."[42] Because the local traditions ultimately were preserved by royal scribes seemingly at work in major cities, we can assume that tribal insistence on their inclusion factored as a precondition of allegiance. Thus, the book of Joshua captures political negotiation in an ever-tipping balance of power.

When Joshua confers property, of course, it is with God's authority, so the presence of other peoples sets a limit on tribal and national power alike. God acknowledges the continued existence of Philistines, who pose the biggest threat, "namely, the five lords of the Philistines—the Gazites, the Ashdodites, the Ashkelonites, the Gitties, and the Ekronites" (Josh 13:3). Their presence delimits the span of the Promised Land in its southern reaches and makes for an ongoing contest. Sidonians, in turn, set the northern limit such that the massive victories declared in early chapters over kings of south and north become balanced against the recurrent skirmish required to hold the southern and northern frontiers. After conceding to the soft borders between Israel and these groups, God pledges further dispossession after the tribes settle their apportioned lots (Josh 13:6). This generates the particular border tension born

42. Gottwald, *Tribes of Yahweh*, 172.

from the aspiration for expansion and the acknowledgment of formidable opponents.

The tribes, at least a core five, appear as both strong and constrained by their neighbors. Nili Wazana helpfully explains the sociological arithmetic in which subgroups become absorbed into an equation of two and a half tribes east of the Jordan River and another two and a half to its west. The five central groups are divided such that the eastern tribes—Reuben, Gad, and Half Manasseh perceived as mixed-blood frontier dwellers—are mirrored by "another group consisting of two and a half tribes, yet never designated as such—Judah and the House of Joseph, encompassing Ephraim and the other half of Manasseh."[43] It is important to note that the tribal designations are themselves composite, existing as broad categories to encompass a stream of alliances. This trend is nowhere clearer than in the House of Joseph made up of two subtribes with a fraught connection. However, when all five of the larger tribes stand before Joshua bin Nun, who recognizes their patrimony, the picture is one of cohesion.

As a collective character, the People of Joseph, split between the tribes of Ephraim and Manasseh and forming the key constituency of the northern Kingdom of Israel as Judah does for its southern kingdom, perfectly illustrates the nature of the tribe as a social unit. The north was fertile, wealthy, more religiously open, and less concerned about its dividing lines. The literary scholar Gabriel Josipovici reads the difference between north and south through the Genesis family drama involving Joseph and his brothers, save Benjamin. Joseph may outshine his brothers, flourishing in the Egyptian empire, but Judah's moral authority prevails (Gen 37:26–27).[44] To Josipovici, the eclipse of Joseph's power by Judah's steadfastness bespeaks the historical-geographical destruction of the Kingdom of Israel by the Assyrian Empire around 722 BCE and the attendant push for the survival of Judah and the south. The narrative effects of

43. Wazana, "'Everything Was Fulfilled,'" 18.

44. Gabriel Josipovici, *The Book of God: A Response to the Bible* (New Haven, CT: Yale University Press, 1990), 85. Both Reuben and Judah raise an objection to killing Joseph in cold blood in Genesis 37, which suggests—like the mention of the Stone of Bohan son of Reuben in Judah's border list (Josh 15:6)—an association between the two groups. Frank Moore Cross suggests that when the tribe of Judah eclipsed Reuben, an additional layer favoring Judah was added to these traditions; see "Reuben, the Firstborn of Jacob: Sacral Traditions and Early Israelite History," in *From Epic to Canon: History and Literature in Ancient Israel* (Baltimore: Johns Hopkins University Press, 2000), 53–72.

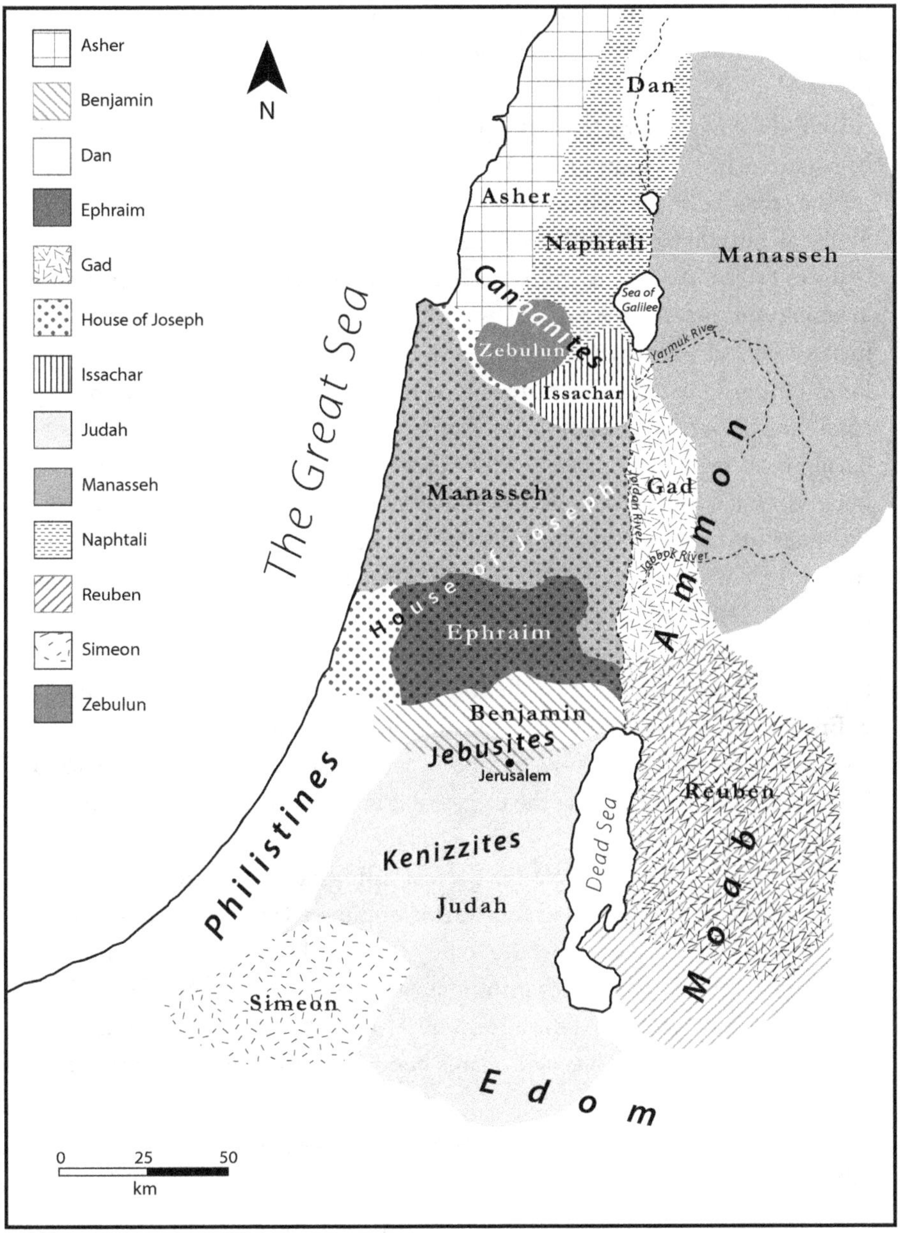

FIGURE 2.1. Map of Tribes and Peoples in Ancient Israel, Roni Blushtein-Livnon.

this cataclysmic event include the subordination of the People of Joseph's traditions and critical charges against northern syncretism and assimilation. With this in mind, it is highly possible that southerners collated the documents and shaped the story of Israel, but the political movement toward confederation began in the north (Judg 5:14–18).

The tribes of Manasseh and Ephraim are anthropomorphized as the sons of Joseph born in Egypt, with the younger Ephraim, following a pattern, slated to prevail (Gen 48:5, 13–14, 17–20). But, according to the phrase-coining scene in which "shibboleth" becomes a password that distinguishes between eastern men of Gilead absorbed into the tribe of Manasseh and western men of Ephraim (Judg 12:1–6), these brother tribes hate each other with simmering passion. An ancient tradition in the book of Judges even accuses Ephraim of having roots in Amalek, Israel's primordial enemy, but upholding its military duties within a northern confederation all the same (Judg 5:14). The book of Joshua, showing a profound desire to synthesize and integrate, gives them some joint borders (which could drive the aforementioned resentment) (Josh 16:1–8; 17:8–10); an Ephraimite enclave within the territory of Manasseh (Josh 16:9; 17:9); and the shared challenge of Canaanites in the city of Gezer (Josh 16:10). Like Jerusalem in the south, the prominent city of Gezer stands in Ephraimite lands "until today" (Josh 16:10).[45] The text brings up Gezer as a sign of Ephraim's failure as an autonomous tribe, then provides consolation in class terms by insisting that the Canaanites in question are subdued through "forced labor" (Josh 16:10).[46]

The term "Canaanite" accrues quite a different connotation when the People of Joseph describe their formidable opponents with iron chariots who rule in nearby Beit Shean and the Valley of Jezreel (Josh 17:16). In no way subordinate, these Canaanites intimidate and cause the People of Joseph to bewail the deficiency of their allotment.[47] In a challenge to their agency, Joshua responds, "If you are such a large people cramped on the Mountain of

45. Like Jerusalem, contradictory traditions surround Gezer. Joshua 10:33 and 12:12 allege that Joshua razed the city, but Joshua 16:10 and Judges 1:29 portray it as still Canaanite. In 2 Samuel 5:25, David drives out the Philistines from Gezer.

46. Along with these Canaanites, "the Archites at Atarot" and "the Japhletites as far as the border of Lower Beth-horon and Gezer" (Josh 16:2) interrupt the contiguousness of Joseph.

47. In an ironic subversion of the word "one," so often used in the first part of Joshua, Ephraim and Manasseh lament having "one" allotment and "one district" for the two of them (Josh 17:14).

Ephraim, then go to the forest and clear some space there among the Perizzites and Rephaim" (Josh 17:15). The exchange between Joshua and the People of Joseph reveals that no national army rushes out to aid local initiatives and that the mode of settlement, whether through negotiation, accommodation, or skirmish, depends upon the group in question. The Tribe of Manasseh, for example, simply cannot expel neighboring Canaanites no matter the level of imposed oppression (Josh 17:12–13). In the context of Joshua, this bespeaks tribal failure, but I suggest that we understand it as expressing not only the endurance of Canaanites, but also that the politics in question produced its own set of divisions. That is, the very unification of Manasseh and Ephraim as the House of Joseph meant that some groups either chose not to join or, because of their class position, were not extended an invitation. In our passage, the term "Canaanites" seems to hold both meanings. Acknowledgment of Canaanites reverberates in the text, causing recapitulation, even exacerbation, of the primal split between Ephraim and Manasseh (Josh 17:14). When they complain both as individual tribes and as a unified House of Joseph, the upshot is that their shared territory is too small. Since the Canaanites simply cannot be dispossessed, Joshua's solution is twofold: they must expand the frontier by cutting down forests and domesticating the land (Josh 17:18), and he will designate two different allotments for Ephraim and Manasseh (Josh 17:17). Still, these solutions are presented alongside the impossible demand to expel the Canaanites despite their might and iron chariots (Josh 17:18). Without this unreasonable order, the unity of Ephraim and Manasseh, not to mention the book of Joshua itself, seems to have no purpose. In sum, when Joshua promises that the brother tribes will not inhabit the same district, we see a dynamic in which facing allegedly external Canaanites brings up the internal instability in the House of Joseph. At such a moment, the very premise of unity comes into question and then is quickly countered by articulating truculent enmity toward the Canaanites.

At smaller scales, settlement appears to be more contingent. A truncated hero story, for example, tells how a warrior named Machir, the firstborn son of Manasseh, personally conquered the fertile plains of Gilead and Bashan east of the Jordan (Josh 17:1).[48] We also meet a Manassite female clan led by five

48. Machir's initiative distinguishes him from "the remaining Manassites" comprised of clans named Abiezer, Helek, Asriel, Shechem, Hepher, and Shemida.

sisters named Mahlah,[49] Noa, Hoglah,[50] Milcah, and Tirzah,[51] who find themselves in the position of being the only possible inheritors of their family's land.[52] Tradition has it that in order to prevent the loss of their patrimony, the sisters strike a deal with Moses in which women gain the right to legitimately own land so long as they have no brothers and promise to marry their tribesmen (Num 27:8). According to Joshua 17, these "daughters of Manasseh" claim their portion "in the midst of his sons," such that a female clan interacts with others under the umbrella of the Tribe of Manasseh (Josh 17:6). Beyond these more colorful and allusive geographic descriptions, the Manassite territorial picture conforms to the conventions of Joshua. Despite the markers of clear borderlines (Josh 17:7–10a), tribal claims overlap at key sites (Josh 17:10b–11),[53] and Canaanites persist despite imposed submission (Josh 17:12–13). The static borderlines, as we have seen, express a dynamic social reality.

The Map

After the five main houses assume their place in Joshua's map, the text moves to seven smaller tribes—Benjamin, Simeon, Zebulun, Issachar, Asher, Naphtali, and Dan—assembled at the shrine of Shiloh. The fortunes of these tribes appear more uncertain insofar as they depend on a survey project conducted by their own mapmakers. As we have come to expect, this degree of tribal autonomy becomes balanced by actions of the central authority. That is, the tribes may commission their own reconnaissance, but they must return with valid reports to be compiled by Joshua. From their records, Joshua establishes

49. Tamara Cohn Eshkenazi sees the site of Abel-meholah on the western edge of the Jordan as related to the name "Mahlah." See Cohn Eshkenazi, ed., *Torah: A Women's Commentary* (New York: Union of Reform Judaism Press, 2008), 972. To Eshkenazi's suggestion we can add the strategic marriage of Merav, daughter of Saul, to Adriel the Meholathite (1 Samuel 18:19; 2 Samuel 21:8).

50. Hoglah's name appears as a place in the Judahite boundary list (Josh 15:6). Along with Noa, it also appears as a place name in the Samaria Ostraca. See Zechariah Kallai, *Historical Geography of the Bible: The Tribal Territories of Israel* (Leiden: Brill, 1986), 56.

51. Tirzah, mentioned in other biblical passages as a place in the Northern Kingdom (1 Kings 14:17; Song of Songs 6:4), is identified by scholars as Tell 'el-Far'ah near Nablus.

52. The five women are also known as daughters of Zelophehad son of Hepher, son of Gilead, son of Machir, son of Manasseh. A seemingly excessive note about "the *male* clans of the people of Manasseh son of Joseph" (Josh 17:2) alludes to the female claims within the tribe of Manasseh.

53. The tribes of Manasseh, Issachar, and Asher share jurisdiction over towns such as Beit-Shean and Ibleam and the "inhabitants" of towns including "Dor, Ein-dor, Taanach, and Megiddo" (Josh 17:11).

a lottery in which land charters are pooled then randomly drawn by individual tribes. This fascinating scene not only attests to the outsized role of geographical study in establishing land claims (foreshadowing a global history of imperial and national mapping), but also deftly grants legitimacy to regional forms of authority as it asserts the necessity of a federal structure.

The plot that holds these lists of cities, borders, and strangers together provides key evidence for how the groups acceding to the Israelite confederation bring their traditions to bear on the image of national territory and how, in turn, these traditions are woven into the larger narrative about a national homeland. As well as an ingenious technique of harmonizing autonomous areas as parts of a whole, the survey expeditions point to the discursive dimension of territorial acquisition. This means that groups or individuals must first write or speak the name of a place before it can assume the desired character. For this reason, the book of Joshua punctiliously gathers place names in order to bring Israel into being. As we will see in the next chapter, the same technique and the very same names are revived when the Zionist movement restores the state in question. The expedition that Joshua commissions points to the form and function of the book as a kind of survey. The stalwart general instructs the representatives of seven tribes to produce a document outlining seven acceptable parcels; just write the book, he tells them, and the place will come into being. What the surveyors do for the seven tribes, the book of Joshua does for all the groups designated as the People of Israel—create a narrative justification for both presence and limit. Without the survey, the tribes possess no territory, and without the book of Joshua, there is no national homeland.

Tension between an integrated whole and aggregate parts runs through the episode as it presses unity with all the familiar motifs: "The whole community of the People of Israel gathered together at Shiloh where they assembled at the Tent of Meeting. The land lay conquered before them" (Josh 18:1–2).[54] Everyone in the assembled group figures as a potential settler, and Joshua urges them to the task: "For how long will you avoid going out to conquer the land that Yahweh, God of your ancestors, has given you (Josh 18:3)?" To anyone paying attention, the contradiction jumps off the page. How can a conquered land lie fallow before them at the same time that they must go to war to conquer it? Add to the mix the assurance that God grants the land as a perpetual gift and

54. Joshua 18:1 marks the significant place where the word נכבשה/*nichbeshah* is used. The root of this word will grow into כיבוש/*kibbush*, the word that signifies both conquest and occupation.

the place in question seems impossibly complex. The text solves the problem by differentiating between a national war whose success is attributed to God and the recurrent skirmishes required by settlement. At several junctures, however, this distinction breaks down, and settlement emerges as a continuous form of war.

Joshua orders three surveyors from each tribe to "get up, walk about the land, describe it as your own territory, then return to me" (Josh 18:4). Unlike the sacrosanct borders of Judah or the People of Joseph's battle with the forest, the seven tribes must write themselves into the interstices of already defined southern and northern regions. Moreover, with Judah and Joseph out of the equation, the seven tribes cannot bear the name "all Israel," so they are labeled as "the people of Israel according to their divisions," a locution that captures both unity and difference (Josh 18:10). Mention of Israel here carries the double meaning of constituents of the northern kingdom and members of an emerging nation.[55] Scholars have noted how the seven groups from the Canaanite north gathered at Shiloh bear the traces of an ancient tradition absorbed into the book of Joshua.[56] Such a covenant among the seven may well be the basis for the consolidation of tribes into Israel. Among Joshua's borderlines we can recognize the processes through which seven groups allied to become Israel, a host of others merged as Judah, and numerous clans became the tribe of Ephraim and the half-tribe of Manasseh uncomfortably joined as the House of Joseph. These three main units, as well as their subdivisions, all remain players jockeying for territory and influence even when arrayed under the banner of all Israel.

The main themes evident in the surveys compiled by Joshua include the strategic importance of Benjamin, the subsidiary position of Simeon within the tribe of Judah (Josh 19:9), and a lurking disparity between the tranquil description of territories belonging to Zebulun, Issachar, Asher, and Naphtali, and a counter-tradition of ongoing contest with Canaanites in these regions (Judg 1:30–33). L. Daniel Hawk neatly summarizes the structure of the six tribal allotments that follow Benjamin: "The first and last tribes (Simeon and Dan) have inheritance but no boundaries. The second and fourth (Zebulun and Naphtali), however, have clear (if abbreviated) boundaries and separate sections for the towns. The middle tribes (Issachar and Asher), however, mix boundary descriptions

55. That Simeon ultimately becomes absorbed by Judah somewhat troubles this assessment.

56. Aharoni, *Land of the Bible*, 215; Israel Finkelstein, "Saul, Benjamin and the Emergence of Biblical Israel: An Alternative View," *Zeitschrift für die Alttestamentliche Wissenschaft* 123, no. 3 (2011): 355; Gottwald, *Tribes of Yahweh*, 173.

together with town lists."[57] In other words, the notion of a blind lottery promotes an image of symmetry and peace in tribal lands. The greatest friction arises from the preservation of a trace legend about the tribe of Dan.

> The People of Dan lost hold of their frontiers so they went up to fight with Leshem [Laish, Judg 18:7]. They captured it, subjected it to the sword, and claimed it. After they settled there, they called Leshem Dan after Dan their ancestor. (Josh 19:47)

The truncated story of how the Danites captured and inaugurated territory reveals a local process of marking land through naming, as well as the fact that tribes can as easily lose as they can gain land. It would stand out as markedly different enough from the conquest story as to undermine its authority were the editors not so clever. They expertly distinguish between a great war that unequivocally establishes national sovereignty and the contingent nature of settlement. The fact that during settlement sovereignty wavers in uncertainty provides the editors with the perfect out: the tribes fail to uphold the sublime resolve of the army when they sit at home. In this way, the contradiction eases and the kernels of local traditions remain in place in national annals.

Joshua's roster of boundaries concludes with characteristic resolution, framing all that remains disputed with assurances that "God gave Israel the whole country which He swore to their ancestors," "God delivered all their enemies into their hands," and "everything promised came to pass" (Josh 21:41–43). Such declarations weave the disparate parts into a coherent image of space, time, and nation.

Civil War

In sociological terms, Israel's antithetical relationship to the Canaanites sets a boundary with an external group that, in turn, defines the nature of its internal affiliations. Once the boundary is set through stories of war and oaths of enmity, the book turns inward to detail affiliate tribes and territories. The equation might hold together perfectly if the tribal section did not continually collapse the essential difference such that the other peoples of the land appear as proximate neighbors whose presence is stitched through the territories. Beyond the fact that Canaanites declared eliminated persist, they simply don't

57. L. Daniel Hawk, *Joshua in 3-D: A Commentary on Biblical Conquest and Manifest Destiny* (Eugene, OR: Cascade Books, 2010), 175.

seem that different. Certainly, the conjuring of their fearsome iron chariots intimidates and the insinuation of their subservience implies a stratified class system, but these also seem like stereotypes intended to produce a cultural separation where a geographic one does not exist. Content that admits how specific locales do not support the national vision creates the editorial challenge of overriding their contradictory force.

Surprisingly enough, the editors of Joshua do so through a story about how the tribes reach the brink of civil war. However much civil war or its near miss may seem to threaten national unity, the literary scholar Nasser Mufti has explained how the figuration of war as fought between brothers ultimately joins antagonists in common purpose and contrasts them with exterior foes.[58] Because Mufti's initial examples derive from nineteenth-century British literature, the brothers at odds ultimately become legitimate citizens or, at the least, the colonial figures of record like the Boers of South Africa. The colonized subjects, in contrast, become marked as unable to wage a "civil" war with their colonizers. In our case, brotherhood is established between eastern and western tribes that, in turn, categorizes outsiders as Moabites, Jebusites, and Canaanites. Mufti names this "socialization of one's own people through a will-to-difference with a more or less cultivated outside."[59] As we apply his theory to Joshua 22, let us pay particular attention to the rhetoric of averted civil war as an illumination of the book's overarching project to conjoin certain groups and demonize others.

The story of negotiations over an altar at the Jordan River is one of the best in Joshua, but, because I have analyzed it at length elsewhere, I only briefly summarize here.[60] Following the lottery at Shiloh, the wealthy tribes of Reuben, Gad, and half of Manasseh travel home across the river. Soon upon arrival, they build "a highly visible altar" that seems to outdo the one from which they have just departed. Infuriated, the western tribes reconvene at Shiloh to prepare for war. As a warning, they send an esteemed delegation of ten chieftains and the (apparently long-lived) priest Phineas to charge the easterners with treachery, rebellion, and impurity. Their calmly florid response suggests that the two and a half tribes dissemble when they insist that their altar is a mere symbol of their inclusion in Israel. Projecting their concerns beyond the present dialogue, they justify their replica altar as a way to shield their children from future accusations

58. Nasser Mufti, *Civilizing War: Imperial Politics and the Poetics of National Rupture* (Evanston, IL: Northwestern University Press, 2017), 17.

59. Mufti, *Civilizing War*, 7.

60. See Havrelock, "The Other Side," in *River Jordan*, 106–123.

of nonbelonging. The expression of desired filiation in the future placates the western delegation, reestablishing fraternal bonds in the present. The eastern tribes clearly intend for their children to remain in Israel, so both banks of the river erupt into praise for the God who forestalls civil war.

In the next generation, full-fledged civil war will erupt between eastern and western tribes (Judg 12:1–6) and between Benjamin and "all the People of Israel" (Judg 20:1) with Judah in the infantry (Judg 20:18). The rift between north and south endures long enough to erupt into the schism between the Galilean followers of Jesus and the Temple emissaries in Jerusalem, with ramifications for the long history of Christianity and Judaism.[61] But, in the days of Joshua, members of the People of Israel are defined as those with whom negotiation precedes attack. Even if civil war ensues, the covenanted first step is to initiate dialogue. After such a bloody contest with the people of the land, who really has the energy for civil war? Best to accept the intergenerational pledge of allegiance. So, reconciliation becomes the outcome of the first confrontation between brothers in arms. True to Mufti's assessment of nationalism, this ancient case attests to a national formation that relies on a discourse of both "self-perpetuation" and "self-division."[62] The picture of a united Israel depends upon the representation of civil conflict that ultimately produces the tribes as brothers with common interests and enemies. As a nationalist imaginary par excellence, the book of Joshua exposes internal discord in order to contrast it with perpetual war.

How Does It End?

Joshua parts twice from his people with a lengthy speech summarizing the dramatic events of his era. As we will see, this doublet understood by biblical scholars as the product of different literary sources was vital to Prime Minister David Ben-Gurion's theory of eternally indigenous Jews who united with a revolutionary vanguard from the Diaspora. However tailored to his own political agenda, Ben-Gurion's interpretation picked up on the dual agenda of the book of Joshua—asserting a narrative of unity and enlisting constituent groups. Let us now turn to how the book tries to wrap up these dual agendas and where their reconciliation remains incomplete.

61. Daniel Boyarin, *Border Lines: The Partition of Judaeo-Christianity* (Philadelphia: University of Pennsylvania Press, 2004).

62. Mufti, *Civilizing War*, 15.

Unity and cohesion ring as the clarion calls of the first speech: "all Israel" gathers to hear Joshua (Josh 23:2), in all directions enemies sit subdued (Josh 23:1), all other nations have been banished from their presence (Josh 23:3–4), all of the land rests under Israel's control (Josh 23:5–6), and everything promised has reached fulfillment (Josh 23:3, 14). In another verse with deep resonance for modern Israel, God describes its land as stretching "from the Jordan to the Mediterranean," and including "nations that still remain," despite the fact that God resolves to eventually drive them out (Josh 23:4–5). This unique scenario of both complete and partial success results from God's fighting on Israel's behalf, what we would name holy war (Josh 23:3, 10). Because God brought everything to pass, Israel must now uphold its part of the covenantal partnership (Josh 23:16). The key imperative in this regard is to "be very steadfast in both heeding and doing all that is written in the book of the Torah of Moses, do not veer from it to the left or right" (Josh 23:6). To never stray from the Torah means, in this formulation, "never intermixing with these peoples that remain" (Josh 23:7).

The prohibition against intermingling with "these peoples" turns the self-congratulatory speech into a confession of national failures and causes the declaration of total destruction to fall flat. Had all the inhabiting nations actually been destroyed, then there would be no need to forbid contact with them. Thus, the iteration of creed grates against the claims of the conquest. In harping on "the nations that remain," this most nationalist of speeches admits to a varied social world with numerous groups opposed to the project of nationalization. Because the text does not want to traffic in coexistent political structures, the difference becomes rendered in religious terms—the nation of Israel shows (or should show) total fidelity to the God who supports them, while the other nations worship errant gods.

Correct religious practice, in turn, promises to yield political effects: "If only you cling to Yahweh your God as you have done up to today, then God will banish nations strong and great from before you and no man will stand up to you as it has been up to today" (Josh 23:8–9). Attachment to God not only produces social cohesion, but also military success to the point that harmony of worship and unity of war become mutually supportive. When not engaged in war, collective rites will bind the people together. In order to press the principle, the converse is presented: "If you should turn away and cling to these remaining nations—these still in your midst—and marry them so that you intermix, then know for sure that Yahweh your God will not continue to banish these nations from before you" (Josh 23:12–13). To fraternize, not to mention commingle, with those outside the polity is construed as undoing the conquest and its attendant amity. Alliance with these other peoples is "an ensnaring trap" that will bring irritation and pain until it eventually leads to the loss of the land (Josh 23:13). Exactly as "every good thing" transpired in the recent past, so could "every bad thing" erupt with equal measure. With the same lightning speed of the conquest, the land could slip from Israel's hold (Josh 23:16).

The second address so expertly condenses the plot of the Bible that many scholars insist that Joshua once served as the sixth book of the Torah. Content and form align when Joshua marks the People's covenant with God in "a book of divine instruction," attesting to the undeniable power of literary record (Josh 24:26). The differences between the two parting speeches quickly become apparent. His battles are won, so Joshua now behaves like Moses enacting covenant and inscribing law. In contrast to the prior audience of "all Israel" (Josh 23:2), Joshua gathers "all *the tribes* of Israel" at the holy site of Shechem (Josh 24:1). He arrays the people "before God" (Josh 24:1), engages in prophecy (Josh 24:2), recites collective history, and delivers law (Josh 24:25). Memory seems to have altered the nature of conquest since the peoples of the land—"the inhabitants of Jericho, the Amorites, Perizzites, Canaanites, Hittites, Girgashites, Hivites, and Jebusites"—not Israel, are blamed for starting the war (Josh 24:11). Moreover, the army plays a smaller role in this version where God sends "the hornet" before the troops to dispel opponents (Josh 24:12).

The land stretches before Israel like a tabula rasa, offering its gifts without labor or imprint by the people. Providence alone granted the People "a land for which you did not labor, cities that you did not build yet dwell in, orchards and olive groves that you did not plant yet from which you eat" (Josh 24:13). Rather than supporting a complicated present of multiple claimants, this history describes a ghost-land haunted by its expelled builders and planters. In line with our analysis, we should understand the insistence that God bequeathed Israel an already developed land as a nationalist strategy for discounting claims both prior and alternate to specific lands, farms, and cities. By figuring as soldiers alone and thus alienated from the past, Joshua's warriors are uncannily distanced from the land that they conquer.

Their future hinges on a choice: worship idols and "the gods of Amorites in whose land you dwell" or Yahweh. Joshua pledges his fidelity and that of his household (causing us to wonder if Joshua has a wife) to Yahweh as precedent (Josh 24:15) and presents a bevy of reasons: God brought Israel's ancestors out of Egypt, performed great miracles, nurtured the people "on every path we walked and amidst all the peoples through whom we passed" (Josh 24:17), and expelled other peoples from the land (Josh 24:18). Israel follows its leader, pledging, "We too will worship Yahweh because He is our God" (Josh 24:18). Joshua responds with skepticism, warns of the presence of a "holy, jealous" God (Josh 24:19), and assures a "response of malice" in which "God will destroy you after having done you well" should Israel vacate its pledge (Josh 24:20). Echoing the revelation at Sinai, the People resolve to "worship Yahweh our God and to listen to His voice" (Josh 24:24).

Joshua establishes the covenant between the nation and God in writing, as well as in his final memorial stone (Josh 24:26). The stone attests to unity "beneath the terebinth that was in God's temple" in Shechem (Josh 24:26). As with his other stones, this one serves as "a witness, which heard all of God's speech that He spoke with us" and a reminder not to transgress the terms of covenant (Josh 24:27). With the stone firmly planted, Joshua disperses the people to their respective lands (Josh 24:28). The book concludes by acknowledging the power of narrative to create social cohesion even amidst political instability. Joshua's legacy rests safely in the hands of elders who know "everything that God did for Israel" (Josh 24:31) and can therefore lead the People, but the rifts beneath the covenant, as well as the alliances across territory, already run in multiple directions.

3

The Joshua Study Group at the Home of David Ben-Gurion

We have called it Israel since the days of Joshua the son of Nun.

—DAVID BEN-GURION, SPEECH BEFORE THE ANGLO-AMERICAN COMMITTEE OF INQUIRY, MARCH 11, 1946

IN 1958, Israel's prime minister determined that the time had come for his ten-year-old state to read the book of Joshua. By "reading," David Ben-Gurion meant living in the sense that contemporary Israeli citizens would realize biblical promises as the reborn People of Israel sovereign in their ancient homeland. This image of historical fulfillment involved a set of distinct choices on the Prime Minister's part: Ben-Gurion decided that the *Tanakh*—or Hebrew Bible—was the most relevant text for modern Israel, with the militant book of Joshua holding supreme importance.[1] The book's modern truths, however, would not be apparent absent their interpretation in the context of modern Israel. In the name of creating a collective, authoritative interpretation, Ben-Gurion convened an elite group at his home to parse the details before they spread the gospel of Joshua among the people. The study group's meetings coincided with the tenth anniversary of the State of Israel and, as I will argue, resulted in a popular narrative that coded the events of 1948 in the language of Joshua. This chapter focuses on the crucial period when Ben-Gurion fused the public culture of Israel with biblical tales of ceaseless conquest. It marks

1. I will refer to the Hebrew Bible as both the *Tanakh* and the Torah, as did the members of Ben-Gurion's study group.

the key point of alignment between Joshua and modern Israel when occupation became a definitional part of the Jewish State.

Language attests to the impact of the group's interpretation. The word for the Israeli Occupation (כיבוש/*kibbush*) derives from the biblical term for Joshua's systematic wars against Canaanite peoples.[2] The word for settlement in the book of Joshua (נחלה/*nahalah*) forms the root of the word for Jewish settlements in Occupied Territories (התנחלות/*hitnahalut*). Through use of the word, settlers (*mitnahalim*/ מתנחלים) assume their identity and present their "fortified cities" as avatars of the sanctified parcels of land bestowed to biblical tribes (Joshua 19:35).[3] The inseparable valences of conquest/occupation (כיבוש/*kibbush*) and tribal allotments and militarized settlement (נחלה/*nahalah*), in combination with the selfsame word for contested borders (גבול/*gevul*), mark the formative influence of Joshua in Israel. The linguistic context further sets the stage for lived reality insofar as figuring the Jewish citizens of Israel as the reincarnation of Joshua's army exalts the male soldier while assigning to the Palestinians the role of the Canaanites.[4] As in other cases of colonization, biblical tropes proved expedient in resolving the paradox of justifying dispossession and discrimination amidst claims of liberal democracy. However secular Ben-Gurion's interpretations, they still appealed to an authority higher than international law as they advanced political claims.

Similar to the editors of Joshua, the elite group that gathered in Jerusalem produced a narrative with two functions: absorbing constituents into a highly centralized state, and denying the social realities that did not conform to the vision of that state. The analogies drawn by Ben-Gurion and his cohort endured at the same time that their enterprise resembled their source text: a war story intended to unify disparate groups as a nation even as the groups in question lacked unity on the ground. The citizenry of Israel was comprised of diverse immigrants who spoke different languages and practiced unique variations on Jewish traditions alongside Palestinian communities that remained subject to military rule after the war. Ben-Gurion wished for religious commonalities to give way to secular national bonds and for distinct political positions to dissolve into commitment to the state. As they narrated the story of

2. The use of the word in Joshua 18:1 suggests a completion of the conquest.

3. Michael Feige, *Settling in the Hearts: Jewish Fundamentalism in the Occupied Territories* (Detroit: Wayne State University Press, 2009), 48, 73–76.

4. See Yael Zerubavel, *Desert in the Promised Land* (Stanford: Stanford University Press, 2019), 82–83.

Israel's founding war through Joshua, Ben-Gurion and his colleagues looked to blend Jewish immigrant communities and obscure—even overpower—a complex social reality that did not line up with ethnonational aspirations. By justifying and valorizing war as the essential moment of Jewish redemption, their story fused national destiny with perpetual conquest. However, parallel to the ways Joshua unwittingly attests to its failure to produce an integrated nation, so Ben-Gurion's study group reveals the degree to which war stories can produce more war but cannot efface material differences in the name of national cohesion. The institution of the Israeli armed forces left its imprint on every enlisted member but did not annul Jewish ethnic or religious affiliation, class difference, or political position. Fractures only deepened beneath the modern biblical veneer. Furthermore, displaced Palestinians remained present, and defining them as threatening enemies and infiltrators all but ensured that the War of Liberation, whose tenth anniversary was commemorated in 1958, would never draw to a close.

As Ben-Gurion's chosen interpreters gathered to synthesize 1948 and the book of Joshua, they brought a set of pressing questions of their own. What is the best way to conquer and transform a foreign homeland? Is it best to eradicate a previous culture through a coordinated, systematic war effort or through a slow process of colonization and skirmish? Or, in other words, what takes priority in the book of Joshua: conquest or settlement? Is the general the real hero, or does heroism lie among local settlers tenaciously expanding their territory? Can the peace treaty pick up where war left off and serve as an effective mode of securing control? What is the correct status of non-Jewish citizens? How can land become territory, and how can the ancient past affirm the quotidian imperatives of the modern state? What is the nature of Jewish claims to the land and the proper relationship between native and immigrant? These questions and the fierce debate around them crystallized into five key themes of Israel's conquest story.

The first theme is that of the Jewish army reborn after centuries of quiescence and the brush with extinction in Europe's industrialized genocide. Such survival and national reanimation is rendered possible due to a determined command structure and high morale shared by all the troops. At Ben-Gurion's home, Yigael Yadin—former chief of staff of the Israeli Defense Forces and starchaeologist excavator of the ruins he declared left in Joshua's wake—voiced the theme of miraculous victory obtained through tip-top military organization. His interpretative strategy claims that to have fought a war is to understand the book of Joshua. The second theme is that of collective settlement, which reflects practices of Labor Zionism in the kibbutz and moshav. The miracle in question is the transformation of landscape through the labors of a unified social group that, as in Yadin's conquest story, brings about the end of a prior society. The fact that indigenous people disappear in both the account of conquest and that of settlement did nothing to soften the cutthroat debate between Yadin and his fellow archaeologist Yohanan Aharoni, who advocated for the settlement paradigm. The third major theme is that of the peace treaty as a technique of aligning Israel with its neighbors. Critics of the Oslo Accords will not be surprised that the version articulated by the biblical scholar Menaham Haran describes the treaty as an effective mode of political suppression. The fourth theme is territorialism, the intense connection to the land matched with a single-minded push to transform it. As expressed by the geographer Ben-Zion Luria, Israeli territorialism depends upon a combination of biblical excavation and Palestinian removal. Ever the politician, Ben-Gurion consolidated these themes in the straightforward and direct question: who belongs in Israel?

The prime minister's answer surprisingly draws on native claims as he makes the point that civilizational advancement best qualifies a people for sovereign rule. In a wild interpretation that ultimately caused the religious parties to call for his censure, Ben-Gurion explained that the book of Joshua shows there to have been two groups of ancient Israelites: the elite pioneers who returned from the Diaspora with Joshua and the more backward native Hebrews who lost their way by blending in with their neighbors. The study group incorporates these central themes in an overarching narrative that fuses European nationalist and settler-colonial concepts with a biblical book written by an ancient, protonational party that advocated for political centralization. As the nation of Israel took form in a war story, the themes hardened into political tenets that foreclosed other, less militarized social configurations.

Independence Day 1958

Israel's dogged prime minister met the tenth anniversary with many of the same worries he had harbored since the prestate days along with a new set of anxieties. Foremost among them stood the question of how to forge a modern nation out of a welter of Jewish immigrant groups who shared no mother tongue. In the 1940s, he had approached the challenge in a Soviet manner by creating state institutions intended to impress national identity on the individual and bind him to the whole. The military was Ben-Gurion's signature institution into which he infused biblical elements, heightening the existential significance of the Israel

Defense Forces, born amidst the war. But, by the 1950s, memories of Israel's founding war only went so far. Two-thirds of the Jewish population were immigrants without firsthand experience of the 1948 war who faced stark daily trials of absorption, livelihood, and housing. However much Ben-Gurion's biblical images were "seared into the consciousness" of the generation who experienced the war, they needed to be refreshed for those who had not.[5] Thus the commemoration of 1948 amidst the pomp and circumstance of 1958 needed to hit existential notes of biblical redemption in the name of producing a cohesive Israeli citizenry and motivating future sacrifices.[6]

Ben-Gurion portrayed immigrant absorption as the actualization of the prophecy of ingathering exiles from the "four corners of the earth" who "stream in by the thousands and ten-thousands to the State of Israel" because of "a messianic urge." Ingathering these exiles constituted "a supreme mission" of "making desolation bloom, conquering the forces of nature on land, on sea and in the air, giant-scale housing projects, large scale irrigation works and power plants, the building of a diversified economy," as well as "an education program."[7] He approached the practical challenge by establishing a highly centralized and discriminatory system of immigrant absorption that favored Ashkenazi Jews at every turn while lauding its momentousness in his familiar biblical idiom.[8] Unlike the self-selecting Zionist pioneers of the prestate era, the immigrants arrived as ethnic groups instantaneously arranged along a class

5. "The nightmarish fears of impending destruction, the successful counterattack against civilian population—with whom they had uneasily coexisted since the beginning of the modern Zionist experience—were all subsumed in a powerful and unambiguous biblical image: the divinely ordained conquest of Canaan by Joshua, at the head of the tribes of Israel." Neil Asher Silberman, *A Prophet from amongst You: The Life of Yigael Yadin: Soldier, Scholar, and Mythmaker of Modern Israel* (Reading, MA: Addison-Wesley Publishing Company, 1993), 146.

6. Ian Black describes the Independence Day parade on April 24, 1958, in West Jerusalem as "deliberately emphasiz[ing] the armed might of the Jewish state" as King Hussein "inspected the reinforced units he had carefully deployed to counter-balance the unusually heavy Israeli presence" just to the east of the armistice line. *Enemies and Neighbors: Arabs and Jews in Palestine and Israel, 1917–2017* (New York: Atlantic Monthly Press, 2017), 162–163.

7. David Ben-Gurion, "Uniqueness and Destiny," in *Ben-Gurion Looks at the Bible*, trans. Jonathan Kolatch (Middle Village, NY: Jonathan David Publishers, 1972), 33.

8. Discrimination was practically the case, although not part of Ben-Gurion's rhetoric: "There is, however, no basis to the assumption that the Jews of North Africa or Turkey, Egypt, Persia or Aden are different in their make-up and nature from the Jews of Lithuania, Galicia, and America. Rich resources of pioneering ability are hidden within them as well; resources of bravery and creativity." "Uniqueness and Destiny," 36.

hierarchy.[9] The "whitest" Jews from the most Westernized countries—Germany, France, England, the United States—formed the elite together with Russian and Polish pioneers of the prestate era. Ashkenazi Jews enjoyed positions of leadership and a better standard of life in an austere country; Sephardic Jews from Mediterranean cities were cosmopolitans mostly living beneath the elite, followed by Jews from Muslim or Asian countries called *Mizrahi* or "Eastern," and destined, from the government's point of view, for frontier towns.[10] These broad ethnic divisions were further stratified by country of origin, so that a German Jew had a different experience from a Romanian Jew, and an Iranian Israeli faced a set of challenges different from a Moroccan. Thus, intra-Jewish ethnic distinction was reinforced, even as Jewish nationalism was supposed to erase these differences.

The political integration of 1950s Israel pivoted on ethnic nationalism: the United Nations had granted the state in response to the Holocaust and postwar crises of Jewish displaced persons, Arab states had joined together in opposing the Jewish State, and ethnic Jewishness constituted the primary condition for Israel's sovereignty, as well as its citizenship. The Jewish character conferred on the state meant that the assertion of Arab sovereignty constituted a challenge to the nation and that Arabness itself was nationally suspect. For the Arabs absorbed by Israel as citizens, this entailed living under martial law from 1949 to 1966, as well as confiscation of property and restriction of movement.[11] On this count, distinguishing Jews from Arab countries from Arabs within the country was vital at the same time as these Jews were largely relegated to a lower class position than their Ashkenazi counterparts. The Arabs

9. On the level of state policy, stratification determined eligibility. Avi Picard has argued that rather than ethnic criteria, Ben-Gurion distinguished eligibility on the basis of age and skill and proved ready to discount infirm or older Jews no matter their point of origin; see "Building the Country or Rescuing the People: Ben-Gurion's Attitude towards Mass Jewish Immigration to Israel in the Mid-1950s," *Middle Eastern Studies* 54, no. 3 (2018): 382–399.

10. Avi Picard describes the "From Ship to Village" policy that coincided with the spike in immigration from North Africa in 1954. The policy made agreement to residence wherever the Jewish Agency chose a precondition to their immigration. The destinations in question were either agricultural settlements or the "development towns" that served them; Picard, "Building the Country," 389.

11. "Arab lands constituted a majority of privately owned real estate in Israel. . . . Between 1948 and 1953, 370 new Jewish settlements were established—350 on land classified as abandoned. At least 250,000 dunams of the land so classified were in fact owned by Arab residents of Israel who had been assigned 'absentee' status by the government under the Absentee Property Act of 1950." Ian Lustick, "Zionism and the Idea of an Arab Minority," in *Arabs in the Jewish State: Israel's Control of a National Minority* (Austin: University of Texas Press, 1980), 56–57.

granted Israeli citizenship—Israeli Arabs or Palestinian Citizens of Israel—in large part lived in enforced poverty and thus did not even figure on the same class spectrum.

Living in many "cities that you did not build and eating from vineyards and olive groves that you did not plant" (Josh 24:13), Israelis tried not speak of those who had built and planted them. For their part, Palestinian exiles just beyond the armistice lines in Lebanon, Syria, and Jordan had no right to return or to reclaim their property, though they often crossed over to try to recover belongings, harvest ancestral lands, or engage in acts of revenge. By labeling all of these acts "infiltration"—a word that served as a rhetorical recapitulation of dispossession—Israelis attempted to externalize the challenge they posed to the state by linking them to the negotiation and control of borders.[12] In 1949, "Ben-Gurion launched what he called the 'War on Infiltration,' a massive bureaucratic, military, and ultimately legal campaign against Palestinian return, resettlement, and overall presence. For the next seven years, this campaign, more precisely named the 'War on Return,' became a frightening and fate-altering staple of Palestinian daily life in Israel."[13] The Israeli public's fear of infiltrators and its desire for definitive borders indirectly lent support to brutal military reprisals on communities charged with harboring them. In the 1950s, the war supposedly won extended into daily life. This put the onus of reconciling the paradox on the commemorative narrative of Israel's tenth anniversary.

By formulating the Joshua narrative, Israel's elite looked to counter the portrayal of 1948 as the *Nakba*, or Catastrophe, that began circulating publicly with the 1958 release of historian Arif al-Arif's first volume *Nakbat Bayt al-Maqdis* (The catastrophe of Jerusalem). As much as the notion of the *Nakba* encoded the ruinous Palestinian losses, it advanced a biblical allusion of its own to the devastating loss of holy Jerusalem in which Palestinians figured as ancient Jews and Israelis as Romans. Fearful that the Palestinian narrative might gain international traction, Israel's elite looked for biblical analogies tight enough to keep Palestinians outside the space of the nation once and for all.

12. Meron Benvenisti speaks of the period from 1949 to 1956 as a miniwar involving Israeli military forces, Palestinian guerrillas armed by Arab countries, and Palestinian refugees. The term "infiltrator," Benvenisti notes, concealed the fact that "most of the infiltrators were former inhabitants of the abandoned villages and that their reasons for returning were in most cases personal and economic or even sentimental." *Sacred Landscape: The Buried History of the Holy Land Since 1948*, trans. Maxine Kaufman-Lacusta (Berkeley: University of California Press, 2000), 218.

13. Shira Robinson, *Citizen Strangers: Palestinians and the Birth of Israel's Liberal Settler State* (Stanford: Stanford University Press, 2013), 74.

On the subject of war, Ben-Gurion looked to bury his recent blunder of attacking Gamal Abdel Nasser's Egypt in 1956 and thereby subjecting Israel to widespread international censure. Israel had colluded with the former colonial powers, England and France, to thwart Nasser's nationalization of the Suez Canal. During the same period, Israel was engaged in nationalizing infrastructure that remained in British hands and protesting continued British military support of the Jordanian Arab Legion, so, despite the pronounced enmity of Egypt and Israel, Nasser and Ben-Gurion were in a certain sense pursuing parallel goals. During the Suez Canal War, Ben-Gurion's justifying biblicisms failed spectacularly. Dubbing the war "Operation Kadesh" and restricting Israel's participation to the Sinai Peninsula, Ben-Gurion appealed to the narrative of Exodus in which the People of Israel spend much of their sojourn in a place called Kadesh-Barnea. Amidst tactics of halting raids from Gaza and opening the Suez Canal to Israeli shipping, Ben-Gurion declared the establishment of a "third kingdom of Israel" with the capacity to absorb new territory and populations.[14] Such predictions proved inauspicious.

As a result of the Suez Canal war, Israel gained no territory, secured no borders, and came close to destroying its relationship with the United States. Ben-Gurion, along with Anthony Eden and Guy Mollet, had deceived President Eisenhower and raised the hackles of the Soviet Union. The retreat by Israel and the waning colonial powers elevated Nasser's profile in the region along with his international reputation. Again Palestinians paid the highest price for the military adventure, with a brief occupation of Gaza resulting in an estimated 930 to 1,200 deaths.[15] Ben-Gurion's biblical proclamations seemed to bespeak expansionist tendencies with no regard for international law or American diplomacy. Because there was little heroic inspiration to be gleaned from Israeli military actions in 1956—Israel had attacked Egypt, not escaped as in the biblical story—the commemoration of the 1948 war also served as a piece of brilliant political theater used to distract from the more

14. Yona Hadari-Ramage perceives the "religiously oriented hyperbole" and "soldier . . . directly linked to Joshua Bin Nun" in the Israeli public sphere during the Sinai Campaign as igniting messianic emotions that, after the Sinai was quickly restored to Egypt, mounted and eventually broke the floodgates of reason following the 1967 war. See "War and Religiosity: The Sinai Campaign in Public Thoughts," in *Israel: The First Decade of Independence*, ed. S. Ilan Troen and Noah Lucas (Albany: State University of New York Press, 1995), 357–358.

15. Yezid Sayigh, *Armed Struggle and the Search for State: The Palestinian National Movement, 1949–1993* (Oxford: Oxford University Press, 2000), 65.

recent misadventure. Ben-Gurion found it a fitting time to move past the Sinai chapter and take up Joshua's conquest.

The Joshua study group played a role in both the run-up to and the festivities surrounding Israel's tenth Independence Day celebrations. By way of preparation, it packaged the events of 1948 as a dramatic biblical tale for the thousands of journalists and external observers evaluating the first decade of the Jewish State. The ten-year gap between the events of the war and their commemoration can be explained in part by the exigencies of state-building. Between absorbing immigrants and establishing state institutions, Israeli officials had little time for reflection and commemoration. Ben-Gurion seized the opportunity of the tenth Independence Day to valorize the founding war in the name of unifying a country of immigrants through a national culture more Hebraic than Jewish and burying his recent military blunder in the Suez Canal. He chose Joshua's conquest as the template for remembering the 1948 war largely because he had always cast Zionist successes and trials in a biblical frame and understood the book of Joshua as evidence that national independence was the only possible redemptive outcome of Jewish exile. The 1948 war/Joshua story marks a climax in Ben-Gurion's "bibliomania," when he sought to drown out the less heroic evaluations and political critique of Israeli artists and intellectuals by evoking a text with unquestionable authority.[16] Pressured by the state to contribute their scant public funding and visibly exult in the anniversary, Arab citizens challenged the Independence Day celebrations, with many risking rights and personal safety to call for a boycott.[17] In response, Ben-Gurion enshrined the Joshua narrative in state rituals like the Independence Day Bible Quiz, popular archaeology conferences, and the holiday

16. Ben-Gurion announced that Israel had little use for modern Hebrew literature. Its citizens should instead draw their inspiration from the *Tanakh*. The move makes sense in light of the late 1957 outcry by "seven leading journalists, poets, and playwrights—many of whom had earned their nationalist credentials lionizing or fighting with Zionist paramilitary groups before 1948" regarding the random killing of forty-eight Palestinian citizens from Kfar Qasim at the beginning of the Suez Canal War. "The media floodgates opened one week later, after MAPAI's *Davar* published a poem denouncing the cover-up. Its author was Natan Alterman, a party loyalist and close associate of the premier." Robinson, *Citizen Strangers*, 162.

17. The "'minority' celebrations . . . [to] 'show the world how different races could live together'" for which state officials planned required "five months of verbal and physical confrontations that climaxed on Israel's tenth anniversary." Coercion of lockstep unity ultimately "further polarized its citizens along racial and national lines." Robinson, *Citizen Strangers*, 179, 186.

FIGURE 3.1. Prime Minister David Ben-Gurion attends the first Bible Quiz at the Hebrew University in Jerusalem. His personal secretary Yitzhak Navon and Teddy Kollek sit to his left. President Yitzhak Ben Zvi and Knesset Speaker Yosef Sprinzak sit to his right. Courtesy of the Israel Government Press Office.

cycle of Holocaust Remembrance Day, Memorial Day, and Independence Day that was also established in 1958.[18]

Embedding Joshua in Israeli culture gave the conceptual structure of occupation a life of its own. Ben-Gurion's Joshua project commenced in 1958—nine years prior to the Six-Day War and subsequent occupation of the West Bank, Gaza Strip, and Golan Heights—and outpaced the Old Man, as Ben-Gurion was known, in the giddy mass messianism following the 1967 war. When Ben-Gurion insisted upon the repatriation of territory to Egypt and Jordan, it was already too late to call troops back from the front. This marks what Anita Shapira calls the ironic reversal of the biblical territorialism unleashed by Ben-Gurion.[19] His insistence that territories conquered in 1967—absent the city of Jerusalem and the water-rich Golan Heights—be restored to Arab countries in exchange for peace agreements met with public refusal to forfeit hallowed biblical lands.

18. Yael Zerubavel, *Recovered Roots: Collective Memory and the Making of Israeli National Tradition* (Chicago: University of Chicago Press, 1997), 216.

19. Anita Shapira, "Ben-Gurion and the Bible: The Forging of an Historical Narrative," *Middle Eastern Studies* 33, no. 4 (1997): 670.

Related legacies of Ben-Gurion's interpretation of Joshua are militarism defined as the exemplary expression of nationalism and the identification of the state with the army, which not only conferred a distinctly male cast on the young country, but also meant that each generation pursued more thorough militarization rather than de-escalation of the conflict.[20]

Biblical Interpretation at the Prime Minister's Home

The interpretations of Ben-Gurion and his group mark a dramatic turn in the history of Jewish interpretation, in which biblical events are taken as directly relevant to the contemporary scenario. So interpreted, the Bible operates to sanction and justify the actions of the state as legitimate and, to a certain degree, blessed. Scholars have commented on this Protestant turn in the Israeli reception of the Bible and understood it to be part and parcel of a concerted project of nationalist state-building. The Prime Minister tasked his group with reading a text historically unimportant to Judaism in an altogether novel manner. He assembled generals, ministers, and justices together with archaeologists and biblical scholars to forge a modern Israeli form of biblical interpretation that would employ the scientific mode of biblical criticism advanced in European academies while stripping it of anti-Semitic biases about the lower evolutionary status of Jews. In fact, such biases were not stripped but rather redirected so that the embedded assumptions about evolutionary hierarchy now pertained to Jews and Arabs. By taking up nationalist forms of biblical commentary, Israeli interpreters imported a set of European ethnonational beliefs into the text and the land. To the degree that Ben-Gurion's group did not break free from the biases of modern biblical criticism, it also did not transform the other tradition that the Old Man wished to dismiss: Judaism. Diaspora Judaism, in his eyes, represented a near two-millennial mistake of eschewing war and territorialism in favor of cultural survival and religious existence.[21] He wanted no part of it in the official state narrative, but with so much yeshiva learning in the room, it, of course, seeped in.

20. Although my dating of Israel's militarism differs from that of Uri Ben-Eliezer, I agree with his definition that it comes into being "only when the use of military force acquires legitimation, is perceived as a positive value and a high principle that is right and desirable, and is routinized and institutionalized within society." *The Making of Israeli Militarism* (Bloomington: Indiana University Press, 1998), 7.

21. In her essay on the study group, M. T. Wacker describes Ben-Gurion's thoughts on Jewish commentary: "In exile, the Jewish people became the people of the book but through the

According to Ben-Gurion, the Torah had been misinterpreted because of its decontextualization, meaning that correct understanding required that the descendants of the ancient Israelites have sovereignty in the land of its authorship. The *Tanakh* was their patrimony, but scholastic interpretation had distanced them from its essence. As prime minister, he saw himself as responsible for identifying and releasing the essence of the Jewish people and the homeland, with the *Tanakh* holding the key to their unalloyed reality. But these essences could not simply rise to the surface at any occasion; they required certain conditions for discernment.

> The *Tanakh* was, without a doubt, one of the main causes of the formation of our national character, yet this cause came from within—from the midst of the nation. The greatness of the *Tanakh* is the greatness of Israel's spirit, it is a product of this spirit, a product of the spirit of the *heroes* of our nation.[22]

Approaching Scripture in an avowedly secular manner, Ben-Gurion still perceived in its pages the revelation of a sublime national spirit, of an indelible connection to territory, and of the bond among Jews. He reasoned that God had not given the Jews the Torah; rather they had produced it as a reflection of an exemplary national spirit. This very spirit needed to soar again among "a free Jewish nation in its country capable of studying the eternal creation whose every page exudes the air of the land and the atmosphere of Hebrew independence and its struggle with the entire world for its historical uniqueness and destiny."[23] He believed that an essential aspect of Jewish peoplehood lay dormant until the momentous year of 1948.

In his eyes, nationalism and militarism were not novel characteristics befitting a postcolonial, post-Holocaust moment, but part and parcel of a realized Jewish essence.

---

aggregation of commentators and comments about comments, it became detached from its original meaning. To those, however, who live on their own land, the Bible reveals itself not only culturally but also historically and geographically. This is why the Bible must be taught in schools." Marie-Theres Wacker, "Das Buch Josua—angeeignet durch David Ben-Gurion," in *The Book of Joshua*, ed. Edward Noort (Leuven: Peeters, 2012), 612.

22. David Ben-Gurion, *Biblical Reflections* (Tel Aviv: Am Oved Publishers, 1976), 44 (Hebrew).

23. David Ben-Gurion, "The Welcome Address of Prime Minister David Ben-Gurion to Members of the Study Group," in *Studies of the Book of Joshua: The Discussions of the Biblical Study Group at the Home of David Ben-Gurion. Full Transcription*, ed. Haim Rabin et al., Publications of the Israeli Society for Biblical Research (Jerusalem: Kiryat Sefer, 1971), vii (Hebrew).

> Occupation, settlement, tribe, nation—I doubt if a scattered and divided people that has no land and no independence could know the true meaning of these words and their full content. Those who do not engage in conquest cannot know what is involved in the act of conquest. It is the same thing with settlement. Only with the establishment of Israel in our generation did these abstract concepts assume skin, sinews, and flesh, so that we know their content and essence.[24]

According to Ben-Gurion, Jews could not correctly interpret Joshua before the rise of the State of Israel. Unable to reenact its concepts, these readers missed their meaning. Israeli war and settlement thus embodied Joshua and exhibited the national dimension of the Torah neglected over so many centuries of exile. As the materialization of occupation and settlement proved the veracity of Joshua, it also placed stress on contemporary bodies and locations to signify biblical truths. The War of Independence realized the archetype of Joshua's conquest and thereby liberated the Jewish people from existential threat and confining borders, as well as from the distortions of a tradition that had depoliticized its founding texts. The War of Independence was thus an exemplary act of interpretation and the soldiers were those who unleashed biblical truth.[25]

Ben-Gurion fancied himself an avatar of Joshua.[26] As the minister of defense and prime minister who presided over a foundational war of liberation that banished the people of the land and established "the tribes of Israel" in their place, he saw himself as the loyal disciple of Theodore Herzl, who, by envisioning the Jewish State, served as the modern Moses.[27] Herzl may not

24. Ben-Gurion, "Welcome Address," vii (Hebrew).

25. "Not one of the interpreters of the *Tanakh*, Jewish or Gentile, from the Middle Ages to our times, could have interpreted the chapters of Joshua as did the actions of the Israel Defense Forces last year." David Ben-Gurion, "Address to the Sixth Congress for Knowledge of the Land," *Bulletin of the Jewish Palestine Exploration Society*. Vol. 25, 3–4 (1950): 123 (Hebrew).

26. Haim Gevaryahu said as much; see "Recollections from the Bible Study Circle at D. Ben-Gurion's Home," in *Ben-Gurion and the Bible: The People and Its Land*, ed. Mordechai Cogan (Beer-Sheva: Ben-Gurion University of the Negev Press, 1989), 73 (Hebrew). See also the section entitled "Joshua" in Dan Kurzman, *Ben-Gurion: Prophet of Fire* (New York: Simon and Schuster, 1983), 209–286.

27. At Herzl's burial, Israel Zangwill spoke of him as Moses who glimpsed, only briefly, the Promised Land yet "has laid his hands upon the head of more than one Joshua, and filled them with the spirit of his wisdom to carry on his work." *Speeches, Articles and Letters of Israel Zangwill,*

have initiated Ben-Gurion as his successor as Moses did Joshua, but nonetheless Ben-Gurion saw himself as his disciple par excellence. After hearing Herzl speak in his hometown of Plonsk in Russian Poland, Ben-Gurion recalled, "One glimpse of him and I was ready to follow him then and there to the land of my ancestors."[28] The analogy further portrayed Israel's War of Independence as collective redemption following the devastation of genocide perpetrated by Europeans, and Ben-Gurion took this as evidence that militarized nationalism in the face of Arabs offered the only option for Jewish survival. Time itself rippled through the figuration of territory as the redeemed biblical homeland to which Jewish exiles could now be ingathered. Such associations that would become so natural first needed to be produced and affirmed, such that the hardships, the violence, and the ceaseless struggle would seem destined and conclusive. Biblical associations further allowed the violent dispossession of Palestinians to go unspoken or quickly justified by way of analogy—had not Joshua's wars of restoration required the extermination of the Canaanites? Had not the Israelis as moderns shown more compassion by engaging in expulsion rather than wholesale slaughter? For those uninterested in biblical figuration, the war still provided evidence that might makes right: if a fledgling country could not only defend itself, but also gain more ground when attacked by five countries, then something miraculous was surely afoot.

In the name of a secular state on a civilizing mission, Ben-Gurion pursued a confident narrative characterized by wide consensus, but his chosen methods of interpretation engendered ambivalence in individual interpreters, as well as the group as a whole. The literary product of the twin desires to understand the Bible outside of Christian supersessionism and Jewish diasporism is a most unusual hybrid. A punctilious transcription of the meetings at Ben-Gurion's home, the written collection resembles the Talmud insofar as a group of Jewish male elites reflects on its times and sets the parameters of discourse through biblical interpretation.[29] As it vacillates between German higher criticism with its latent disregard for the Jews and the more benign exceptionalism

ed. Maurice Simon (London: Soncino Press, 1937), 131–132. In his biography of Jabotinsky, Hillel Halkin describes the Herzl-Moses analogy: "Many of his followers also regarded him as a Moses-figure, a Jew raised in Pharaoh's court, as it were, with no sense of connection to his fellow Israelites." *Jabotinsky: A Life* (New Haven, CT: Yale University Press, 2014), 15.

28. David Ben-Gurion, *Recollections* (London: MacDonald & Company, 1970), 34.

29. Dina Stein, *Textual Mirrors: Reflexivity, Midrash, and the Rabbinic Self* (Philadelphia: University of Pennsylvania Press, 2012).

of American Christian scholars, the record of the study session shows the adaptations, rather than the independence, of Jewish national interpretation.

Ben-Gurion invited three recognizable groups to the bimonthly discussions of Joshua: prominent figures in the Israeli Bible Society led by Haim Gevaryahu, who planned the meetings; scholars with university appointments; and the phalanx of doctors, who attended to Ben-Gurion and his wife, Paula.[30] One of twelve chosen disciples lectured at each of the meetings. An assigned respondent contended with the lecturer's thesis, followed by a lively discussion engaging the whole group. The designated lecturer then had a chance to answer questions and reiterate his arguments with closing remarks. Of the twelve, seven (Yohanan Aharoni, Yehudah Elitzur, Menahem Haran, Ben-Tzion Luria, Ya'akov Liver, Binyamin Mazar, and Avraham Malamat) were career academics focused on biblical history, philology, or archaeology. Most contributed to state endeavors in education, culture, or geography, either in an official or honorary capacity. The five politicians took scholarship or publishing seriously enough to consider their contributions grounded in academic methods. In addition to Ben-Gurion, President Yitzhak Ben-Tzvi, former IDF Chief of Staff Yigael Yadin, Acting Chairman of the Jewish Agency Zalman Shazar (later to become president), and Supreme Court Justice Sheneur Zalman Heshin interpreted Joshua in an official register. Numerical symmetry aside, the twelve speakers cannot be said to represent distinct "tribes" in 1950s Israel. All were Ashkenazi, all but one were secular, all were either born in Israel or had immigrated prior to 1948, and all believed wholeheartedly in the Bible's relevance to the modern state. Most had refashioned their identities or, at least, Hebraicized their names in order to manifest the transformation of Jews into the reborn People of Israel.

Ben-Gurion governed single-mindedly, so we should not downplay his investment in group interpretation. He could easily have penned his own commentary on Joshua, which if nothing else would have had political authority. He could have likewise composed a treatise on the book of Joshua through correspondence with the eminent (or what Shlomo Sand calls fundamentalist)[31] biblical critic Yehezkel Kaufmann, whose analysis of the book helped to launch the project of critical Jewish study of the *Tanakh* along with its nationalistic bent.[32] Kaufmann and Ben-Gurion did exchange letters on the subject. That

30. Silberman, *A Prophet from amongst You*, 240.

31. Shlomo Sand, *The Invention of the Jewish People*, trans. Yael Lotan (London: Verso, 2010), 108.

32. In 1953, Kaufmann published a monograph on Joshua entitled *The Biblical Account of the Conquest of Palestine*, which came out in Hebrew in 1956 as what I would translate as *The Biblical*

Ben-Gurion inaugurated a study group says many things. First of all, that he sought widespread public impact and vocabulary that could as easily refer to the modern state as to a golden age of heroic warriors. His initial intention, largely unfulfilled, was for each participant to give public lectures—all the more laudable if they were in peripheral areas—to spread the word about how the Bible was best understood in Israel. On this count, group interpretation was a strategy for cultural influence. This motivation was connected with Ben-Gurion's own experiences in residential-worker collectives of the prestate *Yishuv*. Seeing the commune and the kibbutz as essential to Israel's survival and growth, he likewise believed in collective knowledge production and looked to model it from the highest office in the land. Ben-Gurion had little interest in the theme of holy war, but rather wanted the group to probe "history, strategy, conquest and settlement according to the book of Joshua."[33] The idea was to find an actionable precedent or what Shemaryahu Talmon, a prominent member of the group, called "the strategic probability of Joshua's conquest," of particular value "since the War of Liberation."[34]

Yigael Yadin and the Morale of Conquest

Along with Ben-Gurion, no one had done more to build the army and its image than Yigael Yadin. A strategic creator of the Israel Defense Forces and its former chief of staff, Yadin himself cut the dashing figure of the Israeli warrior. The scholar in him saw symbol as a functional tool that could boost the very element vital for military victory: morale. Just before the 1948 expiration of the British Mandate, Ben-Gurion had asked Yadin to brief a provisional council about the chances of a Jewish victory over multiple Arab opponents.

Story of the Conquest of the Land. What to name this land remained an issue that was somewhat resolved with the posthumous 1985 rerelease of *The Biblical Account of the Conquest of Canaan*.

33. David Ben-Gurion, "Discussion Following Ya'akov Liever's Presentation, 'The Character of the Sources in the Book of Joshua in Light of Their Historical Meaning,'" in *Studies of the Book Joshua*, 56 (Hebrew), 86.

34. Shemaryahu Talmon, "Discussion Following Yigael Yadin's Presentation, 'Military and Archeological Aspects of the Book of Joshua's Description of the Conquest of the Land,'" in *Studies of the Book of Joshua*, 86 (Hebrew). According to Avraham Tzivyon, Ben-Gurion turned to biblical images and symbols during the organization of the Israel Defense Forces in order to inform and express military power; see "'Like All the Nations' and the 'Chosen People,' Ben-Gurion's Bond to the Bible," *Shadmot: Organ of the Kibbutz Movement* 107, no. 82 (1988): 82 (Hebrew).

FIGURE 3.2. David Ben-Gurion participating in a festive meeting of the Bible study group at his home in Sde Boker on the occasion of his eightieth birthday celebration. Courtesy of the Israel Government Press Office.

"The question is," Yadin answered him, "to what extent our people will be able to prevail against that force, considering the morale and ability of the enemy and our own tactics plan."[35]

Soon after, Yadin began a concerted program of morale boosting by infusing multiple aspects of the Israeli Defense Forces with biblical significance and symbols of national destiny. High-ranking officers received the biblical title of *aluf*, the princes or possibly militia leaders of the tribes.[36] Ben-Gurion took part as well, initiating the command structure with the assurance that Joshua's army had been reborn: "With this oath you have sworn to, you have now been united with the long succession of Hebrew warriors from the times of Joshua Bin-Nun."[37] In his classic style, Ben-Gurion collapsed history so that his present moment reflected the biblical past and the span between them became

35. Silberman, *Prophet from amongst You*, 114.

36. Silberman, *Prophet from amongst You*, 125. The IDF's first *aluf* was Mickey Marcus, the US Army colonel who had helped to liberate Dachau and offered to serve in Israel's founding war. Significant for the present inquiry, Colonel Marcus was instrumental in planning Operation Bin Nun (as in Joshua Bin Nun) to displace the Arab Legion from the Latrun fort that blocked the road between Jerusalem and Tel Aviv.

37. Silberman, *Prophet from amongst You*, 125.

filled by an anonymous "succession of Hebrew warriors,"[38] a figuration that erased the dominantly nonmilitary history of the Jewish people. To reflect the rebirth of Hebrew warriors, Ben-Gurion instructed the initiates to change their names to a Hebrew, preferably biblical, idiom. At this moment, "the young man now named Yigael Yadin (né Sukenik) was born again—to begin a far more public phase of his military career."[39] Part of Yadin's public career involved briefings of the foreign press during 1948 that acclimated readers across the world to thinking about war in Israel in light of the biblical record.

Yadin seized the public imagination in the 1950s when he began the excavation of Hazor, the northern city allegedly destroyed by Joshua.[40] As he traveled abroad to fundraise, he voiced the literalism of his Christian predecessors in a decidedly Jewish national key: "I must know about Joshua. I must know if he really conquered it."[41] The former chief of staff's urgency stemmed from his projects of aligning the book of Joshua with modern Israel and mobilizing archaeological proof as a guide and justification for how the state would relate to the nations in its midst. Yadin's affirmation of Joshua's conquest both verified the 1948 war as an indisputable victory and framed the landscape of everyday life as the site of a perennial contest.

Speaking before the study group, Yadin appraised Joshua Bin-Nun's strategy as if he were a peer. The limitations to which he admitted—"It is doubtful if we have here a complete strategic picture"[42]—threw up no barriers. Biblical war stories may not provide actual battle plans, but Yadin still found them to be true military reports from the field. As he saw it, Joshua's overarching strategy was diversion: "The tactics described in the Book of Joshua strive first of

38. Silberman, *Prophet from amongst You*, 125.

39. Silberman, *Prophet from amongst You*, 125.

40. An organizer of the study group, Gevaryahu had a penchant for clearly stating its goals: "What persuaded our esteemed colleagues Drs. Yadin and Aharoni to excavate in Hazor? The wish to understand the Book of Joshua. . . . Our generation has a special connection to archeology. In fact, it is one of the expressions of settling in our ancient homeland." "Recollections," 83. Supporting Gevaryahu's comment, Michael Feige notes, "During the 1950s and 1960s, biblical archaeology was considered to be a central part of Israel's 'civil religion' and was even hailed as 'the national pastime' of the newly established state." "Recovering Authenticity: West-Bank Settlers and the Second Stage of National Archeology," in *Selective Remembrances: Archeology in the Construction, Commemoration, and Consecration of National Pasts*, ed. Philip L. Kohl, Mara Kozelsky, and Nachman Ben-Yehuda (Chicago: University of Chicago Press, 2008), 277.

41. Silberman, *Prophet from amongst You*, 221.

42. Yigael Yadin, "Military and Archeological Aspects of the Book of Joshua's Description of the Conquest of the Land," in *Studies of the Book of Joshua*, 73 (Hebrew).

all to prevent, as far as possible, battles against fortified cities. By means of cunning they get the entrenched men to leave the city so as to fight them in the open field."[43] The conquest may have begun by encircling the walls of Jericho, but Joshua made no habit of depending upon miracles to prevail against walled encampments. Instead, he picked battles that he could win and maximized the power of intelligence: spies, as well as turncoats, proved indispensable. Avoiding densely populated cities, Joshua lured his opponents to the field where they could be matched on grounds of skill.

How is it possible that the long-standing Canaanite culture with its fortified city-states was brought to an end by a migratory band of tribes? To answer this question, Yadin called upon something "we ourselves have experienced: we saw that spirit, morale, is the most important element from a military perspective. There is none more important. Through the strength of this element it is possible to do things which at first seem impossible."[44] To show the potency of morale, somewhat ironically, Yadin drew examples from the scattered yet motivated Arab bands that overthrew the Byzantine Empire.[45] Developing such morale certainly required discipline and a clear command structure, but it also relied on a public culture of cohesion to support solidarity. Morale, or what the Bible names "miracle," was for Yadin a transcendent collective force that can reverse odds and assure swift victory. For all his focus on unity, however, Yadin antagonized the "civilian" Yohanan Aharoni for doubting "the Book of Joshua on the basis of military principles [he] never experienced."[46]

How to Win Joshua's War

The feud between Yadin and Aharoni began at the Joshua-driven Hazor dig. After the excavation closed in 1958, their dispute polarized the discussions at Ben-Gurion's home along lines more consequential than their stated arguments of when to date Israel's conquest of Canaan.[47] Aharoni was the

43. Yadin, "Military and Archeological Aspects," *Studies of the Book of Joshua*, 73 (Hebrew).

44. Yadin, "Military and Archeological Aspects," in *Studies of the Book Joshua*, 78 (Hebrew).

45. Nadia Abu El-Haj shows how nineteenth-century colonial explorers redefined the Islamic conquest "as a simple reenactment of the dynamics of a much earlier one—that of Joshua." *Facts on the Ground: Archeological Practice and Territorial Self-Fashioning in Israeli Society* (Chicago: University of Chicago Press, 2001), 37.

46. Yadin, "Military and Archeological Aspects," *Studies of the Book of Joshua*, 71 (Hebrew).

47. Yadin assigned dates of the "thirteenth and twelfth-eleventh centuries, respectively" to two strata excavated at his famous dig at Hazor, "the last Canaanite city and the first Israelite

FIGURE 3.3. Photograph of Yigael Yadin (R), David Ben-Gurion, and Shimon Perez (L) exiting an army helicopter at the Hazor excavation. Photographed by Moshe Pridan. Courtesy of the Israel Government Press Office.

underdog with only his mentor, Benjamin Mazar, counting as occasional ally. Who would stand against the architect of the Israel Defense Forces? A winning Jerusalemite, Yadin was the son of Eliezer Sukenik, who had played a pivotal role in the discovery of the Dead Sea Scrolls. Yadin joined his father's bookishness with his mentor William Albright's romantic American literalism in a way that made uncovering the biblical past appear as the most vital and wonderful thing that a person could do. The Albright-Yadin relationship marked an early juncture of secular Zionism and millenarian American Christianity that transpired in the august halls of Harvard. The analytic mind of a strategist tempered his flare, but Yadin still struck American audiences as a modern biblical

settlement [then] concluded that Israelite settlement *in the Galilee* had to have begun 'after the conquest of Hazor,'" in "Military and Archeological Aspects," in *Studies of the Book of Joshua*, 95. What all this archaeological evidence verified, for Yadin, "was the historicity of the story of the conquest presented in the Book of Joshua" (95). At the same excavation, Aharoni came to the conclusion that "the destruction of Hazor did not *precede* the process of Israelite settlement in the region. Rather, it succeeded it. The dating of each element in this historical tale (the destruction of Hazor, the initial process of settlement in the ancient Galilee) would have to be reconsidered. The Israelite wars in the Galilee described in the Book of Joshua chapter 11 are wrongly attributed to Joshua." Abu Al-Haj, *Facts on the Ground*, 102–103.

warrior resurrected from the past, even if he did not fancy himself an incarnation of Joshua as did Ben-Gurion and would Moshe Dayan.

Yohanan Aharoni immigrated at age fourteen from Frankfurt to Mandate Palestine amidst the rise of the Nazi party in 1933, finding refuge and experiencing personal transformation as he helped to found a Galilean kibbutz. Here a Jewish refugee named Aronheim became Yohanan Aharoni as a place called Qusqus where Arab families lived among the oak trees became Kibbutz Allonim. Despite Yadin's ribbing, Aharoni was not exactly a civilian, having served in the IDF during the key years of 1948 to 1950. Soon after, he returned to his beloved landscape as antiquities inspector for the Galilee region. The experience fed his dissertation research of walking the Galilee and surveying the landscape for signs of ancient migrations and settlement. Aharoni brought the German scholar Martin Noth's peaceful infiltration theory (which I translate from Hebrew as "quiet settlement") to bear on Israel's geography and argued that the conquest of Joshua had no historical validity. The southern tale from ancient Judah, he asserted, mischaracterized the experience of northern tribes who had arrived in spurts to slowly build their culture.

When Yadin's excavation opened at Hazor, Aharoni easily landed a position as supervisor of excavations at the lower city. He saw himself as the resident expert and resented Yadin's air of unimpugnable certainty. Their clash became as personal as it was intellectual. Beyond elevating the book of Joshua as an essential part of Israel's celebration of its first decade, the passionate fight between Yigael Yadin and Yohanan Aharoni signaled to the public that the obscure little book of the *Tanakh* mattered to their lives.[48] The combination of fanfare surrounding material finds and vitriolic duels between the two men drew interest to the lonely Galilean slope, classified as "the periphery" of Israel where the Ministry of Absorption settled North-African immigrants.

Nadia Abu El-Haj has analyzed how the empirical assumptions shared by the rivals laid the foundation for an archaeological practice that projects

48. Although the fight was vital and personal to both men, it contains an element of splitting hairs. As they debated the nature of ancient heroism, both were deeply involved in the project of appealing to "a scientific endeavor that could potentially validate and reinforce its moral claim to the land, especially against increasing Arab national resistance." Biblical archaeology worked in tandem with the secular Zionist movement to create "a continuous connection to a heroic and glorious past and countered anti-Semitic images" of Jews "as parasitic, lazy . . . and unable to fight." Nachman Ben-Yehuda, "Excavating Masada: The Politics-Archaeology Connection at Work," in Kohl, Kozelsky, and Ben-Yehuda, *Selective Remembrances*, 251–252.

modern ethnic categories and state imperatives onto stones, gates, and pitchers. She explains the kind of circular logic in which events described in the Bible guided interpretation of material finds, which in turn verified the historicity of the events themselves. A similar logic had governed the finds of Christian archaeologists working at the end of the Ottoman or during the British Mandate period, which were used to justify European colonialism in the Middle East.[49] As Christian imperial aims shifted to Jewish settler-colonial goals, "a tale best understood as the modern nation's origin myth was transported into the realm of history" as the "ancient Israelite social collectivity emerged as historical fact."[50] Inasmuch as Aharoni and Yadin cocreated this historical fact, they each inflected it according to what Neil Silberman calls "their own understandings of modern processes of territorial conquest and nationhood."[51] Where Yadin imagined a victory definitive enough for the prior inhabitants to never again reestablish themselves, Aharoni envisioned pockets of Canaanite autonomy under overarching Israelite sovereignty.

Building upon Abu Al-Haj's analysis of how the adversaries deployed the empirical language of archaeology to assert the factuality of the ancient/modern state and its necessary militarism, I will focus on the archaeologists as interpreters in order to show how the terms of their debate set the parameters of mainstream political discourse such that the conflict at hand could be understood as either apocalyptic or quotidian. In the apocalyptic scenario, a declared, concerted war on the Palestinians would ultimately cause them to disappear or submit, whereas in the quotidian version, a less confrontational slog of settlement would, one day, achieve similar ends. The study group pondered these options by considering "the decisive question" of what came first in the days of Joshua: conquest or settlement.

The frame of interpretation, as much as the bloodthirsty content of Joshua, informed the conclusions at which the opponents arrived. Yadin and Aharoni culled different source texts: the chief of staff's exegesis dwelled on the decisive battles waged by Joshua in the first twelve chapters of the book, whereas the kibbutznik hewed to the tribal geographies enumerated in the book's second half and, more particularly, to the book of Judges, where local skirmishes among tribes are solved by charismatic leaders. The content in question is

49. See Rachel Havrelock, "The Ancient Past That Oil Built," *The Bible and Critical Theory* 11, no. 2 (2015): 51–60.

50. Abu Al-Haj, *Facts on the Ground*, 103.

51. Silberman, *Prophet from amongst You*, 237.

markedly different: in the first half of Joshua, Israelites gruesomely murder Canaanites of all stripes, and in the second half—particularly when taken with the stories in Judges—a host of neighboring peoples with too many gods annoy the tribes who are stuck with them all the same. There is no disputing that war constitutes the main theme of these books, and that witnesses in other tongues amplify motifs of enmity and revenge. However, extant realities again go far in explaining why the Israeli elite interpreted Jewish Scripture as a tale of ethnic competition.

Where Yadin advocated for the singular victory of Joshua over multiple opponents, which like 1948 "was possible only through innovative leadership and unified command," Aharoni saw the gradual settlement expansion reminiscent of kibbutzim.[52] To Aharoni, the conquest was actually an assortment of local battles that inevitably erupted as tribes migrated to zones where others dwelled. Aharoni's interpretation proved a tough sell to a group assembled in the name of composing a national creation story to commemorate Israel's tenth anniversary. What public wants to be told that they need to work harder in order to hopefully one day prevail in a ceaseless struggle, much less one gathered for a fireworks display? Perhaps such a narrative had worked for socialist worker collectives and the more idealistic branches of the Labor movement, but it could hardly stir a country of immigrants.[53] Better to claim that the miraculous war of establishment had concluded swiftly, attesting to the superiority of the victors, and that the enemy could not rise again. Ironically, the simple fact that Israel's war was hardly over necessitated the story of total victory in the first place—citizens needed to stay ready and willing to enlist in the army. With the conflict yet to reach any sort of resolution and the consistent resistance of Palestinians to the posture of defeat, both Yadin and Aharoni's strategies, on their own terms, can be analyzed as failures.

In his role of statesman, Yadin negotiated armistice lines with neighboring Arab states, thereby achieving some territorial stability for the young state, but these were hardly official borders. Ben-Gurion, like all prime ministers who followed, grew to appreciate how flexible boundaries can be easily overrun, but the fluidity meant that nearly every community in Israel hovered on a

52. Silberman, *Prophet from amongst You*, 237.

53. It is noteworthy that Ben-Gurion, who believed in the spartan living and collective labor of the kibbutz more than he believed in any theological tenet, voiced no support for Aharoni's theory. This point goes to show how canny of a politician the prime minister was and that he well understood what could gain broad national appeal.

tenuous border of sorts. In such a precarious state with undeniable evidence that the Palestinians were not in fact subdued, Yadin's certain account of Canaanite eradication struck an assuring note.

Yadin claimed that his archaeological discoveries corroborated that Joshua waged "a single, one-time conquest" to erase the culture of Canaan.

> It is a fact that in every Canaanite city which has thus far been thoroughly excavated (further I shall briefly refer to Ai and Jericho), without exception we witness an indisputable phenomenon: a cultured Canaanite city, a fortified city, a city with sanctuaries,—be it Lachish or Bethel or Hazor—ceases suddenly to show signs of life. It is a conclusive fact from an archeological point of view that these Canaanite cities were all destroyed during a single period. These cities were destroyed, burned, and their inhabitants did not return to rebuild them. If one of them was restored, then it was only in a poor and wretched manner.[54]

He punctuated his address with the insistence of its factuality; there are "no exceptions" to the "indisputable phenomenon" and "conclusive fact" that he describes. Armed with such certain material evidence, he upheld that the excavated sites in question were Canaanite cities razed by the tribes of Israel following in lockstep behind their leader. Rock walls and pottery shards attested to the fact that "every city" "without exception" met its end during a single spurt of war. Over the wreckage, the People of Israel built their new society. His definitive dating of the war to 1200–1250 BCE lent the entire Exodus cycle the authority of a history in which Canaanite culture gave way to the ostensibly more pure monotheistic society formed by the descendants of liberated slaves.[55] When it came to the effect on the vanquished, Yadin's rhetoric grew more evocative, dwelling on the annihilation whose ashes can only host the most "poor and wretched" forms of restoration. The total victory in a sweeping war meant that the Canaanites were either extinguished or subdued. If and when Canaanite revival occurred, it simply attested to systematic cultural subjugation. Such overblown rhetoric belied the tremulous Israeli wish

54. Yadin, "Military and Archeological Aspects," *Studies of the Book of Joshua*, 75–76 (Hebrew).

55. Of course, a live argument underlay Yadin's remarks. Where he contended that Joshua and his troops destroyed Hazor in an impressive battle soon after they crossed the Jordan, his rival Yohanan Aharoni perceived "Israelite destruction of the city at the end of a concerted process." Yohanan Aharoni, *The Land of the Bible: A Historical Geography*, rev. ed., trans. A. F. Rainey (Philadelphia: The Westminster Press, 1979), 227.

that a successful war of establishment could mark the definitive end of a prior society.

Yadin never drew an explicit connection between the total destruction of Canaanite culture and the expulsion of Palestinians, but the analogy was clear enough. His mobilization of biblical language aimed to morally exonerate, even justify, his contributions to Plan D—*Tochnit Dalet*—a tactical strategy for territorial expansion that both explicitly and implicitly set the stage for large-scale Palestinian dispossession amidst the war.[56] Plan D, along with other war plans, extended biblical allusions into the realm of modern violence.[57] For example, the strategy to raze the Arab villages around Jerusalem in the name of isolating and penetrating the city was coded as Operation Jebusite, as if the goal was to avoid a replay of Joshua's failures.[58] Ben-Gurion, Yadin, and their inner circle formulated Plan D to give the Haganah the footing from which to stage "aggressive defense."[59] The phrase "aggressive defense" represents the sort of contradictory locution that would come to express the ethos of the Israeli military, as if to say, "We are only defending ourselves, but it requires extraordinary acts of aggression." The conflating of aggression with defense makes it difficult to determine how to live alongside nonnationals and to distinguish between open hostility and civil disobedience. Israel's existential need for self-defense in 1948 was undisputedly profound, but, at the same time, Plan D is the smoking gun showing how territorial appropriation and Palestinian displacement were bound up in the very definition of survival.

The motivation for Plan D cannot be understood without reference to the map of partition promulgated by the United Nations prior to the outbreak of war. In his introduction to the plan, Yigal Sukenik (soon to be Yadin) wrote, "The objective of this plan is to gain control of the territory of the Hebrew state and defend its borders. It also aims at gaining control of the areas of Jewish settlement and population outside the borders of the territory allotted to the Jewish state by the UN partition plan."[60] The Partition Plan realized a Western

56. See Walid Khalidi, "Plan Dalet: Master Plan for the Conquest of Palestine," *Journal of Palestine Studies* 18, no. 1 (1988): 4–33.

57. Some of Plan D's component operations bear the names of biblical judges such as Jephthah, Gideon, and Barak.

58. Interestingly enough, a plan preceding D was named "Operation Joshua" to honor the memory of the fallen Haganah commander Joshua Globerman, but, I believe, also analogizing the ancient and modern wars.

59. Ben-Gurion's description as quoted in Silberman, *Prophet from amongst You*, 102.

60. Silberman, *Prophet from amongst You*, 102.

scheme of territorial division according to variant centers of Arab and Jewish population that had first been proposed in the late 1930s, following the Palestinian Revolt. From a geographic perspective, the patchwork of autonomy made little sense, but Ben-Gurion took sovereignty where he could get it in order to launch expansion. Plan D outlined how such expansion would occur: Jewish fighters would have to hold on to what partition had conferred while using sites of Jewish settlement beyond the UN boundaries as points of territorial enlargement. Resident Arab communities were categorized as either resistant, which served as a precondition for expulsion, or nonresistant, in which case they could remain in place under military rule.

The terms for removal of the population also derived from the Bible: *tihur,* a key term for purification, encoded a sense of religious duty in ethnic cleansing, and *Biur Chametz,* the removal of leavened products from the home as part of Passover cleaning, suggested that ridding the landscape of existing communities paved the way for national liberation.[61] The Israeli military absorbed territory in the north, east, and southwest, enlarging the country by 23 percent (from the 55 percent of Mandatory Palestine conferred by the United Nations in 1948 to the 78 percent resulting from postwar armistice agreements), but the language used in official quarters still suggested that the abiding presence of Arabs conferred impurity and brought trouble.

Palestinians experienced Plan D as the *Nakba,* the catastrophic end of their society that brought the expulsion of approximately seven hundred thousand people and massive, collective losses of property. Until the 1990s, when Palestinian commemoration of the *Nakba* inflected public narrative and the Israeli archives opened to allow corroboration of Palestinian accounts, the Israeli public largely dismissed the Palestinian catastrophe as an inevitable outcome of war or an indication that Palestinians were weak or uncommitted to their land because they had left voluntarily. The 1958 study group offers a window into how the Israeli elite discussed Palestinian expulsion at the time and how they coded the events for the general public. Similar to his narration for the foreign press during the war, Yadin's language merged the events of 1948 with the Bible. Israeli troops had simply razed Arab communities and cleared them of their inhabitants in the manner of Joshua with the Canaanites. To do otherwise would be to lose the war. Wrapping assurance around his analogy, Yadin emphasized the sudden and complete nature of Canaanite destruction.

61. See Black, *Enemies and Neighbors,* 115–116.

In conclusion, Yadin took hope from Joshua about the divided Jerusalem of his day.

> I cannot prove this, but allow me to say that there was victory in Jerusalem—they defeated the king, attacked the city, but did not rule over it. There is a difference between penetrating cities, raiding them and their inhabitants and settling in those cities. These are two completely different things.[62]

As the group met, Jerusalem was a boundary city with a jagged, uncrossable line drawn between the Israeli west and the Jordanian east. The Old City with its repository of the ancient Jewish past was off-limits, although Yadin could remember the more integrated landscape before the war. As they parsed the book of Joshua in a partitioned city, not one interpreter cited Joshua 15:63—until today, Jerusalem remains divided between the People of Judah and the Jebusites. Instead, their interpretations portrayed the situation as only temporary. By way of polemic, Yadin's reading insists that simply because Jerusalem was not immediately settled does not mean that they conquered the land in a gradual fashion. He differentiates conquest and settlement as two separate stages of control in which the second requires success in the first. Beyond the scholarly debate, Yadin's distinction represents a mystifying public assurance that settlement builds upon conquered ground when, in fact, settlers in Israel simply move to the next theater of war. Through this reasoning, Yadin claimed past Israeli victory in Jerusalem in his prediction of future war.

How to Settle Joshua's Land

In contemporary parlance, the founding of Israel marks an instance of "settler colonialism," the takeover of land and extraction of resources by a nonlocal group connected in some way to empire or Western powers. In 1958, Israel's connection to the West could still be uneasy, and no member of Israel's elite considered himself an imperial colonizer, however much the term "settler" was celebrated at the time.[63] From an internal perspective, the project was an exceptional case of Jewish nationalism. That said, employing the framework of settler colonialism reveals how the Joshua study group bracketed the act of

62. Yadin, "Military and Archeological Aspects," in *Studies of the Book of Joshua*, 99 (Hebrew).

63. Shira Robinson deftly details how Israel formed "as a liberal settler state within, rather than outside, changing global norms of republican sovereignty after 1945." *Citizen Strangers*, 8.

settlement from the definition of conquest while, at the same time, recognizing it as an essential component of war.

Where Yadin identified the morale of an army as the key to ancient Israel's success, Aharoni cited a solidarity reminiscent of the kibbutz movement. Amidst the disruption of immigration and the difficulty of life in a small, besieged state, it made sense to contextualize settlement as a form of Jewish heroism. The prestate settlers described themselves as "pioneers" (the very term for the biblical Joshua's infantry) who cultivated virgin land and withstood all matter of hardship in the name of collective redemption. The accounts from early collectives and kibbutzim are replete with references to Joshua, and, in the spirit of revival, many of their names derive from the book.[64] As a kibbutz member committed to the ideology of collective labor, Yohanan Aharoni recognized his values in the biblical text, as well as in the Old-New Land over which he toiled. At the study group meetings, he tried to advance the image of settler as true hero only to be attacked for the perceived slight to the iconic soldier. The group preferred its heroes in uniform and its battles decisive. The blocking of Aharoni's account of ancient settler-heroes thwarted a broader public narrative celebrating regular acts of homesteading that include women and confessing the degree to which they built on the mass expropriation of others' property. When the formal settler movement arose in the 1970s, their pointed distinction between war and settlement placed settler violence not only outside the scope of sanctioned war, but also beyond the scope of law. This situated the settlers in the Israeli imagination as literal and figurative outliers whose perennial combat marks an aberration rather than official state warfare.

Antagonism is as palpable in Aharoni's address as it is in Yadin's. Stepping up as "the citizen-civilian described by Yigael Yadin,"[65] he wraps admonishment about personal biases around a charge of absurd literalism: "Can we accept the conquest as reality or actual history as it is narrated in Joshua?"[66] Yet, for all the insistence on historical precision, Aharoni still perceived ancient processes of settlement as reflecting his ideological commitments.

64. See Rachel Havrelock, *River Jordan: The Mythology of a Dividing Line* (Chicago: University of Chicago Press, 2011), 245–250.

65. Yohanan Aharoni, "The Settlement of the Tribes of Israel in the Land," in *Studies of the Book of Joshua*, 79 (Hebrew).

66. Aharoni, "Settlement of the Tribes of Israel," in *Studies of the Book of Joshua*, 220 (Hebrew).

> Was Jericho conquered? Was Hazor conquered? Of course they were. I do not cast doubt on the fact that they were conquered. The question is: when did this conquest begin? Was it the first step of settlement and penetration of Canaan?[67]

Aharoni finds it difficult to believe that the tribes miraculously crossed the Jordan and immediately began waging massive battles. A victory over a major city like Hazor was, in his view, the crowning event of a long process of struggle. Yadin's experience devising strategy and directing an army, Aharoni implies, is neither the sole nor the superior prism through which to view territorial accomplishment. "I could bring endless historical analogies—of infiltrations and conquests that were not always singular wars but transpired in different ways and involved stratagems that followed different courses."[68] A comparative historical view showed Aharoni that conquest need not involve war between standing armies but could entail persistent attempts to prevail over others within a circumscribed place.

Aharoni contended that a grand military conquest never occurred. Instead, Israelite tribes moved incrementally into woodlands, wilderness, and the interstitial zones of Canaan where they pursued "permanent settlement and agricultural labor in the different parts of the Land."[69] The obsession with borders evident in the book of Joshua results from the experience of living on the frontier and a protracted settlement process of slow habituation and absorption. Joshua's detailed, somewhat relentless boundary lists—along with the contradictory traditions in the book of Judges—record the semiregular migrations of the tribes and their constitutive clans and families. The contesting claims that emerge from these boundary lists reflect a dynamic process of migration, land seizure, and pushback. For a considerable amount of time, territorial control stood in flux. Amidst the fluctuation, a pattern developed in which the Canaanites held sway in cities of the valleys and the Israelite tribes constructed their world on the heights of mountains. Attentive to "the details of the settlement of each one of the tribes," he concluded, "a number of tribes succeeded in gaining control of certain Canaanite cities, other tribes added Canaanite cities to their possession, while yet others 'dwelt among the

67. Aharoni, "Settlement of the Tribes of Israel," in *Studies of the Book of Joshua,* 81 (Hebrew).

68. Yohanan Aharoni, "Discussion Following Yadin's Presentation, 'Military and Archeological Aspects,'" in *Studies of the Book of Joshua,* 81 (Hebrew).

69. Aharoni, "Settlement of the Tribes of Israel," in *Studies of the Book of Joshua,* 220 (Hebrew).

Canaanites' as a result of a certain dependence." The varied nature and uneven successes of the settlement project fly in the face of Joshua's "homogeneous and quick campaign of conquest."[70]

If the battles were continuous and their successes partial, how did the triumphal book of Joshua come to be? Aharoni answered that the book's editors gathered accounts of disparate events that occurred between the thirteenth and twelfth centuries BCE and organized them as stages of Joshua's conquest.[71] In fact, long before the editors of Joshua wove the stories together, they were multiply transformed by the transmission process of oral tradition. The editors took these received traditions—some no doubt historical or containing a historical kernel—and stitched them together to create the mini-epic of Joshua's war, dramatized further by its connection to the Exodus.

Aharoni's interpretation dismissed the idea of a miraculous conquest led by a stalwart general, which seemed to initially dispel a sense of Israel's exceptionalism. He explained that the groups ultimately unifying under the banner of Israel migrated and settled just like other groups in the period. They told stories about their origins and arrivals that were passed down, ending up in the hands of ambitious scribes. Insofar as the book of Joshua records such processes, according to Aharoni, it presents a historical record that can be confirmed by other witnesses to the period. Its unique aspect derives from how the distinct tribal groups experienced the historical shift and adapted themselves to it. Although he promotes the idea that the people of Israel ultimately develop a cohesive and superior culture, Aharoni both universalizes and fragments Israelite history. As they pursue immediate goals of survival and stability, his tribes look similar to other social groups in their time and place. The collectivity necessary to meet their goals is highly localized while linked to parallel projects across the region.

Aharoni's Israelite tribes sound quite a bit like the founders of Galilean kibbutzim.

> On the one hand, the Israelite tribes learned from the Canaanite inhabitants as true and diligent students, and, on the other hand, they were not swallowed up by the superior culture surrounding them. . . . Eventually,

70. Yohanan Aharoni, "Discussion Following Yehudah Elizur's Presentation, 'The Plan for Conquest of the Land in the Book of Joshua,'" in *Studies of the Book of Joshua*, 8–9 (Hebrew).

71. Aharoni perceived evidence that Israelite tribes began to arrive as early as the fourteenth century BCE but did not challenge their neighbors until after their settlements gained footing.

> they realized an original, independent culture and their own borders despite the fact that they borrowed so much from the Canaanites in the land.[72]

Canaanite neighbors instructed the Israelites on how to survive in the wilds of Canaan, and eventually the Israelites expanded from the wilderness to the borders of Canaanite cities. Many of the early kibbutzim—Degania, the first kibbutz, for example—preserved memories of arriving at a strange location and learning local means of survival from the resident *Felaheen* (Palestinian peasants). In the story of Degania, Jewish immigrants come to a place called Um Juni, where their Arab neighbors teach them how to build brick ovens, plant crops, and produce dairy products.[73] As these neighbors are valued, romanticized, and pitied, the pioneers work toward a separate culture of exclusively "Hebrew labor" and the unspoken goal of their absence. The overarching approach, which Aharoni attributes to the Israelite tribes, was to behave "as true and diligent students" while avoiding being "swallowed up" by a surrounding culture—learn from the natives, but don't be like them in order to eventually surpass them.

The patient, persistent project of settlement, for Aharoni, meant that Canaanite cities with long-standing cultural traditions of their own went unincorporated. "The transformation of the land of Canaan into the Land of Israel is not the result of a one-time conquest of a settled land, but first and foremost the result of acquiring and settling uninhabited lands."[74] In the archaeological record, Aharoni found evidence of advanced Canaanite urban centers as well as vacant lands where the tribes of Israel asserted themselves. He could thus imagine an empty land conquered by Hebrew labor without denying the Canaanite presence or accepting the conquest as portrayed in Joshua. Conquest, for him, was a slow process of penetration, acclimation, and expansion. Aharoni constructed his argument in a logical and careful way without the sweeping gestures of Yadin, yet still framed it in terms of colonization as redemption. A founding member of a kibbutz, Aharoni viewed the herculean process of converting "backward" lands into "new earth" as "one of the great revolutions in the history of the Land of Israel" that ultimately "changes the face of the land

72. Aharoni, "Settlement of the Tribes of Israel," in *Studies of the Book of Joshua*, 232 (Hebrew).

73. Havrelock, *River Jordan*, 248–250.

74. Aharoni, "Settlement of the Tribes of Israel," in *Studies of the Book of Joshua*, 233 (Hebrew).

of Canaan from one end to the other."[75] In place of a conquest by soldiers, Aharoni perceives disparate moments of quiet, persistent collectivism that create "the Land of Israel."

Necessity prompted the gradual yet extensive historical shift. "We see around the 13th century and the beginning of the 12th century a tremendous push on the part of the different tribes of Israel toward settlement. This push—as if from a lack of choice—occurs under particularly difficult conditions and circumstances."[76] As if describing the motivation for Jewish immigration to Israel, Aharoni explained that the tribes settled the often-inhospitable land because they had nowhere else to turn.[77] Persecuted by other groups, forced to constantly move, the tribes located wild, untrammeled tracts of land and put down roots. Because this process did not end their torment, the tribes banded together, protected their holdings, and worked to enlarge them.

No matter how strong the bond among the tribes, the landscape never became socially or ethnically homogenous. For example, despite the fact that the tribe of Manasseh absorbed Canaanite cities, the important city of Shechem (modern-day Nablus) never became Israelite. Instead "the Canaanites ruled the city within the framework of the treaty among the tribes of Israel."[78] The tribal system, out of necessity, had provisions for other sites of sovereignty. The enemy that shaped tribal alliances and necessitated a joint war effort never totally disappeared. Here again a contemporary scenario seems to influence Aharoni's sense of the past: large Arab cities such as Nazareth and Umm al-Fahm and mixed Arab-Jewish cities like Haifa withstood the 1948 war, comprising a significant feature of the Israeli Galilee.[79] As Aharoni formulated his thesis, Palestinian inhabitants of Galilee were subject to military law and

75. Aharoni, "Settlement of the Tribes of Israel," in *Studies of the Book of Joshua,* 233 (Hebrew).

76. Aharoni, "Settlement of the Tribes of Israel," in *Studies of the Book of Joshua,* 231 (Hebrew).

77. In his response to Aharoni's lecture, Yehudah Elitzur accuses him specifically of this slippage. "If I am not mistaken, his position relates to the modern Israeli settlement of our times (and this is no sin), which began with quiet settlement and ultimately led to military conquest . . . but Joshua did not necessarily 'repeat' what transpired in the Zionist period." *Studies of the Book of Joshua,* 240 (Hebrew). It is worth noting that no speaker who focuses on war is accused of the same slippage.

78. Aharoni, "Settlement of the Tribes of Israel," in *Studies of the Book of Joshua,* 227 (Hebrew).

79. See Dan Rabinowitz, *Overlooking Nazareth: The Ethnography of Exclusion in Galilee* (Cambridge: Cambridge University Press, 1997).

massive expropriation while remaining a present and influential presence nonetheless.

Aharoni also located the perennial Israeli concern with security in the Bible. Three principle factors (weapons, water, and war) enabled settlement in the mountains: the acquisition of iron instruments from the Philistines, the Canaanite technology of collecting rain in cisterns, and the unique idea of collective security.[80] Security concerns in particular influenced Israelite settlement and society, he argued, because protection of the group as a whole necessitated collectivism. Just as the tribes sought to slowly infiltrate Canaanite areas, so the Canaanites persistently tried to penetrate into Israelite territory. In such an environment, pacts of mutual defense sprang into action such that encroachments could be met by "tribal forces to repulse the enemy that penetrated their boundaries."[81] Roving militias allowed settlements to spread across the terrain, but "also constrained the tribes and clans from any inclination to break or split in any significant way from the tribal framework, which was the only framework that promised any protection to the settlers in the different areas."[82] Security concerns thus inflected the development of society by promoting interdependence and requiring fidelity to a common purpose. A strong group ready to defend itself and help its neighbors do the same was the only kind that Aharoni wagered could survive the early days of settlement.

With the Galilee likely in his thoughts, Aharoni described the copresence of Israelites and Canaanites in terms of variant power dynamics based on the particularities of place.

> This development, which originally no doubt displeased the tribes, had extremely positive results over time, which can scarcely be exaggerated. As a result of their inability to overcome the Canaanite centers, the Israelite tribes crowded into separate areas and cleared the forests to cultivate virgin land. This historical necessity left its imprint as the development of a distinct independence and the preservation of the spiritual values of the

80. "Settlement in the hill country was also furthered by the invention of the plastered cistern. . . . This device was not original to the Israelites; it shows up in the Canaanite cities who had always spared no effort to assure an emergency water supply. But the newly arriving tribes took it over very quickly, and it helped them to found small independent settlements, widely dispersed and unrestricted by the limited number of wells." Aharoni, *Land of the Bible*, 240.

81. Aharoni, "Settlement of the Tribes of Israel," in *Studies of the Book of Joshua*, 231 (Hebrew).

82. Aharoni, "Settlement of the Tribes of Israel," in *Studies of the Book of Joshua*, 232 (Hebrew).

> settling tribes. This helped them in a Canaanite surrounding whose material condition was incomparably superior to theirs. The partial military defeat of the settling tribes, in the course of time, turned into the greatest victory, without which it is difficult to imagine the transformation from the Land of Canaan to the Land of Israel.[83]

Although their grand dreams were initially hobbled by Canaanites, the tribes benefitted from the challenge of facing an established civilization on the site of their would-be homeland. Crammed into interstitial spaces, the tribes learned to break out, cut down forests, and plant crops in their place. In contemporary words, they behaved as settler colonials. Hardship fed their resilience until defeat became success. The resolve that the tribes had to develop in order to survive came to serve them more than any other factor. Remaining separate from the superior Canaanite civilization allowed the tribes to preserve "spiritual values" that eased the heartbreak of defeat and exhaustion of frontier labor. Alluding to the Zionist tenet of how the state rose phoenix-like out of the horrors of the Holocaust, Aharoni described the willed transformation of defeat into victory as the means through which Canaan became Israel.

As Aharoni laid out his theory, one can almost feel Yadin mounting his attack. Armed with every last publication of Aharoni's (proving that opponents make avid readers), Yadin accused him of side-stepping his true thesis of conquest by "quiet settlement"[84] involving local skirmishes rather than formal battles. Where Aharoni saw decentralized national origins in Joshua, Yadin perceived the breakdown of a disciplined military society, similar to the one he thought should form the permanent basis for modern Israeli society. Garnering proof through relentless, hostile citation, Yadin lashed out at Aharoni's refusal to accept "the facts" pulled from the earth at Hazor.

> The excavations prove that the process as described in Scripture is completely valid. First there were battles to the end and only afterwards the struggles of settlement.[85]

83. Yohanan Aharoni, "Discussion Following Yehudah Elitzur's Presentation, 'Plan for Conquest of the Land,'" in *Studies of the Book of Joshua*, 9 (Hebrew).

84. Yigael Yadin, "Discussion Following Yohanan Aharoni's Presentation, 'The Settlement of the Tribes of Israel in the Land,'" in *Studies of the Book of Joshua* (Hebrew), 234.

85. Yadin, "Discussion Following Aharoni's Presentation, 'Settlement of the Tribes of Israel,'" in *Studies of the Book of Joshua*, 237 (Hebrew). Yadin further disparages Aharoni for advancing theories based on "little settlements of the Galilee" while denying "the results of four seasons of excavations by two hundred workers and forty-five team members" at Hazor (238).

The former IDF Chief of Staff from Jerusalem refused to cede any heroism to Galilean pioneers and founders of kibbutzim. When Aharoni tried to narrow the terms of disagreement to questions of historical dating, Yadin responded, "The issue is not specific; it is the question of the connection between processes of settlement and conquest in light of the findings at Hazor."[86]

The study group discussants lined up behind the general. Although later scholarship would vindicate Aharoni's theories, if not his dating, at Ben-Gurion's home, only his mentor Benjamin Mazar counted as an advocate—and a partial one at that.[87] With a glum tone but fighting until the end, Aharoni insisted that he had been attacked for the phrase "quiet settlement," which he did not employ in his lecture. He refused to see Israelite history as exceptional or dependent upon an ineffable surge of morale. If only his interlocutors would abandon their secular-national faith in the story of Joshua, they could understand ancient history: "The story of Hazor could be consistent with the history of the period if we give up the simplistic explanation that the city was conquered by an organized military march of all the tribes of Israel as soon as they entered the land."[88]

Whereas the biblical record represents the active, ongoing presence of different peoples, Aharoni and Yadin could only imagine them as disappeared or perpetually receding in power. This suggests that, as much as their rivalry sharpened, both Yadin and Aharoni pursued a paradigm in which a varied cultural landscape gives way to national territory supporting one people alone. They simply saw different paths to getting there. Their debate stipulated that conquest and settlement were separate processes and, at the same time, that these were the only options available in creating the State of Israel. As such options foreclosed other, less martial means of political organization, they also distanced Israel's elite from an honest assessment of their actual social present. The pull of a mythic biblical land motivated "aggressive defense" in one way or the other as it prevented seeing Palestinians as anything other than enemies. It was a biblicist, rather than an archaeologist, who suggested to the group how the state might deal with the peoples who stubbornly remained.

86. Yadin, "Discussion Following Aharoni's Presentation, 'Settlement of the Tribes of Israel,'" in *Studies of the Book of Joshua*, 238 (Hebrew).

87. Archaeologists speak of how the rivalry literally lasted to the grave. At Aharoni's funeral, it is told, Yadin ashed his cigarette before Aharoni's casket was lowered into his grave.

88. Aharoni, "Lecturer's Response," following discussion of his "The Settlement of the Tribes of Israel in the Land," in *Studies of the Book of Joshua*, 247 (Hebrew).

The Nations in Your Midst

It is easy to take the People of Israel for granted and simply assume that the various tribes, clans, and family units are factions of an established nation. In the book of Joshua, however, the story of the Gibeonites who trick the credulous general into alliance exposes the component parts of the social fabric. The exegetical conundrum of the Gibeonites who belong to Israel while not being of Israel provided the modern Israeli commentators the platform to discuss the Arabs in their midst. In 1958, about 180,000 Palestinians fell beneath the umbrella of Israeli sovereignty, with some holding citizenship, others subjected to military law, and most denied access to former lands and property.[89] Those named "Arab Israelis"—a phrase that distanced them from full Israeli citizenship while eliding the Arabness of Jews from Arab countries—experienced the contradiction of simultaneous inclusion and exclusion.[90] As the biblical scholar Menahem Haran held forth on the ancient Gibeonites, Ben-Gurion's group pondered the issue of included outsiders with an eye to how such a group might be prompted to shed their identity and meld with the nation. Their questions regarding how a group of recognized outsiders might fit into the state, how they might cause disruption, and how attendant risks might be mitigated shaped subsequent government policy around non-Jewish citizens in a Jewish state.

Supreme Court Justice Shneur Zalman Heshin opened the proceedings by casting the Israelites and the Gibeonites as nations recognizable in the modern sense who drew up "one of the first, if not the first, non-aggression pacts." Although he claimed this early pact was superior to Israel's recent armistice agreements because "the sanction against the nation that violates the treaty was not determined by a human being, the League of Nations, or the U.N., but by God," Heshin nonetheless criticized it for being an asymmetrical "one-sided non-aggression pact."[91] Joshua pledged amity and protection, but

89. The paradoxical phrase "present absentee" worked in the manner of "aggressive defense" to justify the expropriation of property from those forcibly removed from their homes and lands and blocked from repossession. "In 1954, more than one third of Israel's Jewish population lived on absentee property and nearly a third of the new immigrants (250,000 people) settled in urban areas abandoned by the Arabs." Lustick, "Zionism and the Idea of an Arab Minority," 58.

90. The term has been revised by the citizens themselves to "Palestinian Citizens of Israel" or "1948 Palestinians."

91. Shneur Zalman Heshin, "Introduction to the Gibeonites—Their Place in the Campaign of Conquering the Land and in Israel's History," in *Studies of the Book of Joshua*, 101 (Hebrew).

exacted no reciprocal promise. However much 1948 may resemble Joshua's war, Heshin warned his fellows against emulating his diplomacy.

When Professor Menahem Haran stood to lecture, he showed little interest in the analogy drawn by the Justice—only in passing did he point out that the biblical term for "making peace" conveys a sense of mutual nonaggression (Josh 9:15)—preferring instead to implicitly advance his corollaries. Drawing attention to Joshua's nonviolent mode of dispensing with the threat of internal enemies, Haran asserted that absorption can erase the existence of a people just as definitively as annihilation.[92] As he sketched the eight-hundred-year period during which the Gibeonites moved from a recognized national group to an unmarked segment of Judean society, Haran proposed the peace treaty as a means of eroding an enemy's autonomy.

Haran perceived a kernel of historical truth in the Gibeonite episode, despite its legendary features. The colorful portrayal of Gibeonite tricksters may insinuate that they bested Joshua, but, in fact, he exercised good judgment when drawing a treaty rather than contending with them. Through a pact of nonaggression, Joshua permitted the Gibeonites to remain in their territory as he exacted the price of subordination. When deployed correctly, Haran estimated that a treaty could initiate a longer, more permanent process of subjugation.

> We can distinguish three stages in the history of this collective. The stage at which they were distinctly Gibeonites was the first in their history. The Gibeonites dwelled in their territory, partially enslaved and laboring as hewers of wood and carriers of water in several locations. At a later stage they functioned more as servants in the temple and in service to the king without a unifying origin—"nitinim, and servants of Solomon" as we read in the books of Ezra and Nehemiah. The third stage took place at the beginning of the Second Temple period. In essence, they did not exist as a collective in and of themselves in this period. In fact, they had already disappeared, as no other witness to the workings of the Temple speaks of the existence of "nitinim" in the Second Temple period. We see then that the period of their history lasts for at least 800 years—from the time of the conquest until the early days of the Second Temple. The history of these Canaanites is concurrent then with the history of the ancient nation of Israel as recorded in Scripture.[93]

92. Menahem Haran, "The Gibeonites—Their Place in the Campaign of Conquering the Land and in Israel's History," in *Studies of the Book of Joshua*, 102 (Hebrew).

93. Haran, "Gibeonites," in *Studies of the Book of Joshua*, 109 (Hebrew).

Haran's Gibeonite history unfolds in three stages. First, the Gibeonites remain a subordinate group in their ancestral territory; next, they lose definition as a landless class of temple servants; finally, they blend, without ethnic name or class designation, into the larger collective. Their labor as subordinates ushers in the second stage of their history as servants in the Temple.[94] Before achieving this honor, however, the Gibeonites experienced cataclysmic loss: King Saul dispossessed and scattered them across the land (2 Samuel 21:2), and in the days of Solomon they "ceased to exist as an ethno-territorial collective" and became "absorbed into the new class of Canaanite slaves."[95] As much as one might not like to say such things out loud, Haran insists, "we must look at historical facts nakedly, even if they are not pleasant for us."[96] The naked fact that the group had to behold was that the ultimate disappearance of the Gibeonites motivated Joshua's treaty all along.

As a subservient class of workers, the Gibeonites elevated their status when they volunteered as servants in the Temple. In Haran's version of Gibeonite history, at this point, they became "*nitinim*," a subordinate group providing service for rituals in Jerusalem. Although the new name still marked their difference, their geographic and ethnic affiliation had already eroded. The identification of the Gibeonites with "the *nitinim*"—something of a standard in biblical studies—allowed Haran to explain why it is that biblical traditions speak of non-Israelite temple servants.[97] By the Second Temple period, all traces of the Gibeonites had disappeared. With no "*nitinim*" or Gibeonites to speak of, Joshua's ancient treaty completed its task. Whoever the Gibeonites may have been, they were completely assimilated into Israel to the point where their eight-hundred-year history eventually became indistinguishable from that of the larger group.

The Gibeonite example provided Haran with evidence that conquered cities and regions can be recognized without jeopardizing national security or

94. "The great privilege of dynastic servants at the temple (we see this at the Mosque of Omar and Al-Aqsa, maintained by Samaritans) was a widespread phenomenon in those days." Menahem Haran, "Lecturer's Response," following discussion of his "The Gibeonites—Their Place in the Campaign of Conquering the Land and in Israel's History," in *Studies of the Book of Joshua*, 120 (Hebrew).

95. Haran, "Gibeonites," in *Studies of the Book of Joshua*, 106–107 (Hebrew).

96. Haran, "Gibeonites," in *Studies of the Book of Joshua*, 106 (Hebrew).

97. On the *nitinim* as Gibeonites, see Joseph Blenkinsopp, *Gibeon and Israel: The Role of Gibeon and the Gibeonites in the Political and Religious History of Early Israel* (Cambridge: Cambridge University Press, 1972), 106–108.

cohesion. Furthermore, insofar as such recognition involves subordination, it marks a necessary step toward the dissolution of collective ethnic and national difference. Absorption of this kind appeared to Haran to be as effective as conquest. This seemingly arcane discussion of biblical interpretation, I submit, indicates an early instance of Israeli thinking about the peace treaty as a form of political suppression. In other words, the group considered that a peace treaty, as much as conquest, could subdue or negate potential enemies. Hardly a picture of happy coexistence, at the very least Haran's Gibeonite story grants ethnic others a shared fate. He explained that after ancient Israel collapsed as a nation, the Gibeonites likewise "cease to exist as a living entity."[98] Gibeonite indistinguishability, in fact, attests to Israel's strength as a nation that can establish a treaty with Gibeon and a society into which it can disappear.

In order to illustrate the effectiveness of disappearance through absorption, Haran referred to the modern map of concern to all in the room. I wish I could state with confidence that the Professor of Bible pointed to an actual map hanging in the meeting room, but I have been unable to confirm this fact.[99] I can confirm that there are few contexts for studying the Land of Israel where the map of the Old-New Land does not hang on the wall.[100] Whether or not the group gazed at an image before them or simply saw the reality in their minds' eye of the Galilee and Negev joined by a thin strip running down the middle, they shared an awareness that no line of territorial connection was certain. They lived within coordinates of armistice, not borders. Inside these lines, the presence of Palestinians—however named—seemed to further disrupt the ethno-national character of the territory. On this count, Haran's story of the Gibeonites assured them that the state could gain mastery over nonbelligerent groups without war.

Gesturing toward some form of a map, Haran aligned the biblical city of Gibeon with El-Jib, its satellite Chephirah with the "northwest of Jerusalem, contiguous with our border with Jordanian holdings," Kiryiat-Yearim with Abu-Ghosh ("or, to be more precise, Tel-El-Azhar next to Abu Ghosh"), and

98. Haran, "Gibeonites," in *Studies of the Book of Joshua*, 110 (Hebrew).

99. On July 10, 1960, the *Chicago Daily Tribune* reported on a few items in the room where the study group met: "a replica of the American Liberty bell, given to Ben-Gurion in 1951 by the city of Philadelphia, and a replica of an Israeli mortar shell, given the prime minister by defense workers. But the spirit of the evening was in the large festival candelabrum, inscribed, from Zechariah 4:6, 'Not by might, nor by power, but by my spirit.'" See "Leaders of Israel Hold Bible Study Sessions," *Chicago Daily Tribune*, July 10, 1960.

100. Havrelock, "Maps and Legends," in *River Jordan*, 1–4.

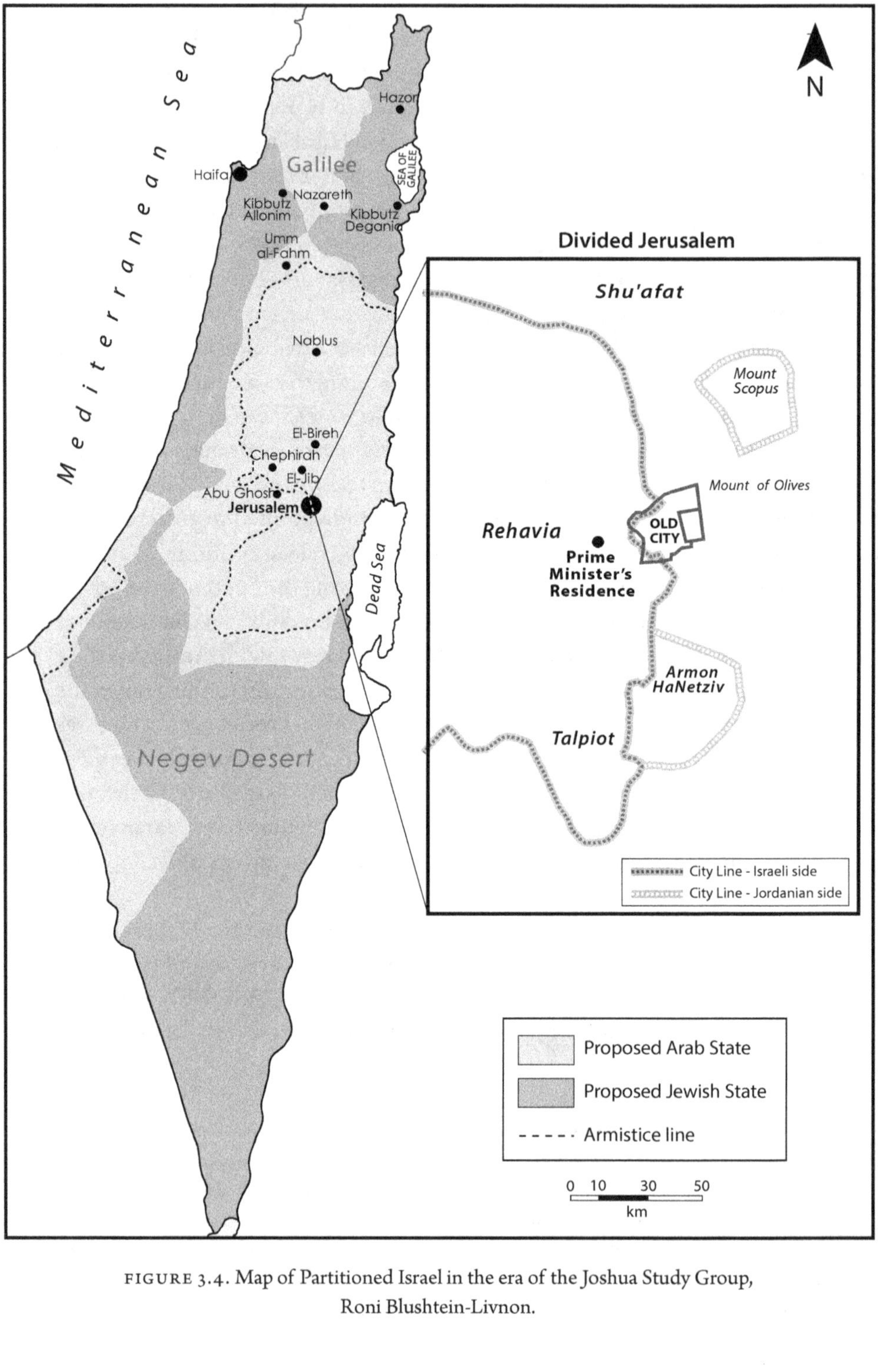

FIGURE 3.4. Map of Partitioned Israel in the era of the Joshua Study Group, Roni Blushtein-Livnon.

Beearot with the Palestinian El-Bireh to the north.[101] Reference to these geographical markers brought him to the overall conclusion that "the Gibeonites were not concentrated in one territorial zone, but part of a confederation of scattered cities," which meant that they had the potential to pose substantial risk to the national enterprise.[102] Considering the strategic importance of the region and the difficulty of ruling a widely dispersed population, Joshua did well to neutralize them as hard laborers in Israel. The contemporary map of Israel illuminated Joshua's treaty such that the Gibeonites became Palestinian citizens and Moses's apprentice appeared as a clever strategist after all.[103]

The implications of Haran's argument become clear through the reference to the city of Abu Ghosh that he identified with the Gibeonite Kiryiat-Yearim. The name of Abu Ghosh alone—the town near Jerusalem "left largely unscathed while other nearby villages were emptied" during the war—communicated to the group the importance of local collaborators.[104] Haran's talk drew an analogy in which the people of Abu Ghosh paralleled the Gibeonites as reliable allies who had been absorbed into the state. The analogy confirmed Abu Ghosh's reputation as loyal to Israel to the point of collaboration and therefore worthy of special treatment. Despite their support of Jewish civilians and soldiers during the 1948 war, most residents fled Abu Ghosh amidst the fighting. Taunted elsewhere as collaborators and threatened by other Arabs, they risked Israeli hostility and blockade as they made their way home. Once back, they received permanent identity cards, which seemingly attested to their patron's embrace and largess.[105] However, as Shira Robinson details, the village's celebration of Israel's first Independence Day coincided with the forcible removal of two recently returned families. As articulated by the District Commissioner of Jerusalem, these modern Gibeonites posed the threat of demographically outpacing the Jews in the area. Nine years later, Haran alluded to the scenario as simply one step on the way to their ultimate disappearance.

In *Itineraries in Conflict*, Rebecca Luna Stein reflects on fieldwork in the numerous cafes and restaurants of Abu Ghosh where she witnessed the value that

101. Haran, "Gibeonites," in *Studies of the Book of Joshua*, 105 (Hebrew).

102. Haran, "Gibeonites," in *Studies of the Book of Joshua*, 105 (Hebrew).

103. Martin Buber remarked explicitly that Zionists treated Arabs as Gibeonites and that "the Jewish state was a disaster and a mirage." Quoted in Yehouda Shenhav, *Beyond the Two State Solution: A Jewish Political Essay* (Cambridge: Polity Press, 2012), 161.

104. Black, *Enemies and Neighbors*, 128

105. Robinson, *Citizen Strangers*, 113.

Israelis place in the city as a safe site of contact with Palestinians.[106] A preferred site for hummus, baklava, and Arabic ("Turkish") coffee in a "friendly" Palestinian village, Israelis commemorate the nonaggression of Abu Ghosh in the 1948 war as they frequent familiar establishments.[107] Stein describes how the owners adorn their restaurants with Israeli flags and other symbols of patriotism in order to sustain the culinary pilgrimage and brisk business. Due to its history of nonbelligerence, Abu Ghosh came to represent Arabs that need not be feared or, to use a biblical phrase, the wood-hewing and water-carrying Gibeonites. Where better to enjoy Arab cuisine? The Gibeonite topology offers one avenue of understanding why Israelis have long frequented Abu Ghosh and are prepared to accept it as nearly an Israeli city. Implicitly, Haran's contrast between Gibeonites and Canaanites advances the argument that conquest by absorption, when possible, is in everyone's best interest.

How to Establish National Territory

Haran's proposition for absorption raised questions of how to distinguish between docile neighbors and internal enemies. On this count, the biblical Joshua's employ of spies seemed to provide the answer. Professor Ben-Zion Luria explained to the group how a web of intelligence networks is key to transforming land into national territory: "The secret of the greatness and success of Joshua" lay not simply in destruction, but in "a clear plan" of how to envision "the state of the People of Israel" while confronting an existing society.[108] Luria's interpretation, which lauds full-blown conquest as the only viable option in establishing Israel, counters Haran with biblical evidence that alliance with others can only weaken Jews and distance them from their brethren.

Biblical studies, historical geography, and national-military conquest merge in the figure of Ben-Zion Luria, who produced the iconic map of the Jewish Land of Israel in which biblical and modern elements became indistinguishable.[109] The

106. Rebecca Luna Stein, "Culinary Patriotism: Ethnic Restaurants and Melancholic Citizenship," in *Itineraries in Conflict: Israelis, Palestinians, and the Political Lives of Tourism* (Durham, NC: Duke University Press, 2008), 97–127.

107. See Robinson, *Citizen Strangers*, 49.

108. Ben-Zion Luria, "The Settlement of the Tribe of Dan," in *Studies of the Book of Joshua*, 250 (Hebrew).

109. In addition to academic research, Luria produced the map through surveys conducted with David Benvenisti, the father of Israeli geography. In the 1920s, Luria and Benvenisti embarked on a comprehensive expedition of the region and project of data collection. Their search

sovereign Israel that he pulled from the earth was militarized and hostile to other layers of material reality, particularly that of the present. The displacement was at once conceptual and real—as he drew the map and published multiple volumes commemorating the Jewish territorial past, Luria compiled the intelligence needed to defeat Palestinian villages and establish Jewish communities in their stead. Almost anticipating the territorial maximalism that followed the Six-Day War, he and his partner David Benvenisti published *The Atlas of the Bible and the Cities Listed in Scripture* in 1966, which stressed that obscure biblical locales form an essential part of the state.[110] However, in 1958 and perhaps thereafter, Luria remained haunted by the other peoples present in the land.

In addition to manifesting the Land of Israel through symbolic acts of naming and mapping, Luria pursued the replacement of Arab villages with Jewish settlements. Well before Israeli forces destroyed hundreds of Arab villages in 1948, Luria envisioned how academic study could facilitate their disappearance.[111] As a staff member at the educational department of the Jewish Agency, Ben-Zion Luria recommended that the Jewish National Fund (JNF)—responsible for acquiring lands for Jews to settle—undertake a detailed registry of all Arab villages, which would "greatly help the redemption of the land."[112] Yossef Weitz, head of the JNF settlement department, saw the immediate application of such a study as a "national project," and Yitzhak Ben-Zvi—Ben-Gurion's coauthor of the Zionist historical geography *Eretz Yisrael*, the second president of Israel, and member of the Joshua study group—proposed the dual project of scrutinizing existing villages while exposing their "Hebraic origins."[113] Here stands a clear application of the colonial paradigm in which underground discoveries discount the claims of those living above.[114] With

for antiquities and signs of the ancient Jewish past was simultaneously a study of how rapidly and completely the landscape could be transformed by Jewish nationalism.

110. Ben-Zion Luria and David Benvenisti, *The Atlas of the Bible and the Cities Listed in Scripture* (Jerusalem: Ahiasaph, 1966).

111. Walid Khalidi cites between 290 and 472 destroyed villages; see *All That Remains: The Palestinian Villages Occupied and Depopulated by Israel in 1948* (Washington, DC: Institute for Palestine Studies, 1992), xv–xvi.

112. Ben-Zion Luria, "The Intelligence Service and the Village Files, 1940–1948," prepared by Shimri Salomon, *The Bulletin of the Hagana Archives* 9–10 (2005), as cited by Ilan Pappe, *The Ethnic Cleansing of Palestine* (Oxford: Oneworld Publications, 2007), 17.

113. Pappe cites Ben-Zvi from Hagana Archives, File 66.8 in *Ethnic Cleansing of Palestine*, 18.

114. The origins of archaeology and mining are alike in this respect: using scientific forms of unearthing subterranean treasures, agents of colonial power or early oil companies sought to

the Village Files, Luria and his cohort envisioned how geographic information could conjure the Jewish past from beneath the ground to upend the Arab present.[115]

According to Ilan Pappe, the combined topographical mapping and surveillance for the Village Files built the scaffolding for the war strategy in 1948. After early exposure to the Files for the villages of Sindiyana and Sabbarin, Ben-Gurion authorized the best photographers and intelligence gatherers at his disposal for the project. "By the late 1930s, this 'archive' was almost complete. Precise details were recorded about the topographic location of each village, its access roads, quality of land, water springs, main sources of income, sociopolitical composition, religious affiliations, names of its muktars, its relationship with other villages, the age of individual men. . . . An important category was an index of 'hostility.'"[116] This multiscalar study of landscape, in other words, weighed the assets of the villages and how easily they could be obtained.[117] The perceived hostility gauged in a particular village often grew into a case for the eventual targeting and even destruction of that village.

As time went on, the research for the files tilted increasingly from the conceptual to the applied. After 1943, collection for the Village Files became "even more systematic" and merged with the recruitment and employment of local informants.[118] A subsequent stage focused on "each clan and its political affiliation, the social stratification between notables and common peasants, and

---

establish claims to what lay underground. The operative idea here was that contemporary powers were more connected to the buried past than the people currently living above. In the case of mining, this took form as "concessions," or claims to buried riches. In the case of archaeology, this involved Western countries carrying off archaeological finds to museums where they came to attest to an evolutionary human history. During the Ottoman period, agents of mining companies and colonial powers could often only gain prospecting licenses by claiming to be searching for evidence of the Christian past. This linked the two forms of excavation forever after; see Havrelock, "Ancient Past That Oil Built," 54–57.

115. The focus on "antiquities" and "water sources" in the Acre village file, cited in its entirety by Benvenisti, perfectly illustrates this; see *Sacred Landscape*, 71–74.

116. Pappe, *Ethnic Cleansing of Palestine*, 19. Although he sees the project as consistent with earlier Zionist spatial practices, Meron Benvenisti dates the beginning of the "village dossiers," differently from Pappe, to 1940. *Sacred Landscape*, 71.

117. "More than 600 of Palestine's 800 Arab villages were surveyed." Ian Black and Benny Morris, *Israel's Secret Wars: A History of Israel's Intelligence Services* (New York: Grove Press, 1992), 28.

118. Pappe notes the focus on land, trees, and assets at this stage; see *Ethnic Cleansing of Palestine*, 20.

the names of the civil servants in the Mandatory government."[119] Information in the files from around 1945 focuses on domestic and religious spaces, as well as the characters of its subjects. "Towards the end of the Mandatory period the information becomes more explicitly military orientated: the number of guards (most villages had none) and the quantity and quality of the arms at the villagers' disposal (generally antiquated or even non-existent)."[120] According to Pappe, the "final update of the village files took place in 1947" and "focused on creating lists of 'wanted' persons in each village."[121] Those people with names recorded on these lists were singled out and "often shot on the spot" when their villages were conquered in 1948. Yigael Yadin claimed that the intimate knowledge of the villages made available by the files stoked military confidence that the Palestinians could be easily conquered. Ultimately, Pappe argues, Ben-Gurion employed the Village Files in Plan C (*Gimel*)—the 1946 preparation of "the military forces of the Jewish community in Palestine for the offensive campaigns they would be engaged in against rural and urban Palestine the moment the British were gone."[122] The scrupulous collection of data allowed for a simultaneous rejection of the existing social reality and construction of the biblical past in its place.

The Village Files attest to the fact that Palestinian society was not flatly ignored or perceived to be without content by the Zionist elite. Instead, a team of experts (who became such through their actions) scrutinized the villages and transformed them into carefully calibrated data sets that could equally substantiate Israeli claims or undermine those of Palestinians. The operating assumption further held that a Jewish essence could be extracted from the

119. Pappe, *Ethnic Cleansing of Palestine*, 20.

120. Pappe, *Ethnic Cleansing of Palestine*, 20.

121. Pappe, *Ethnic Cleansing of Palestine*, 21. Gil Eyal views the 1945–1947 files as constituting the singular "Green archive" reflecting "various interests and forms of expertise," including "the needs of combat intelligence: the number of the men in the village, the number of weapons, the topography, and so on. Another set of items had to do with the needs of *hasbara* (propaganda), with which was blended also the old iconographic practice that sought to find in the village traces of the ancient Jews: the year in which the village was established and the place of origination of its inhabitants (in order to prove that many of the Palestinians were relatively recent immigrants), the ancient ruins found in or near the village ('to show its ancient origins'), the meaning and origin of the village's name (some of the files used Ben-Gurion and Ben-Tzvi's book as reference), and so on. Another important interest was buying land from the villagers and settling it." *The Disenchantment of the Orient: Expertise in Arab Affairs and the Israeli State* (Stanford: Stanford University Press, 2006), 85.

122. Pappe, *Ethnic Cleansing of Palestine*, 28.

places in question and distilled into a purely Jewish national place. The distillation process involved the forcible removal of Palestinians, the rejection of Jewish diasporic cultures, and the alignment of modern Israel and its Jewish citizens with the places and people of the Bible. After the wholesale destruction of villages during the war, Luria and Benvenisti again went out to the field as members of the National Geographic Committee responsible for renaming destroyed Arab places according to biblical, talmudic, or otherwise Israeli names and establishing "the continuity of a historical thread that remained unbroken from the time of Joshua Bin Nun until the days of the conquerors of the Negev in our generation."[123]

At Ben-Gurion's study group, Ben-Zion Luria spoke to "The Settlement of the Tribe of Dan" in the name of reconciling conflicting accounts about the tribe's settlement. One set of biblical sources places Dan along the plain of the Mediterranean coast (Josh 19:40–46; Judg 14–16), and another pair of biblical traditions locates the tribe at the headwaters of the Jordan River (Josh 19:47; Judg 18).[124] Luria dramatized the discrepancy by asking how it is possible that Samson, a famous Danite, contends with Philistine rivals along the Mediterranean coast and then, a mere two chapters later, his kinsmen wander in search of territory to settle. Wasn't Samson's victory definitive? Luria answered the question through a unique reconstruction of biblical history in which he made a few basic claims. Primarily, he asserted that the tribe of Dan engaged in a separate conquest prior to Joshua's that formed part of a wider regional pattern: "there were waves of Hebrew conquerors that came before Joshua."[125] These earlier waves of migration attest to Israelite priority in the land and to the fact that Joshua's armies were forces of nationalist unification rather than colonialism. Prior to Joshua's concerted campaign, however, the tribes lacked "collectivism" and therefore saw their territorial fortunes wax and wane. Because tribes like the Danites "had not yet crystallized as a unified nation and lacked a national-state plan or a national-religious plan," they achieved neither

123. Benvenisti, *Sacred Landscape*, 12.

124. The JNF Naming Committee—in which Luria seems to have played a part—showed more certainty about the location of the biblical tribe during a 1949 dispute over the name of a Jewish place built on the ruins of the village of Yazur. The Jews settling the place chose the name *Mishmar ha-Shiv'ah* to commemorate the seven soldiers who fell in the battle at Yazur. The naming committee insisted on *Azor*, which "was in the territory bequeathed to the tribe of Dan in the time of Joshua Bin Nun." In this case, remembering the war took precedence over remembering the Bible. The place was named *Mishmar ha-Shiv'ah*; Benvenisti, *Sacred Landscape*, 32–33.

125. Luria, "Settlement of the Tribe of Dan," in *Studies of the Book of Joshua*, 249 (Hebrew).

stability nor longevity. Joshua, in contrast, "did possess a clear plan: to destroy the inhabitants of Canaan and to establish in their place a state for the People of Israel."[126] The properly nationalist Joshua, to Luria's eyes, fulfilled a preexisting plan of eradicating the Canaanites and building a new state in their place.

Luria emphasized militarized nationalism as the very thing that granted the biblical Joshua success. The tribe of Dan—his counterexample—never crystallized as a nation and therefore faced repeated military setbacks and ultimate loss of their patrimony. As much as Luria discounted nonnational political options, so he rejected Jewish identities other than that of the nationalized Israeli. The tribe of Dan again exhibits the problem. Although "among the first settlers in the land of Canaan," the people of Dan "mixed and melded with the Canaanites."[127]

> Instead of destroying the Canaanites, the tribe of Dan decided to take part in their voyages on the seas. One must note that such voyages on Sidonian ships would not have been possible for the first generation of conquerors from the tribe of Dan, but the second generation had already, of course, partly blended with the Canaanites and learned to appreciate their considerable surplus wealth.[128]

To Luria's eyes, the tribe of Dan erred by drawing close to Sidonian neighbors on the coast and jumping at the first opportunity to enjoy their adventures and luxuries. Although the first generation of Danite immigrants did not enjoy such an opportunity, the door opened after the Danites assimilated. Sidon marked the name of the confederation of peoples in the Lebanon mountain range that bordered and often opposed the tribes of Israel in biblical narrative, but it is clear that Luria imagined them as the cosmopolitan merchants of a Mediterranean port town. The affiliation with Sidon rendered the tribe of Dan particularly vulnerable during the two-pronged invasion of Canaan.

The idea of double invasion stands as Luria's most inventive historical reconstruction: he maintained that Joshua invaded Canaan from the east at the same time that the Philistines attacked from the sea. Despite the homonym of Philistines and Palestinians, Luria correlated the Philistines and the Hashemite Kingdom of Jordan, which, like Israel in 1948, invaded the land and assumed territory that the United Nations had designated for Palestinians. The

126. Luria, "Settlement of the Tribe of Dan," in *Studies of the Book of Joshua*, 250 (Hebrew).
127. Luria, "Settlement of the Tribe of Dan," in *Studies of the Book of Joshua*, 255 (Hebrew).
128. Luria, "Settlement of the Tribe of Dan," in *Studies of the Book of Joshua*, 255 (Hebrew).

directions may have been reversed—the Philistines came from the west and the Israelites from the east, whereas Israel and Jordan in the 1950s halted to the west and east, respectively, of an armistice line—but Luria identified two distinct national entities that assume their form through a major war of conquest. With the biblical examples, Luria emphatically rejected cohabitation even when it confers mutual economic benefit.

For Luria, the Danites' great mistake was not annihilating the Canaanites and instead continually wandering in search of a safe place to settle. This allowed the Philistines to prevail over the mixed cities on the coast, affording the Danites the sole option of enslavement. The Danites instead abandoned their homes and moved to camps at the base of the mountains close to Zorah and Eshtaol (from which Samson ultimately rises).[129] There, many tribespeople lost their lives. Only a "small remnant [*sheerit haplaitah*]" of Dan remained that migrated north and ultimately allied with Joshua's conquest, their final bulwark against extinction.[130] Assimilation, acceptance, and intermixing factor as acutely negative forces in Luria's vision; only antagonism toward other groups can bind the tribes together and enable them to establish secure, integrated territory. Both the priority of the tribe and its shortcomings emerge in the interpretation, which lauds full-blown conquest as the only viable option in establishing Israel. Where Joshua mobilized a state by enlisting all the tribes against the Canaanites, the tribe of Dan "maintained close relations with Sidon" and "lost their sense of solidarity with the rest of the tribes of Israel."[131]

Worthy of note is the fact that biblical texts do not record these Danite failures. Instead, Luria's evidence relies on passing mention of different locations ascribed to the tribe. The explanation of semiregular migrations proposed by Aharoni never surfaced as a way to reconcile contradictory verses. Along with any conscious or subconscious moral quandary about the violent dispossession of Palestinians, the theory of how nationalism rescued the tribe of Dan allowed Luria to ignore the second half of the book of Joshua in which the tribes of Israel blend with their neighbors. If, as his thinking goes, the tribe of Dan was mortally imperiled by other peoples, then Joshua's conquest actually constituted a form of protection. Through analogy, this interpretive turn suggested that destroying Palestinian villages constituted a form of defense since the danger they posed was existential. Otherness, in this instance of

129. Luria, "Settlement of the Tribe of Dan," in *Studies of the Book of Joshua*, 257 (Hebrew).
130. Luria, "Settlement of the Tribe of Dan," in *Studies of the Book of Joshua*, 256 (Hebrew).
131. Luria, "Settlement of the Tribe of Dan," in *Studies of the Book of Joshua*, 251–252 (Hebrew).

biblical interpretation, figures as enmity and mirrors "the dominant attitude of the Jewish leadership that the Arabs living in Israel were . . . an intrusion by the enemy into Israeli territory."[132]

In his critique of ancient regional alliances, Luria set parameters for modern Israel: it is properly national and statist, its isolationism requires hostility toward neighbors, and it should avoid alliances construed as corrosive. For Luria, alliance or cohabitation signaled weakness, danger, or impending loss. This reading of Joshua coincides with Luria's map of a cohesive Israel, where contact with others is spatially impossible. His vision of the state required the erasure of Palestinians and therefore a permanent state of war. In the group conversation that ensued, Luria's broader argument passed without question or interrogation. Instead, the commentators debated biblical grammar and whether or not it is historically possible that Joshua and the Philistines invaded the land at the same moment.

Ben-Gurion and the Eternally Indigenous Jew

Those imagining the ancient/modern Jewish state, as well as those engaged in actualizing it, still had to contend with the issue of priority in the land.[133] Even before Zionist settlers faced the priority of Arab inhabitants, the issue had plagued Jewish politics. To what place did Jews rightly belong? The notion that Jews were wanderers or latecomers in multiple countries of the Diaspora had long accompanied acts of their disenfranchisement and dispossession. European national obsessions with authenticity and origins directly influenced Jewish political focus on the Bible and the Scriptural homeland, as well as an interpretive stance claiming that the Bible was essentially historical and relevant to the present.[134] Viewing the Bible as innately historical was not unusual in the 1950s, but believing that a Jewish collective was reanimating its truths in real time constituted a particular Israeli position. Both secular and religious leaders took hold of the Bible as the deed to the land and proof of its singularity as the Jewish homeland.

132. Lustick, "Zionism and the Idea of an Arab Minority," 54.

133. Gil Eyal formulates this as "the question of *right*—Who has the right to the land? Is this right divisible?" Noting that "the denial of the existence of an Arab or Palestinian nation was only one strategy in this debate," he shows how the answer to "the question of right was intrinsically tied to the position they occupied in the internal Zionist polemics." *Disenchantment of the Orient*, 82.

134. See Sand, *Invention of the Jewish People*.

Although his interpretive authority derived from his position as prime minister and minister of defense, Ben-Gurion attended to the text itself, combining fidelity and free imagination.[135] His interpretations were novel (fitting, he thought, amidst epochal events) but attentive to the actual words on the page. Essence could provide background and illuminate truth, but it could not negate the content of biblical verses. Admitting "how easy it will be to question my hypothesis," he insisted that "the establishment of the State and the War of Independence cast a new light on our distant past. Questions that I had never pondered as I read the Bible, were aroused within me with an intensity that allowed me no rest."[136] At the same time that the declaration of statehood and founding war clarified the meaning of Joshua, they also provoked questions about conquest and settlement. The kinds of questions that allowed Ben-Gurion "no rest" show him to be more than a hack exegete pursuing political gain. In many ways, Ben-Gurion's interpretations illustrate the contradictions at the heart of biblical studies. His insistence on modern, scientific methods gave him license—like so many biblical scholars—to reconstruct history in his image. But as a Jewish reader trained in a Polish *heder*, Ben-Gurion combined this scientific discourse with a midrashic method that discovers meaning through a literary framework that reads texts in light of other texts with no progressive plot. He and his interlocutors named the combination of biblical studies methods and traditional Jewish exegesis the Israeli school of biblical interpretation and then employed it to read their own experiences and desires in Joshua.

The contradictions between the first and second halves of the book of Joshua were not lost on Ben-Gurion; in fact, they formed the basis of his unique historical chronology. "The locations that are supposed to be settled listed in the second part of the book are, largely, not even mentioned in the conquest narratives of Joshua 2–12."[137] How is it, he asked, that the sites of settlement and conquest do not coincide? As in his own times, Ben-Gurion reasoned that several different maps of a place can coexist. Because aspiration, reality, and variant territorial conceptions all determine representations of

135. Ben-Gurion's stands as the last word on Joshua, delivered at the twelfth study group session on April 4, 1959. The group continued discussion of the prime minister's thesis at a follow-up meeting on April 18, 1959.

136. David Ben-Gurion, "The Priority of Israel in Its Land," in *Studies of the Book of Joshua*, 312 (Hebrew). English readers can find a translation of his presentation in David Ben-Gurion, "The Antiquity of Israel in Its Land," in *Ben-Gurion Looks at the Bible*, 55–109.

137. Ben-Gurion, "Priority of Israel in its Land," in *Studies of the Book of Joshua*, 312 (Hebrew).

place, multiple versions of homeland circulate simultaneously. The prime minister recognized particular value in the multiple representations of homeland captured in the book of Joshua.[138]

One place in particular stood out to Ben-Gurion for its unique settlement history—the biblical city of Shechem, contemporary Nablus. Shechem is Abraham's first stop on his tour of the land promised him by God. He marks his arrival in the land of the Canaanites by building an altar at the terebinth of Moreh (Genesis 12:6). After Jacob returns home following an extended journey, he purchases land in Shechem to settle his family and build an altar (Gen 33:19). The program of maintaining social difference while settling among Hivites hits a definitive limit when Dinah, Jacob's daughter, is raped by the local prince. All the same, Moses urges the People of Israel to return to Shechem and build an altar in a ritual recapitulation of national revelation (Deuteronomy 27:1–8). Ever the faithful disciple, Joshua does as Moses instructed, emulating the revelation at Sinai by reading the Torah aloud to the People arrayed on Gerizim and Ebal, twin holy mountains (Josh 8:30–35).

The textual repetition of the word "all" suggested to Ben-Gurion the national fulfillment at hand: Joshua gathers "all of Israel," reads "all the words," according to "all that is written in the scroll of the Torah." Not one word of "all that Moses commanded" was left unread by Joshua before "all the community of Israel" (Josh 8:33–35). The totality of this gathering and symbolic import of Shechem aroused Ben-Gurion's interest in this early history of the Palestinian city of Nablus. He wondered specifically how Joshua could convene such an assembly in plain view without having conquered the city. Where are Joshua's Canaanite foes during the mass gathering of Israel? Why doesn't the king of Shechem come out to oppose him? Ben-Gurion never denied the shortcomings of Joshua's conquest—after all, Joshua constituted his primary analogy to

138. While primarily invested in territorialized nationalism, Ben-Gurion never fixated on a particular set of borders. In 1918, Ben-Gurion and Yitzhak Ben-Zvi wrote *Eretz Yisrael*, a book in Yiddish that insists upon the very physical nature of the liturgical Jewish utopia. They remained uncommitted to any particular boundary system, dissuading their readers from considering "the ideal boundaries that are promised to us according to tradition" or "historic borders that have changed many times and evolved by chance." Gideon Biger, *The Boundaries of Modern Palestine, 1840–1947* (London: RoutledgeCurzon, 2004), 58. Although the connection to the land has a biblical basis, its borders would depend upon "the cultural, economic and ethnographic conditions of the population that lives there today" (58). For Ben-Gurion, the Bible served to foster Jewish unity, but it was the practice of immigration and settlement that would determine the contours of the nation.

the 1948 war, which also left "so much more to be conquered." Rather than ignore the biblical record of Israelite cohabitation with other peoples, he realigned the ethnic categories of the Bible.

According to his "national Torah," two distinct groups comprised the ancient People of Israel—an elite pioneering group who received the law at Sinai and marched across the Jordan with Joshua, and a more populous group of Hebrews indigenous to Canaan. The pioneers, descended from the successful Joseph, formed a compact social unit, whereas the Hebrews of Canaan were nearly indistinguishable from their neighbors. Joshua's elite corps had been exposed to the advanced culture of the Egyptian empire and chosen by God to receive the law at Sinai, yet their knowledge and skill amounted to little until they returned to the land of their fathers and devised a state. While these elites experienced fluctuating fortunes in Egypt and found their true nature in the wilderness, the bulk of their kin remained in Canaan and blended with their neighbors. Shechem, in Ben-Gurion's eyes, served as the long-standing cultural and spiritual center of Hebrew Canaan to which Joshua brought his people in the name of reunion with their native counterparts.[139] There, the diasporic elite encountered their indigenous compatriots and incorporated them into the national army. The project of reunification, combined with an effective campaign against non-Hebrew natives, improved the prospects for both groups. Ultimately, David King of Israel established a much superior capital in Jerusalem.

Lest one think that turning the native Hebrews of Canaan against their neighbors was a bad idea, Ben-Gurion stressed that the natives reaped the greatest benefit. Mixing with neighbors, Ben-Gurion explained, indicates backsliding

139. In addition to focus on biblical texts regarding the city of Shechem, Ben-Gurion arrived at this position through theorizing with his best friend and early writing partner, Yitzhak Ben-Zvi. In search of a peasant class on which to hang Romantic nationalist notions, Ben-Gurion and Ben-Zvi landed on the fellahin, farmers, and other inhabitants of rural Palestine. They claimed that the fellahin were the descendants of ancient Israelite farmers bonded to the land at their core. Along the way, this group mixed with invaders and migrants alike, thereby eroding the connection to their origins. These origins, to Ben-Zvi, were unquestionably either Jewish or Samaritan. The Samaritan association is key because they are a group in continuous residence that claims to have been in Shechem/Nablus, since Joshua convened the tribes of Israel there. See Yitzhak Ben-Zvi, "Joshua and the Book of Joshua from a Samaritan Standpoint," in *Studies of the Book of Joshua*, 127–164 (Hebrew); Ben-Gurion and Ben-Zvi, *The Land of Israel in the Past and the Present*, trans. D. Niv (Jerusalem: Yad Izhak Ben-Zvi, 1979), 201–209 (a Hebrew translation of their 1918 Yiddish volume edited by M. Eliav and Y. Ben Arieh); and Jonathan Marc Gribetz, *Defining Neighbors: Religion, Race, and the Early Zionist-Arab Encounter* (Princeton, NJ: Princeton University Press, 2014), 121–126.

from monotheism, which he interpreted as an expression of the sublime national spirit rather than a purely religious concept.[140] By forgetting their God, the natives lost the spirit and achieved nothing. Joshua revived them, bound them to their people, and enabled them to achieve the independence befitting their collective essence. In singling them out from their neighbors, the pioneers uplift the natives and restore them to the ranks of the chosen people.

Ben-Gurion arrived at his theory through probing questions that rehearse the reasons for the Zionist movement. Foremost, he asked why anyone would abandon countries of advanced culture for the backwater of Canaan. Abraham left Mesopotamia, "a rich and cultured land, to go to a poor and backward land," and the People of Israel—although with little choice due to Pharaoh's vow to destroy them—similarly emigrated from an advanced society to its hinterland.[141] Ben-Gurion did not, as one might suppose, call upon oppression as the reason that Israel must have its own country.[142] Instead, Israel deserved its land because it has always been the land of the Hebrews. Hebrews were indigenous to the land, and the wanderers of the Bible had always come in search of them with a clearer, purer conception of identity that only privileged members of the Diaspora could cultivate.[143] Abraham journeyed to find these Hebrews, Jacob reunited his family with them in Shechem, they sustained Joshua's troops during the long march of conquest, and the earth itself bears traces of them.

Ben-Gurion flouted the model of rights based on victory presented in Joshua in order to insist upon rights based on priority.

> My first assumption is that the Jewish people or even the Hebrew people was born in Israel and grew up in Israel, even before the days of Abraham, as one of the nations of Canaan, and, at that time, was scattered in the south, the central sector, and the north, with its spiritual and perhaps political center in Shechem.[144]

140. This shows Ben-Gurion's debt, as well as his revision, to Yehezkel Kaufmann's theory that the uniqueness of the Israelites arose from their monotheism.

141. Ben-Gurion, "Priority of Israel in its Land," in *Studies of the Book of Joshua*, 322 (Hebrew).

142. Such a reading of the exodus is consistent with Anita Shapira's observation that Ben-Gurion did not want the Holocaust to provide the justification for the State of Israel. He preferred ancient precedent as validation; see Shapira, "Ben-Gurion and the Bible."

143. See also Zerubavel, *Desert in the Promised Land*, 37–42.

144. Ben-Gurion, "Priority of Israel in its Land," in *Studies of the Book of Joshua*, 323 (Hebrew).

His reading marked a surprising intervention in the discourse of primacy. Hebrews—Jews even—belong to the land because of nativity! Rather than conquerors of Canaan, Hebrews were legitimate members of a Canaanite federation, where "Canaan" signifies an umbrella term similar to Israel with "a double meaning in the Torah and in the Book of Joshua. It is both the name of one of the peoples of Canaan, like the Perizzites, Girgashites, Hivites, Jebusites, etc., and is also the general name for all of the peoples of Canaan, including Hebrews."[145] Insofar as Hebrews belong to the land, Joshua did not initiate a conquest so much as a civil war that redeemed the indigenous Hebrews from the clutch of incorrect worship and backward culture. From a political standpoint, the problem with the native Hebrews rested in the decentralized system that Joshua corrected by establishing a centralized state. This state was not merely a set of bureaucratic institutions, but the agent of cultural revival. As a prelude to establishing this state, Joshua brought his message to Shechem, the current capital and historic birthplace of the monotheistic Hebrews.

At first, Ben-Gurion's positions seem almost counterintuitive. Why bring up native claims when the legitimacy of the State of Israel depends upon the denial of Palestinian indigenous rights? Ben-Gurion himself had approved and presided over the repeated and thorough expulsion of Palestinians and subjected those incorporated by Israel to military rule.[146] Why give voice to a mode of territorial claim so threatening to the Zionist enterprise when discussing a book that justifies holy war? I suggest that Ben-Gurion arrived at his interpretation because the notion of historical fulfillment figured so prominently in his thought. Ten years into statehood, Ben-Gurion desired its justification through history rather than war. Of course, he was a politician singularly driven by the project of nation building, but he was also a thinker who wanted to settle the issue of Jewish belonging. On this count, he claimed to have discovered the essence of Jewish belonging in the pages of Joshua. Jews belonged in Israel not simply because the young state prevailed in its war but because they were properly natives of the land.[147] Without stating it outright,

145. Ben-Gurion, "Priority of Israel in its Land," in *Studies of the Book of Joshua*, 323 (Hebrew).

146. Ben-Eliezer, *Making of Israeli Militarism*, 170–181.

147. At multiple levels, Ben-Gurion's interpretation played with fire. We will later see the degree to which he was called to account for its religious implications, but let us note how the prime minister waded into the question of nativity at a time when "Israel officials generally avoided the word *natives* that might have implied a colonial relationship between Jews and

Ben-Gurion discounted Palestinian claims by dating Jewish ones to a considerably earlier era. Palestinians may have been present when the modern waves of Jewish immigration began, but they did not possess the same historical-spiritual link. Should Palestinians cite their own sense of Canaanite ancestry, then Ben-Gurion could point to coextant ancient Hebrews. His reading replicates acts of physical Palestinian removal during the war and postwar period by erasing non-Hebrew peoples from biblical concern or, at least, dismissing any sovereign or ethnic claim associated with them. But, whereas non-Hebrew natives could only have a corrosive influence, Ben-Gurion viewed knowledge gained in the Diaspora as the necessary component of nation building.

Oh, Pioneers

Ben-Gurion's interpretation enabled him to solve the exegetical crux of the two speeches with which the book of Joshua ends. Joshua bids his people farewell in both chapter 23 and 24, but reestablishes the covenant between Israel and God only in chapter 24. Why are there two separate speeches but only one covenant ceremony? Where the historical linguistic approach—source criticism—answers the problem of repetition by attributing the speeches to scribes from different periods, Ben-Gurion perceived two separate audiences addressed by the great leader on his deathbed. "A thorough study of chapter 24 must lead one to the conclusion that the gist of this chapter was neither written later, nor added, but includes the main contents of the Book of Joshua and, in any case, is its earliest and most reliable portion."[148] Not only did Ben-Gurion refuse to marginalize Joshua's last speech as a later addition, but he also insisted that it contains the most important kernel of truth. Importantly, the Prime Minister heralded Joshua as a prophet (an ascription not provided by biblical texts) who instituted a sacred covenant at Shechem that united backsliding native and elite pioneer Hebrews.

In chapter 23, Ben-Gurion suggested, Joshua encourages the community that escaped Egypt—the new immigrants (*olim hadashim*—the newly ascended—as in the Israeli context)—to uphold the Torah given to them by Moses. "Chapter 23 does not even mention the exodus from Egypt, because

---

Arabs, a bond that could be broken only through a change in sovereignty." Robinson, *Citizen Strangers*, 50.

148. Ben-Gurion, "Priority of Israel in its Land," in *Studies of the Book of Joshua*, 197 (Hebrew).

those who came from Egypt did not need to hear the story."[149] Joshua's immigrant pioneers may have needed encouragement to settle a strange homeland, but they hardly required a rehearsal of their own recent history: "The covenant had long been in effect, and was familiar to the listeners."[150] Furthermore, their identity forged in the wilderness was cohesive and durable: "They were no longer divided into tribes, because those who went down to Egypt and those who left Egypt were united all the while by one faith, one hope; and were led by one teacher."[151] A strong central leader guided the group in using shared experience to overcome social divisions and realize the profound need for unity during a time of conquest. The sense of destiny shared by the recent arrivals woke the indigenous Hebrews from their stupor and catalyzed a revival movement. Absent the new immigrants, Canaan would remain unchanged with its glorious essence dormant.

All attendees at Ben-Gurion's study group would have recognized this dressing of their story in biblical garb and understood that Ben-Gurion intended it to be the widespread public narrative emerging from the group. Although most Israelis would not claim to be immediately indigenous, Ben-Gurion's insistence upon Jewish priority in the land—articulated in the very title of his talk—became a favored appeal to biblical texts. The story further coded Joshua's cadre as the Ashkenazi Zionist vanguard, which included the very figures sitting around Ben-Gurion's table. Under the fearless leadership of their modern-day Joshua, this ideological elite catalyzed nationalism through state institutions. Their transcendent unity of national purpose needed to be impressed upon younger generations and recent immigrants through a military regime that permeated all aspects of culture. Without them, the land would remain a place of rural subsistence agriculture and cosmopolitan cities in which Jews would resemble their neighbors, never fulfilling its destiny as the State of Israel. Their actions, as dramatized by Ben-Gurion, manifested the very process of modern Jewish redemption.

In its mythic tenor, this parsing of Joshua expresses three core principles of Ben-Gurion's defining statism (*mamlakhtiyut*): immigration, acculturation, and centralization. He believed that a country built on successive waves of Jewish immigration required a definitive culture for the immigrants to assume. The Judaism that formed the basis for immigration and statehood was utterly

149. Ben-Gurion, "Priority of Israel in its Land," in *Studies of the Book of Joshua*, 328 (Hebrew).

150. Ben-Gurion, "Priority of Israel in its Land," in *Studies of the Book of Joshua*, 193 (Hebrew).

151. Ben-Gurion, "Priority of Israel in its Land," in *Studies of the Book of Joshua*, 199 (Hebrew).

FIGURE 3.5. David Ben-Gurion, prime minister of Israel, inspecting troops in Tel Aviv along with General Yigal Allon (far left) and General Yigael Yadin (second from left), October 8, 1948. United States Holocaust Memorial Museum, courtesy of National Archives and Records Administration, College Park.

deficient in his eyes by virtue of its two-thousand-year eschewal of nationalism. In place of religious practice, immigrants needed to adopt an Israeli national identity. His insistence upon acculturation intersected with the principle of centralization insofar as Ben-Gurion believed that he was personally responsible for forging national culture. Hebrew language formed an important part of this culture, as did military service, but living an interpretation of the Bible was the sine qua non. Just as Joshua transformed the Hebrews by way of the texts brought from Sinai, so biblical narratives of nation and war could make the Jews of the Diaspora into proper Israelis.

Ben-Gurion reflected his image of Joshua by forging exiles into an army and gathering the tribes as a nation in their homeland. His crossing of the Jordan, so to speak, was more daunting insofar as homecoming was not a singular event, but rather a staggered process of "new exodus from many Egypts."[152] The "many Egypts" from which immigrants hailed needed to be overcome

152. Ben-Gurion, "Uniqueness and Destiny," 32.

through biblical culture, nationalist reeducation, and military service. Moreover, Jewish humanity itself required reconstitution; Ben-Gurion named the prenationalized waves of immigration "human dust" that needed to be "cleansed, refined and purified from harmful, foreign dross in the melting pot of Jewish brotherhood and through military discipline."[153] He expressed loathing for everything diasporic through the mixed biblical metaphor of the dust out of which God creates Adam and the—shall we say—baptism of immigration and rebirth of "the material and spiritual soldier."[154] However, "the melting pot" and "military discipline" could not alone effect the necessary transformation because the people are not comprised solely of elites adapted for such changes. There are recalcitrant "natives" whose experiences fall short and therefore must be immersed in ritual commemoration and public culture.

Native Reeducation

In chapter 24, which describes the covenant ceremony at Shechem, Joshua "starts his remarks with a lecture on the ancient history of the nation," as Ben-Gurion was prone to do.[155] The biblical leader then chastises the Hebrew tribes who had degenerated into Canaanite idol worship and recounts the history of the elite in order to provide them with a model of correct behavior. For those who never left the land and never knew Moses—the veterans or long-standing residents (*vatikim*, as in modern Hebrew)[156]—the covenant at Shechem serves as Sinai. The revelation shakes them—however temporarily—from their idolatrous oblivion. More importantly, it creates motivated leadership among "the

153. Ben-Gurion, "Uniqueness and Destiny," 43.

154. Ben-Gurion, "Uniqueness and Destiny," 34.

155. With an eye on the textual problem that the biblical city of Shechem, where Joshua twice gathers the tribes, does not appear in the list of conquered cities, Ben-Gurion explained that Shechem did not need to be conquered because Hebrews already lived there. "Priority of Israel in its Land," in *Studies of the Book of Joshua*, 319 (Hebrew).

156. The use of contemporary Hebrew words scrambles the analogy a bit: in Israel, the *vatikim*, or longtime Israelis, were the early generations of pioneers. Anat Helman speaks of them as "the state's new, wide, and heterogeneous dominant social layer." Their privilege stood in contrast to "the new immigrants (especially, though not solely, those who came from Muslim countries)." I suggest that in Ben-Gurion's analogy the *vatikim* of Joshua map onto immigrants from Muslim countries and the elite returnees onto members of the Second Aliyah. See Anat Helman, *Becoming Israeli: National Ideals and Everyday Life in the 1950s* (Lebanon, NH: Brandeis University Press, 2014), xv.

elders of the old settlement."[157] The recruitment of these elders facilitates the mass transformation from tribalism to nationalism.

Ben-Gurion detected inferiority in the native Jews at multiple levels: they lived a tribal life, harbored foreign gods, and were not "the least bit aware of God's covenant."[158] The combination of nativity and tribalism suggests that Ben-Gurion had Middle Eastern—aka *Mizrahi*—Jews in mind. As much as he sought to strip immigrants from Muslim countries of their religiosity and to foster nationalism in its place, Ben-Gurion entertained most of the romantic conceptions of orientalism. He considered Jews from Middle Eastern countries to be indigenous, pure of heart, hard-working, simple folk able to withstand deprivation better than their Ashkenazi counterparts. At the same time, he perceived the taint of the Arab: because "they had been raised in backward countries that were in decline," they would "find it difficult to integrate into the society and the army" and not enjoy the easy ride that "the Ashkenazi Jews had."[159] Ben-Gurion's civilizing mission involved the fear that Jews from Muslim countries would thwart the country's European nature along with a sense that "the human dust" in question might be the easiest to reshape. Non-European Jews ultimately became "for Ben-Gurion, a symbol of the state's success in creating the new man."[160] Although the state's existence depended upon the Ashkenazi pioneering elite, Jews from Muslim countries could reflect both the earliest claims and most dramatic transformations.

At the same time, the discovery of native Hebrews in the pages of Joshua recalls Ben-Gurion's prestate idea that rural Palestinians were actually Jews who had remained in the land following the Roman exile and eventually converted to Islam.[161] Zionist immigration, according to this model, could have awakened the memories of the native inhabitants of Palestine and brought

157. Ben-Gurion, "Priority of Israel in its Land," in *Studies of the Book of Joshua*, 76 (Hebrew).

158. Ben-Gurion, "Priority of Israel in its Land," in *Studies of the Book of Joshua*, 191 (Hebrew).

159. An interview of Tom Segev by Ofer Aderet, "In Bed with Israel's First Prime Minister: Historian Exposes David Ben-Gurion as You Never Knew Him," *Haaretz*, February 22, 2018, https://www.haaretz.com/israel-news/.premium.MAGAZINE-in-bed-with-israel-s-first-pm-david-ben-gurion-as-you-never-knew-him-1.5824681.

160. Anita Shapira, *New Jews, Old Jews* (Tel Aviv: Am Oved, 1997), 243.

161. Gribetz analyzes the idea held by Ben-Gurion and Ben-Zvi in its early form as multiple wish fulfillments. In claiming rural Palestinians as Jewish descendants, Zionism "attained greater demographic feasibility," discounted urban Palestinians (largely anti-Zionist) as belonging to the emerging collective, and discovered "*ideal* Jews, the prototypes of the treasured New Hebrew, Jews who had never abandoned the Land of Israel and never stopped tilling its soil."

these lost tribes back to their people. This was no longer a practical program for him in the late 1950s, but "Ben-Gurion's idea that many of the Arabs inhabiting present-day Israel stem from these tribes" meant that "the events of the time of Moses and Joshua can occur again today; the Arabs, who are flesh of our flesh, can adapt once again, assimilate and return to our midst."[162] If Palestinians were actually descendants of the tribes of Israel, then the land could rightfully belong to Israel by means of ancient writ, victorious conquest, and continuous habitation.[163] Ultimately, Ben-Gurion surrendered his vision of Palestinians joining the Jewish national cause, yet still maintained that Jews were and had always been properly native to the land.

The vision of indigenous Jews helped Ben-Gurion to reconcile different stages of his thinking about Arab communities in Palestine. In the 1920s and early 1930s, he advocated a federation encompassing Iraq, Transjordan, and Palestine—the British holdings of the formerly Ottoman Middle East. The federation would be Arab with provisions for a Jewish state or for autonomous Jewish regions if Jewish immigration were permitted throughout the federation.[164] No Arab who wanted to remain in a Jewish region would be dispossessed and, if Iraq factored as part of the federation, then no Jew would be dispossessed from an Arab region. In practical terms, his federation idea came to an end with the Palestinian Revolt of 1936–1939. From this point on, Ben-Gurion accommodated British partition schemes while resisting their attendant limitations on Jewish immigration and sovereignty. The recent cottage industry of Ben-Gurion biographies offers different perspectives on his position regarding Arabs in Palestine after the revolt. In the collaborative biography with David Landau, Shimon Peres claimed that until 1947 Ben-Gurion insisted that the Arab inhabitants would not be driven off their lands or out of the state—Jews would settle only in open spaces, redeeming uncultivated land—and his thinking changed only during the war.[165] In contrast, Tom

---

Defining Neighbors, 125. See also Tom Segev, *A State at Any Cost: The Life of David Ben-Gurion*, trans. Haim Watzman (New York: Farrar, Straus and Giroux, 2019), 138–139.

162. Zeev Tzahor, "Ben-Gurion's Mythopoetics," *Israel Affairs* 1, no. 3 (1995): 67.

163. In the late 1920s and early 1930s, when Ben-Gurion explored ways to coexist with Palestinian communities, he refused to perceive them as part of a distinct people or a parallel national group; Ben-Eliezer, *Making of Israeli Militarism*, 2.

164. Shabtai Teveth, *Ben-Gurion and the Palestinian Arabs: From Peace to War* (New York: Oxford University Press, 1985), 129.

165. Shimon Peres portrays him as an enthusiastic architect of the two-state solution in *Ben-Gurion: A Political Life. In Conversation with David Landau* (New York: Nextbook/Schocken,

Segev cites a statement from the 1930s in favor of a forced transfer of Arabs beyond the eventual boundaries of a Jewish polity.[166] Michael Bar-Zohar's earlier biography shows how Ben-Gurion discounted Palestinian claims by asserting that the supposedly voluntary abandonment of their lands showed the lack of "a sense of nationality" and "feeling for the homeland and soil."[167] Belying these claims is of course the very Joshua-like destruction and evacuation over which Ben-Gurion presided.[168] In the conquered areas that remained standing and populated, he established a repressive military rule restricting freedom of movement, organization, and expression that formally endured until 1966.[169] His idea of collective, continuous Jewish presence in the homeland seems to go hand in hand with legitimizing expulsion and exclusion. Conjuring up indigenous Hebrews from the pages of the Bible in the 1950s was most pointedly a technique of circumventing Palestinian claims as if to say, we are more indigenous than you, and your nativity—if it exists—is simply a component of our own. The convoluted nature of the argument looked for straightening through the citation of biblical authority.

Despite his identification of two distinct Hebrew groups, Ben-Gurion was obsessed with proving the cohesiveness of the ancient nation. In his mind, the People of Israel had no competing or coextensive identities. "There was no tribal way of life," argued the prime minister; the tribes were simply interchangeable administrative divisions.[170] Rather than a tribal order similar to the structure of Arab societies, Ben-Gurion asserted that ancient Israel's divisions were more like those of the Israeli military.

> What the *Tanakh* tells us about the tribes pertains to the divisions like those we established in the Israel Defense Forces—the Golani Brigade, the

---

2011). Prepared to accept British partition schemes, Ben-Gurion found the international recognition that accompanied the United Nations partition of Palestine all the more acceptable.

166. Segev, *State at Any Cost*, 254.

167. Michael Bar-Zohar, *Ben-Gurion: The New Millennium Edition* (Tel Aviv: Magal Books, 2003).

168. Leah Mazor provides another Joshua reference made by Ben-Gurion over the course of the 1948 war. Inveighing against the plunder of Palestinian property, he equated the plunderers with Achan who confiscated taboo property and himself with the disapproving Joshua; "The Rise and Fall of the Book of Joshua in the State School System in Light of Ideological Changes in Israeli Society," *Iyyunim ba-Hinnukh ha-Yehudi* 9 (2003): 31 (Hebrew).

169. "As far as we know, after the War of Independence Ben-Gurion never visited an Arab village." Anita Shapira, *Ben-Gurion: Father of Modern Israel*, trans. Anthony Berris (New Haven, CT: Yale University Press, 2014), 181.

170. Shapira, *Ben-Gurion*, 368.

> Alexandroni, etc. According to the *Tanakh*, there were no tribes at first; each tribe did not develop with its own leaders and its customs and then unify as a single nation. . . . There was no schism or difference among the tribes. . . . Everyone conquered the land together—under one leader. Suddenly this leader died and the tribes arose.[171]

This passage aptly illustrates Ben-Gurion's circular hermeneutics. First, he framed the history of the modern state in terms of biblical narrative and defined exodus, conquest, and settlement as events of the present. Then he used this mythicized Israeli present to interpret Scripture. In this way, the tribes of ancient Israel became units of the Israeli army, and the example of the army proved the unity of ancient Israel. Wishful thinking characterizes both sides of the equation insofar as biblical texts admit to tribal tension sometimes erupting into civil war, and unification of the Israeli armed forces proved an ongoing struggle for Ben-Gurion, requiring both concession and conflict with right-wing militias like the Irgun and left-wing formations like the Palmach. Because empirical reality prevented Ben-Gurion from insisting that there was "no schism or difference" in Israel or its army, he insisted upon the uniformity of Joshua's army and then projected his desire onto Israel's armed forces. While making himself central to the necessary unity, Ben-Gurion also absolved himself of future dissolution by identifying tribal fragmentation only after Joshua's death.

Anxiety about what might occur following a great leader's death permeates Ben-Gurion's stated certainty regarding Israel's unity.

> Even though the people was divided into twelve tribes in the days of Moses and Joshua, it was united and always worked and fought as one national unit, and heeded one leader: first Moses and afterwards Joshua. Only after the death of Joshua do we find the nation split and divided into tribes, with every tribe fighting separately, or in a confederation of tribes, as in the days of the prophetess Deborah.[172]

Against the grain of biblical studies, Ben-Gurion imagined tribalism as a devolution (most likely to occur during the reign of a woman) following a golden age of national harmony. Further anxiety about ideological, as well as ethnic, differences among the newly forged Israelis pervades Ben-Gurion's interpretation.

171. Shapira, *Ben-Gurion*, 367–368.

172. Ben-Gurion, "Priority of Israel in its Land," in *Studies of the Book of Joshua*, 320 (Hebrew).

Such differences seem to him the very forces that could undermine the centralized state.[173] Deliverance, in his view, could only be achieved through *mamlakhtiyut*[174]—centralized state institutions, policy, and culture—because the state figured "as the only political and symbolic entity that could bind together the fragmented Jewish people."[175] Such a view not only put outsized pressure on Ben-Gurion, but also conferred the job of nationalization on the state. As detailed in Uri Ben-Eliezer's study of Israeli militarism, the armed forces assumed the cultural project of unification and, in turn, inflected all aspects of the state with a military character.[176]

The Old Man turned to Joshua as a source of political consolation, as well as historical legitimation for modern state-building. The two inferred audiences that he recognized in the end of the biblical book substantiated a series of claims. Canaan had always been a land inhabited by Hebrews. Not only did Joshua find compatriots there who were ready to take up arms, but Abraham also traveled to Canaan because of the presence of like-minded residents. Biblical founders made the pilgrimage to the city of Shechem—the modern-day Palestinian city of Nablus under Jordanian control in 1958—because it was "the spiritual, or political, capital of the Hebrew nation."[177] For Ben-Gurion, this proved that the link between modern Jews and the land transcends the spiritual and historical dimension. Jews are indigenous to this land, and their separation from it caused centuries of trauma. Ben-Gurion defined the indigenous nature of Jews in a very particular way. On the one hand, the fact that most tribes never left establishes the indelible link between the People of Israel—which Ben-Gurion easily glossed as "Jews"—and the land; on the other hand, the local tribes "were closer in spirit to their Canaanite neighbors," a backward group that required redemption though "the return of the elite among the Hebrew people to the land."[178]

173. This indeed proved to be the case; see Eliezer Don-Yehiya, "Political Religion in a New State: Ben-Gurion's *Mamlachtiyut*," in *Israel: The First Decade of Independence*, ed. S. Ilan Troen and Noah Lucas (Albany: State University of New York Press, 1995), 171–194.

174. Nir Kedar, *Mamlakhtiyut: Ben-Gurion's Conception of Civil Society* (Jerusalem: Yad Yitzhak Ben-Tzvi, 2009).

175. Helman, *Becoming Israeli*, 13.

176. Ben-Eliezer, *Making of Israeli Militarism*, 200.

177. Ben-Gurion, "Priority of Israel in Its Land," in *Studies of the Book of Joshua*, 321 (Hebrew).

178. Ben-Gurion, "Priority of Israel in Its Land," in *Studies of the Book of Joshua*, 326 (Hebrew). "The minority of Jews who went to Egypt was, in my opinion, the Hebrew intelligentsia,

The prime minister's story diverged from the plot of Joshua at a significant juncture. Where the book of Joshua exaggerates the People of Israel's decimation of the Canaanites as a compensatory measure, Ben-Gurion downplays the expulsion of Palestinians as "the flight of the Arabs from the confines of the State."[179] It should be noted that "the confines of the State" as Ben-Gurion thinks of them did not exist prior to the war and that "the flight of Arabs" also entailed forcible removal and confiscation of property. Here, the prime minister departs from the claims of the book of Joshua exactly where they more closely resemble the 1948 war.[180] As it speaks out loud about conquest, Ben-Gurion's interpretation also seeks to obscure the very conquest at hand. The larger problem that rests at the heart of Ben-Gurion's project is likewise evident in his interpretation of Joshua: Joshua may have mobilized elite pioneers and rallied the backward tribes, but he did so in order to wage constant war with the other peoples of Canaan. The message was not universal, but exclusivist, allowing no place for those who resisted the nationalization of Israel. Joshua's conquest entailed violent denial of the social reality in the land.

Inasmuch as identification between Joshua's conquest and the founding of modern Israel held as a public narrative, Ben-Gurion's interpretation met with a series of failures. His notion of a split People of Israel in antiquity was deemed outrageous. After his 1960 presentation of the theory at a press conference, the National Religious Party brought a vote of no confidence in the prime minister before the Knesset. Menachem Begin, Ben-Gurion's right-wing challenger, pounced on the perceived slight of the religious population, publicly drawing "parallels between Ben-Gurion the poor historian and Ben-Gurion the failing politician, as well as between the biblical Exodus and the Israeli withdrawal from Sinai three years earlier."[181] Just as Ben-Gurion tried to mobilize the Bible to support his positions, so it could be turned against him. Ultimately, Ben-Gurion survived the vote with only six Knesset members

many of whom knew the Egyptian language from the outset, as is clear in Joseph's conversations in Egypt and the dialogues of Moses and Aaron with Pharaoh" (385).

179. Ben-Gurion, "Lecturer's Response," following discussion of his "Priority of Israel in Its Land," in *Studies of the Book of Joshua*, 371 (Hebrew).

180. M. T. Wacker explains, "The speaker here leaves no doubt that the Arab villages and cities are identical to the Canaanite enemies of Israel during the time of Joshua; and the warring children of Israel of the Bible are identified with the Jewish armed forces before and after the founding of the state." Wacker, "Das Buch Josua," 630.

181. Magen Broshi, *Bread, Wine, Walls and Scrolls* (New York: Sheffield Academic Press, 2001), 33.

supporting his censure, sixty-one opposing, and six abstaining. Still, there were several Joshuas waiting in the wings to displace "the Old Man."

On a more profound level, the repressed returned in the decades following the tenth anniversary. The very ethnic and ideological tribes that Ben-Gurion feared came soon enough to characterize public and political life in Israel. Despite the investments in national unity based on a secular biblical Jewish culture, collective solidarity eluded the state founded by Ben-Gurion. Protégés in the military like Moshe Dayan took territorial aspiration to maximalist dimensions, locking Israel into a formal occupation that compromised its claims to being a democratic country. The right wing did not fall into formation, but instead rose to power by addressing the frustrations of *Mizrahi* Israelis long barred from joining the ranks of the Ashkenazi elite. Its resurgence mounted to the point of destroying Ben-Gurion's party and silencing its secular majority. Ben-Gurion's statism dressed in biblical metaphor failed to shape and unify a society of Jewish immigrants and disenfranchised Arab citizens. Processes of conquest and settlement alike became brutal to the point where Joshua's battles, not his covenants, provided justifying precedent. Gush Emunim marched into a kind of extra-Israeli space they named "Judea" and "Samaria," and Israeli Jews remembered where they came from and engaged in identity politics. Palestinian resistance required that Israelis individually articulate where they stood on policies of displacement and occupation. The tribal order, so to speak, held and then intensified after Ben-Gurion's death. Ben-Gurion's pitched fear of a fragmented period following the noble pioneers (*halutzim*/חלוצים), in other words, the Joshua Generation was realized.

4

The Tribes of Joshua Land

> Unlike the biblical tribes of Israel, these groups do not spring so much from bloodlines, but from loyalties to ethnic groups, religious brethren or ideology, and they erupt into plain view during election seasons.
>
> DAVID M. HALBFINGER, "A MOSAIC OF GROUPS COMPETES IN ISRAEL'S ELECTION," *NEW YORK TIMES*, SEPTEMBER 17, 2019

THE CRASHING DOWN of Jericho's walls remains the most resonant image of the biblical conquest. Having crossed the Jordan to conclude their long march to freedom, the offspring of slaves encircle the Canaanite city until God shakes its foundations and opens them a future in its spoils. Beyond the immediate plotline, the toppling of the elaborate edifice communicates that the dispossessed can overcome even the most entrenched society and establish something new. However extreme the People of Israel's drive for purity and commitment to annihilate Jericho's residents, something about a rampart's fall confers both narrative satisfaction and political hope. As we have seen, Ben-Gurion and the midcentury elite cultivated this hope in tandem with biblical romance around Jericho—as well as Jerusalem, Hebron, and Nablus—through public ritual, educational curricula, and the conflation of the ancient past and modern nationalism. The romance fed a kind of territorial messianism such that visiting, not to mention conquering, Palestinian cities symbolized redemption that could be religious as easily as it could be secular. Less than a decade following the Joshua study group, the Israeli army conquered the West Bank from Jordan, unleashing widespread Jewish messianism with global repercussions.

This chapter traces the interpretation of Joshua in both the run-up to and aftermath of the 1967 war to consider how an ancient epic framed by falling walls and tribal coexistence, ironically enough, came to justify a massive fortification complex and quotidian strategies of occupation.[1] Citation of Joshua by generals and settlers extends the biblical content and its 1950s interpretation to predictable limits at the same time that its virulence far exceeds Ben-Gurion's realpolitik and the cautioning of biblical scholars to understand the book of Joshua in its original context.[2] Ben-Gurion secured Joshua's place in Israeli culture by giving the public a language for territorial expansion, military rule, and perennial war without having to quite confess their true cost and requisite brutality. His study group—which marked a golden age of political influence for biblical scholars—promoted interpretations supporting a strong central government, a robust military at the ready, and a culture of opposition to Arabs. Its central message, largely dependent on Ben-Gurion's rhetorical command, conveyed the necessity of national unity supported by a cohesive Israeli culture binding each and every wave of Jewish immigrants.

The sociologist Baruch Kimmerling deemed Ben-Gurion and his peers successful in forging a unified national culture that largely overcame the ethnic, religious, and ideological commitments of its constituent groups. This culture endured, Kimmerling argued, until the conclusion of the 1967 Six-Day War, when distinct political responses to the occupation of the West Bank, Gaza Strip, Golan Heights, and Sinai Peninsula fractured Israeli society along latent fault lines.[3] Characterized by deep rifts, Israeli society has come to depend upon recurrent war and a massive wall complex intended to bind Israeli communities as much as to exclude Palestinian noncitizens. By separating Israel proper from major Palestinian cities and ideological settlements alike, the wall also operates to create a state of exception to its east and preserve the image of a liberal democracy to its west. The distinction comes into view in numerous geographic, legal, and economic ways. We will consider it here in terms of the book of Joshua, which, absent some street names and public art from

1. Julie Trottier, "A Wall, Water and Power: The Israeli 'Separation Fence,'" *Review of International Studies* 33, no. 1 (2007): 105–127.

2. The cautious biblical scholars include Moshe Greenberg, "The Use of Talmudic Midrashim as an Educational Resource in the Study of the Book of Joshua," in *The Treasure and the Power*, ed. M. Greenberg (Haifa: Oranim, Hakibbutz Hameuchad and Sifriyat Poalim, 1986), 15–16 (Hebrew); Yairah Amit, *The Rise and Fall of the Bible's Empire in Israeli Education. The 2003 Syllabus: Retrospect and Prospect* (Israel: Reches, 2010); and Yair Zakovitch, "On the Problem of Teaching the Book of Joshua Today," *Iyyunim ba-Hinnukh ha-Yehudi* 9 (2003): 11–20 (Hebrew).

3. Baruch Kimmerling, *The Invention and Decline of Israeliness: State, Society, and the Military* (Berkeley: University of California Press, 2005).

FIGURE 4.1. Joshua mosaic on 1 Joshua Bin Nun Street in Tel Aviv. Mosaic artist Mordechai Yoeli. Photographed by Kevin Dwarka.

earlier decades, is little mentioned west of the wall but remains an active, living point of reference to the east.

The different stances on the book of Joshua enforce Kimmerling's theory that Israeli public culture broke into subnational groups following the Six-Day War. In this chapter, we will see how the dissipation of Ben-Gurion's desired national unity comes into focus through subsequent interpretations of his most beloved biblical book.

Joshua, the Sequel

In 1967, General Moshe Dayan assumed the Joshua avatar—displacing Ben-Gurion—when he conquered the West Bank and brought the People of Israel to the Jordan River through Israel's victorious Six-Day War.[4] Dayan led no biblical study groups, but instead strutted about newly occupied territory claiming antiquities and formulating biblical interpretations like a chieftain. In his widely popular book, *Living with the Bible,* the minister of defense and "prime architect of policy in the occupied territories" enunciated the shift toward greater militarization with the backhanded compliment that Ben-Gurion was "the Moses of our time" and the Palestinian leaders whom he met on his West Bank rounds like the tribal leaders of the Bible.[5] Moses/Ben-Gurion deserved credit for "his mission of leading the nation, the entire House of Israel," but Dayan's stature as the military leader who achieved territorial continuity was undeniable.[6] Counter to his mentor's 1958 interpretation, Dayan maintained that the 1948 war did not resemble Joshua's conquest.

4. On the third day of the war, IDF troops crossed the Jordan River on the Allenby Bridge. Dayan ordered them back and the bridge blown up to indicate "his objective of severing the western and eastern banks of the Jordan." He went on to blow up the King Abdullah and Damia bridges as well, later ordering their repair. See Mordechai Bar-On, *Moshe Dayan: Israel's Controversial Hero* (New Haven, CT: Yale University Press, 2012), 136, 141.

5. Bar-On, *Moshe Dayan,* 143. The book's chapters begin "with a biblical description and immediately continue with stories of the Israel Defense Forces." Leah Mazor, "The Rise and Fall of the Book of Joshua in the State School System in Light of Ideological Changes in Israeli Society," *Iyyunim ba-Hinnukh ha-Yehudi* 9 (2003): 37 (Hebrew). Moshe Dayan, *Living with the Bible* (New York: William Morrow & Company, 1978), 77: "Like Moses, Ben-Gurion was a unique figure: 'I do not know what the nation wants,' he once told me, 'but I believe I do know what is desirable for it.' Ben-Gurion's rule, like that of Moses, was marked by clashes with his people."

6. Dayan, *Living with the Bible,* 53.

> Israel's War of Independence, unlike the Joshua campaigns, was fought when the Jews were already settled in the land. The battles were conducted from and within the country itself. . . . Furthermore, the War of Independence started with a combined Arab assault on the Jewish community, and only as the campaign developed did Israel go over from defence to attack.[7]

Seizing the reigns of the hero myth, Dayan bumped the founding elite back to the position of liberated slaves to portray native-born sabras as the Joshua Generation. His self-valorization pivots on diminishing the national achievements of 1948 as simple results of resident communities defending themselves from Arab attack. In contrast, the true conquest of the modern day entailed an offensive attack on lands absent any local base or militias. The combined interpretation of Joshua and rewriting of 1948, of course, was aimed at the elevation and normalization of occupied territories, but it is worth noting the shift of understanding in which emulating Joshua requires acquisition of resolutely foreign territory.

Whether or not we find Dayan a more appropriate Joshua, his single-authored book amplified the contradictions of the source text more than Ben-Gurion's collective interpretation. In no uncertain terms, he articulated that Occupation requires that war seep into all aspects of daily life. "We are the biblical generation of the settlement, following the Joshua conquest, and the helmet and sword are essential requirements. There will be no life for our children unless we dig shelters, and without the barbed wire fence and the machine-gun we shall be unable to build a home, plant a tree, pave a road and drill for water."[8] Cementing the analogy between the Six-Day War and Joshua's conquest, Dayan identified Israelis of the late 1960s with "the biblical generation of the settlement" who will achieve nothing without "the helmet and the sword." Where Ben-Gurion would have let the reference speak for itself, Dayan left nothing to the imagination as he explained that occupying territory entails perpetual war. Under these conditions, life itself—a home, a tree, a road, and water—requires technologies of combat: shelters, barbed wire, and machine-gun.

In the same breath, Dayan voiced an easy comfort with Palestinian communities. Confronting the biblical charge that the Israelite tribe of Zebulun failed to capture Nahalal—a town in the book of Joshua after which Dayan's

7. Dayan, *Living with the Bible*, 105.

8. Speech at Roi Rotenberg's funeral following an attack on Nahal Oz, near the border with Gaza; Dayan, *Living with the Bible*, 165.

moshav was named—he wrote, "The Canaanites were not strangers to me. I reckoned it had been possible to live with them and maintain good neighborly relations, just as we in Nahalal lived with our Arab neighbors at Ma'alul and Ya'apha, and with the el-Mazarib Bedouin who dwelt behind Tel Shimron."[9] Never naming Palestinians, Dayan spoke of "Canaanites" and collapsed the distance between the biblical and the prestate past. Verbal tense is important here insofar as he nostalgically reflects on how it had once "been possible" to live with Arab neighbors. The halcyon memory, however, elides the history of establishing the Nahalal workers' settlement in a ring of exquisitely planned concentric circles beside the Palestinian town of Ma'alul. In retrospect, it appears that Nahalal's rings were always intended to enclose and overtake Ma'alul, which indeed met with total destruction during Operation Dekel in the 1948 war.[10] The town of "Ya'apha" mentioned by Dayan is Yafa an-Naseriyye, also captured in Operation Dekel, but spared annihilation. Most residents of Ma'alul fled to Yafa an-Naseriyye, where long-standing community members and newcomers alike fell under Israeli martial law. Dayan disappeared such hard facts of conquest (and his role in them) with his nod to "good neighborly relations," as if familiarity alone turns conquest into what he liked to call "enlightened occupation."

Dayan articulated his closing vision of "enlightened occupation" from the heights of a patrol helicopter. Ever cognizant of his Joshua image, the modern general depicted himself in deep contemplation of the borders he bequeathed to his people.

> The future borders of Israel have been my closest concern since the establishment of the state. What will be the Israel of our own times? From where to where? What portions of our historic land will it contain, and which will be excluded? But with dusk, in the helicopter on my way home, all these considerations vanished. Beneath me as we flew was a land without division between Arab and Jew; a land strewn with villages and cities, fields and gardens; a land bounded in the east by the River Jordan and in the west by the Great Sea, crowned in the north by the snowy peak of Mount Hermon, sealed in the south by the parched wilderness. One land, The Land of Israel.[11]

9. Dayan, *Living with the Bible*, 165.

10. See also Ilan Troen, *Imagining Zion: Dreams, Designs, and Realities in a Century of Jewish Settlement* (New Haven, CT: Yale University Press, 2003), 64.

11. Dayan, *Living with the Bible*, 226.

Dayan saw the question of state borders as his personal purview with his authority leaving its stamp on the "historic land," "Israel of our own times," and "future borders." His merger of past, present, and future carried an implicit argument for territorial maximalism—that the land conform to the very borders achieved in the 1967 war. Justification for such a claim inheres from the "historic land" of biblical times. Rather than develop the argument or evidence, like Ben-Gurion, Dayan simply speaks "a land without division between Arab and Jew" into being. His panoptic glance does not perceive the helmet and the sword but rather a singular, unified Land of Israel whose wholeness results from recognition of biblical borders in a modern landscape. In this way, a military occupation is both identified and concealed within an essentialized biblical topography. Bound up in the identification is the message that Israel's very existence requires Dayan's borders and any loss or reduction of territory would mark the end of nation and people alike. From his vantage point, the villages, cities, fields, and gardens between the River and the Sea exist in a natural balance as part of "one land" reminiscent of Joshua's achievement.

Rather than contend for the title of Joshua, Ben-Gurion—no longer prime minister but still politically prominent—rejected the idea of occupying the West Bank and Gaza.[12] Ecstatic over what he perceived as the repatriation of an ancient capital, Ben-Gurion encouraged Jewish settlement in Jerusalem, as well as in Hebron, where Jews had lived until 1929. Yet, cognizant and even somewhat respectful of both Palestinian nationalism and King Hussein's political aspirations, he cautioned against annexation of the West Bank.[13] Ben-Gurion advocated designating Jerusalem as the capital and absorbing the water resources of the Golan Heights while withdrawing from all other

12. Benjamin Uffenheimer writes that until the Sinai Campaign, Ben-Gurion aspired to expand Israel's eastern border to the Jordan River, in part, to fulfill his Joshua-like destiny. Afterward, he abandoned the plan to conquer the mountain range that stretches from Hebron through Jerusalem to Nablus (Shechem). "Ben-Gurion and the Bible," in *Ben-Gurion and the Bible: The People and Its Land*, ed. Mordechai Cogan (Beer-Sheva: Ben-Gurion University of the Negev Press, 1989), 64 (Hebrew).

13. Shimon Peres recalled his mentor as opposing the restoration of the West Bank to King Hussein, but warning "against annexing it, with its one million Palestinian Arab inhabitants. . . . Some say that he foresaw the dangerous consequences of occupation and that therefore, after 1967, he urged withdrawal from everywhere apart from Jerusalem and the Golan. It is important to stress that his condition for returning the territories was full peace." Shimon Peres, *Ben-Gurion: A Political Life. In Conversation with David Landau* (New York: Nextbook/Schocken, 2011), 196–197.

territories captured in the 1967 war.[14] For him, a majority Jewish population remained vital for Israeli nationalism. Citing a biblical precedent, he contended, "The word Hebrew designates not only a certain identity, but a separation from others."[15] However, the conquest rhetoric Ben-Gurion had unleashed could not be restrained by cautious policy recommendations—the conquering of Nablus, Hebron, Jerusalem, and other biblical lands appeared as the fulfillment of the destiny he himself had foreseen.

Old-New Violence

From 1967 onward, the story of Joshua has been reenacted in the West Bank, a place name that denotes its position west of the Jordan River and the period of Jordanian control (1948–1967) when the Hashemite Kingdom ruled over eastern and western riverbanks. The term shifted after 1967 even as the land mass in question remained the same. The West Bank came to mean territory occupied by Israel to the east of the Green Line, which had been the de facto border between Israel and Jordan drawn with a green pen during the 1949 armistice agreements. Its post-1967 meaning hinges not only on its difference from Israel proper, but also on its distinction from the other territories taken during the war—the Sinai Peninsula, Gaza Strip, and Golan Heights—by virtue of its large aquifer and its biblical significance. Most of the Israeli population may reside near the Mediterranean coastline, but Abraham's altars, Joshua's battles, and the capitals of ancient Kingdoms once stood in the occupied West Bank. Against the resistance of Ben-Gurion and then Prime Minister Levi Eshkol, Moshe Dayan and other military elites acclimated the public to claiming the West Bank as the revived Jewish regions of

14. "So in an irony of history, Ben-Gurion in his old age returned to his original pre-1948 Zionist conception: the yardstick for political action was attainable objectives, grounded on a realistic appraisal of the situation—and not ancient territorial myths. By contrast, his followers were influenced in 1967 by prior Ben-Gurionian dreams hatched in the wake of the War of Independence. His biblical teachings, shaped within the 'smaller' Israel after 1948, served his followers after the 1967 conquests as authorization for the ideology of 'greater Israel.'" Anita Shapira, "Ben-Gurion and the Bible: The Forging of an Historical Narrative," *Middle Eastern Studies* 33, no. 4 (1997): 670.

15. David Ben-Gurion, "The Priority of Israel in its Land," in *Studies of the Book of Joshua: The Discussions of the Biblical Study Group at the Home of David Ben-Gurion. Full Transcription*, ed. Haim Rabin et al., Publications of the Israeli Society for Biblical Research (Jerusalem: Kiryat Sefer, 1971), 323 (Hebrew).

Judea and Samaria, no matter the legal and demographic barriers to doing so. The tension between the Old Man's caution and the daring of Moshe Dayan put peers like Shimon Peres and Yitzhak Rabin in an awkward position—should Israel's political aspirations remain sovereignty in territory with a Jewish majority or shift to control over a land declared biblical and populated by Palestinians?

Long-lasting repercussions aside, the Israeli public's initial response was one of euphoric release from constraining borders. Prior restrictions to visiting the Jordanian West Bank made its opening feel like an expansive restoration, leading Israelis to rush to its locales by the thousands. Traffic went both ways, with West Bank Palestinians searching for ancestral homes and visiting the sea and Israeli shopping plazas, but for Israelis, orientalist perspectives blended with biblical longings to shape the relationship to the territory in particular ways. Moshe Dayan's very public mobilization of Joshua during his own conquest naturally fed the issue of settlement. After all, following his battles, the biblical Joshua turned to settling the tribes. Shabbat trips to Palestinian markets and biblical sites / Muslim holy places sufficed for the majority of Israelis who took to heart Ben-Gurion's warnings about absorbing somewhere between six hundred thousand and seven hundred thousand Palestinians as citizens or subjects. But the 1967 war launched another trend in which the secular Israeli use of Joshua mixed with mystical formulations of homeland promulgated by national-religious thinkers. This ideological marriage blended the religious and the secular in a host of novel ways as it understood biblical dictates as political imperatives and restored the sense of divine commandment to Zionist settlement.[16]

Following Israel's occupation of the Golan Heights, Sinai Peninsula, Gaza Strip, and the West Bank, settlers advanced a highly nationalist interpretation of Joshua that addressed a mere segment of the nation. Size of intended audience notwithstanding, these acts of interpretation proved as impactful as those of the founding elite. Sociologist Baruch Kimmerling has explained that beyond polarizing Israeli society into religious versus secular and occupation versus peace camps, the settler movement also challenged "a hegemonic national identity, dominated by a bureaucratized monocultural system" to the

16. The sociologist Gideon Aran has argued that the settlers derived their ideas from secular Zionism, rather than traditional Judaism, and reinfused notions of divine redemption. *Kookism: The Roots of Gush Emunim, Jewish Settlers' Subculture, Zionist Theology and Contemporary Messianism* (Jerusalem: Carmel Publishers, 2013) (Hebrew).

point of fragmenting "the collectivity into a plurality of competing cultures."[17] Said differently, the settlers used the Old Man's tools to dismantle the national home and build their own enclaves.[18] In the name of privileging a centralized state and a singular Israeli identity fostered by a disciplined military, Ben-Gurion insisted upon the subordination of ethnic, religious, and ideological commitments. As settlers took hold of the nationalist tools, they prioritized a religious vision over citizenship. Beyond the varied responses to the settlers' march on the occupied West Bank, other social groups took their lead to enter a sphere of competition for legitimacy and resources. In this way, the settlers catalyzed the dissolution of civic bonds forged during the first two decades of the state.

Ben-Gurion's own conception of a unitary national identity without "a multicultural social order" to mediate and reconcile social competition fostered the fragmentation, which ultimately reduced the state to "merely a means of resource distribution and redistribution, rather than the central and monopolistic symbol of the collectivity."[19] In this way, the settlers' interpretation of Joshua outpaced that of Israel's founding father. Critics of the settlers dismissed the book itself, further dissipating the union Ben-Gurion had envisioned.[20] Detractors excoriated settler violence in its vigilante and state-supported forms by denouncing Joshua as a figure of "nationalism, militarism,

17. Baruch Kimmerling, *The Invention and Decline of Israeliness: State, Society, and the Military* (Berkeley: University of California Press, 2005), 89.

18. At this point, Mazor also notices a shift in use of the word "conquest": prior to 1967, Israelis spoke of "the conquest of labor," "conquering the desert," even "conquering the beach and the waves"; thereafter, "conquest" became synonymous with *the* Occupation. Mazor, "Rise and Fall of the Book of Joshua," 36 (Hebrew).

19. Kimmerling, *Invention and Decline*, 110.

20. We can view broad cultural changes through the Israeli curriculum as described by Mazor. In 1956, the state designated the first twelve chapters of book of Joshua as a subject for study in tenth grade. As Ben-Gurion's study group met in 1958, it was updated to provide further "pride of place" to Joshua. The educational system did not promote explicit hatred toward the Arabs, and the subject of the *ḥērem*/ban on the nations of Canaan did not form a central subject in educational discourse. Ethical questions were "largely pushed to the margins" because "explicit protest of the book of Joshua was understood as an attack on national responsibilities." Mazor, "Rise and Fall of the Book of Joshua," 35 (Hebrew). In this way, conquest became a seemingly natural, inextricable part of Israeli culture whose validity was difficult to question. By 2003, the dissipation of unity and attendant distinct positions on Joshua became visible as the state school (secular) plan reduced the time devoted to Joshua, ultimately removing it from the public high-school curriculum (42–43). At the same time, public-religious high schools

and lack of regard for individual needs."[21] Knowing well that settlement is war by other means but disapproving of the new settlers' provocations, Ben-Gurion's successors in government felt torn and adopted a conciliatory position. In terms of political survival, this proved a mistake, as Joshua-mania ultimately spelled the end of the Labor Party and hegemony of the state.

In the wake of the 1967 war, the settler movement congealed in a confrontational form, ready to take on the Israeli government and international law through settlement in Hebron, Jerusalem, Shechem (Nablus), and ancient tribal allotments. As the West Bank morphed into Joshua's battlegrounds and the late twentieth century appeared as the stirrings of the messianic era, the settlers named squatting and expropriation acts of redemption. When the Messiah tarried and the Israel Defense Forces met a stinging defeat in the 1973 Yom Kippur War, the movement crystallized as Gush Emunim (Bloc of the Faithful) committed to thwarting the return of occupied territories to Arab countries in exchange for peace agreements.[22] Ben-Gurion's association between the Arab countries that attacked Israel in 1948 and perpetual enemies from biblical times allowed the settlers to insist that no peace with them was possible. Therefore, they argued, continual aggression was the only possible position. When Menachem Begin's Likud took hold of the government in 1977, everyday war became state policy, and the stance of militarized settlement became concretized in the fortress architecture of West Bank communities. Ever since, the state has supported the settlers' struggle through direct subsidy and by deploying the military to protect their incursions into Palestinian areas. On occasion, the state has set limits to expansion, which has worked to preserve the settlers' sense of countercultural marginalization.

Appraising such acts opens questions about continuity and rupture. To what degree did the settler movement introduce something new into Israeli war and politics, what Gideon Aran has called a "countersociety"?[23] Are the dispossession and violence against in situ Palestinians simply natural next

---

increased the amount of study devoted to Joshua, developing ninth-grade lessons for all twenty-four chapters (43).

21. Mazor, "Rise and Fall of the Book of Joshua," 39 (Hebrew).

22. Reuven Firestone describes how the crushing defeat of the 1973 war stoked, rather than curbed, "messianic, militant activism," insofar as fear that negotiations might trade occupied lands led to increased commitment to settling them. *Holy War in Judaism: The Fall and Rise of a Controversial Idea* (Oxford: Oxford University Press, 2012), 269.

23. Gideon Aran, "Jewish Zionist Fundamentalism: The Bloc of the Faithful in Israel (Gush Emunim)," in *Fundamentalisms Observed* (Chicago: University of Chicago Press, 1991), 304.

steps following the wars of 1948 and 1967 and the regime of martial law? Are settlers, as they often claim, simply the next incarnation of modern Jewish pioneers? And, if so, then what to make of their bourgeois lifestyles sustained by massive state sponsorship? Rather than within the context of Jewish nationalism, are settlers better understood as fundamentalists in the age of late capitalism whose apocalyptic imaginary both reflects and justifies privatization of public assets and ecological degradation?[24]

With such questions in mind, let us turn to settler interpretations of Joshua and how they mark the dissolution of the Israeli collective. With its proliferation of place names that could be appended to settlements and excoriation of tribes who failed to eliminate their non-Israelite neighbors—not to mention its settler-colonial legacy—the book of Joshua became the urtext of the settlers.[25] As much as these interpretations continue in the vein of Ben-Gurion's study group, it is worth exploring how they differ. Where Ben-Gurion convened scholars to pursue an emergent, distinctly Israeli mode of interpreting Joshua, the settlers take biblical verses and scenarios as directly relevant and applicable to the contemporary landscape. There is a tendency, in other words, to circumvent the mediation of interpretation and fuse the landscape described in Joshua with the contemporary West Bank.[26] For example,

24. Settlers have received more state support in the form of military protection, subsidized housing, and infrastructure development than any other Israeli sector at the same time that they dismiss concerns about state law and international censure. This paradox cannot be reconciled easily, but the principle of following the money points to how many backers of the settlers have a vested interest in eroding state power in the name of assuming control of public assets. The larger trend in which denizens of the economic 1 percent or corporate/financial representatives fund or fuel rogue movements positioned in opposition to the state comes into view in multiple countries. As I write, combined movements of religious fundamentalism and rapacious privatization have assumed political power in states throughout the globe. From this perspective, it appears that right-wing religious groups position themselves in opposition to the state as a means of gaining authority that enables them to assume influence or control of the state in the name of redistributing assets. Group members themselves benefit, although in significantly lower proportion to their patrons.

25. On settler-colonialism and Joshua, see Mark G. Brett, "Settler Mandates: Reading Joshua Ethically," in *The Cambridge Companion to the Hebrew Bible and Ethics*, ed. Carly Crouch (Cambridge: Cambridge University Press, forthcoming); and L. Daniel Hawk, *Joshua in 3-D: A Commentary on Biblical Conquest and Manifest Destiny* (Eugene, OR: Cascade Books, 2010).

26. The eminent biblical scholar Moshe Greenberg suggested that the disturbing themes of Joshua provided the opportunity to instruct students about how the Midrash—the interpretive literature written by Rabbis from roughly the first to seventh centuries CE—allows Jewish

neighboring Palestinians are often labeled as Canaanites (or Ishmaelites or Amalek) and the biblical instruction to destroy them understood as sanction for contemporary violence. The net effect of this interpretive stance is a sense of messianic temporality in a biblical space in which acts of settlement have an elevated significance and impact the divine relationship with the world. Scholars have remarked that such hyperliteralism tinged with mysticism signals a Protestant, Evangelical turn in the history of Jewish biblical interpretation, in which individualized understanding, rather than group consensus, dictates the relevance of a text. Analogy breaks down into identification such that settlers see themselves not *like* the tribes led by Joshua but *as* the tribes themselves. God's promise to Joshua that "every spot on which your foot treads I give to you" rings true and pertinent in many ears (Josh 1:3). Further diverging from Ben-Gurion and Dayan who, however coercively, appealed to Joshua's conquest as a paradigm for the entire nation, settlers cite the book to individual or smaller group ends.

As they draw and diverge from secular Israeli politicians, settlers also transmit religious-national traditions that date from the first Chief Rabbi in Mandate Palestine, Abraham Isaac Hacohen Kook (1865–1935). Accepting of the political aspirations and achievements of secular Zionism, Rabbi Kook viewed the land as a mystical entity in a manner more animate than the romantic conceptions of pioneers like A. D. Gordon. Dov Schwartz describes Kook's perception of the land as encompassing "hidden divine layers and concealed celestial depths" with "the actual earth of the Land of Israel (serving as) an "external cover for seething underground contents."[27] Territory was not what met the eye, but rather a text that could be read for signs of cosmic stirrings. In his careful analysis of Abraham Isaac Kook's writings on the subject of war, Reuven Firestone observes how he aligns combat with holiness

ethics to transcend the literal meaning of biblical texts. By emphasizing the Jewish position that the Torah is mediated through interpretation and is *not* directly relevant to current situations, Greenberg suggested a kind of heresy at work in readings like Ben-Gurion's or those of the settlers. Such heresy should not be reproduced in schools, he insisted. Instead, Israeli students should read the book of Joshua as Jews with the implication that the literalism of Zionist biblical interpretation deviates from—or even perverts—Judaism. Several prominent Jewish religious thinkers have argued, like Greenberg, that secular founders like Ben-Gurion undercut the ethical basis of the Jewish state by promoting the centrality of the Bible in the absence of commentary. See Greenberg, "Use of Talmudic Midrashim," 15–16 (Hebrew).

27. Dov Schwartz, *Religious Zionism Post Disengagement: Future Directions*, ed. Chaim I. Waxman (New York: Yeshiva University Press, 2008), 101.

through the observation that war occupied the energies of all biblical heroes.[28] Importantly, in his book *Vision of Redemption*, Kook anticipates a modern incarnation of the conquest and thus initiates a tectonic shift in Jewish legal thought. Traditionally, Joshua's conquest of Canaan held an exceptional place in Jewish law as a "commanded war" in which every Jew is called to fight. Whereas most wars are simply "discretionary," meaning that individuals could easily defer, the conquest alone required total commitment.[29] By delimiting commanded war to a singular biblical instance, Firestone argues that Jewish legal tradition "essentially eliminated the dangerous wild card of holy war because Commanded War was associated with a historical occasion that had long passed."[30] So, when Rabbi Abraham Isaac Kook spoke of the campaign to establish modern Jewish sovereignty as "conquest," he provided revolutionary sanction along with an obligatory call to arms. In a sense, Kook's interpretation goes farther than Ben-Gurion's by suggesting that the war in question is not waged for liberation or independence, but because God wills it so.[31]

Rabbi Abraham Isaac HaCohen Kook's political theology was expanded and applied by his son Rabbi Zvi Yehuda Kook (1890–1982), whom Michael Feige describes as placing "the victorious Zionist project within a religious framework that assigned his followers a privileged position with respect to other groups."[32] Another scholarly trend addresses how Kook the son lacked "his father's originality and depth" as he translated mystical notions into "an aggressive chauvinism that placed state, sovereignty, and territorial dominion

28. See Abraham Kook, *Orot* (Jerusalem: Mosad Harav Kook, 1982), 14–15 (Hebrew); Firestone, *Holy War in Judaism*, 169.

29. Mishnah Sotah 8; Firestone, *Holy War in Judaism*, 74, 89.

30. Firestone, *Holy War in Judaism*, 74. BT Sotah 44b and PT Sotah 8:1.

31. Another parallel between these somewhat antithetical men was the shared aspiration to establish authoritative academies for Jewish study in Jerusalem. Where Ben-Gurion wrapped his hopes in the Jerusalem Society for Biblical Research, Rav Kook dreamt of *Yeshiva HaMerkazit Ha'Olamit*, the Global/Eternal Central Yeshiva, which ultimately came into being as Merkaz HaRav Yeshiva, later to become the theological center of the settler movement.

32. Michael Feige, *Settling in the Hearts: Jewish Fundamentalism in the Occupied Territories* (Detroit: Wayne State University Press, 2009), 27. Gideon Aran identifies the same trend in Kook's religious thought: "everything not conventionally considered Jewish or religious remains outside the realm of relevance or legitimacy." "The Father, the Son, and the Holy Land," in *Spokesmen for the Despised: Fundamentalist Leaders of the Middle East*, ed. R. Scott Appleby (Chicago: University of Chicago Press, 1997), 306.

at the center of its messianic strivings."[33] Rabbi Zvi Yehuda Kook stressed the divine call to occupy biblical lands in the present, "the conquest of the Land of Israel in order to establish our rule in it is a divinely ordained war. . . . Joshua made it plain to the inhabitants of the land: this land is ours. It is under our sovereignty."[34] In Kook's described chain of divine-human relationship, God directed the war of conquest and Joshua enacted divine intervention through declaration of sovereignty. Despite the fact that Kook emphasizes the divine, rather than the human, achievement of the war, he echoes Ben-Gurion in reading sovereignty as an indicator of collective redemption. Kook's unique emphasis falls on the fact that the land is *ours*, not on the basis of nativity or history, but because God willed it so. Fulfilling God's command then requires a victory to establish sovereignty. Once sovereignty becomes an undeniable fact, Kook can countenance non-Jewish inhabitants—as did Joshua after his conquest—so long as they accept and submit to the sovereign power.[35] When Kook spoke of "the inhabitants of the land" who opposed Joshua, Palestinians did not need to be named explicitly.[36] At the same time, Kook believed that Palestinians could still exercise agency and determine their fate in terms of how they chose to position themselves in relation to Jewish power. Kook the son dispensed with the long-standing belief that the Messiah will only come following collective Jewish repentance and ethical behavior and instead declared that Jewish sovereignty marked the onset of awaited redemption.[37] For example, Kook instituted the pious celebration of Independence Day as an occasion of

33. Tamar Ross, "Review of Gideon Aran, Kookism," in *A Club of Their Own: Jewish Humorists and the Contemporary World*, ed. Eli Lederhendler, Contemporary Jewry 29 (Oxford: Oxford University Press, 2016), 302.

34. Yonina Dor and Naomi De-Malach, "'They Did Not Space a Soul'—The Book of Joshua in an Israeli Secular Education Environment," in *Joshua and Judges*, ed. Athalya Brenner and Gale A. Yee (Minneapolis: Fortress Press, 2013), 18–19.

35. Dov Schwartz, "The Conquest of the Land and the Relationship to the Nations Dwelling Therein: Attitudes in Religious Zionist Thought," *Cathedra* 141 (2011): 87. Schwartz argues that Kook the son derived this position from his father, for whom the condition of recognition of Jewish sovereignty replaced the command to destroy the other nations in the land (97).

36. It becomes clear the degree to which the outcomes of the 1967 war changed Religious Zionist thought when comparing this position to that of movement founder Rabbi Isaac Jacob Reines (1839–1915), who forbade imitation of Joshua's army and the conflation of Palestinians and Canaanites; see Warren Zeev Harvey, "Rabbi Reines on the Conquest of Canaan and Zionism," in *The Gift of the Land and the Fate of the Canaanites in Jewish Thought*, ed. Katell Berthelot, Joseph E. David, and Marc Hirshman (New York: Oxford University Press, 2014), 392.

37. Aran, "The Father, the Son, and the Holy Land," 308.

messianic fulfillment, which had the effect of both inciting religious traditionalists and subverting Ben-Gurion's vision of the holiday as a unifying ritual for all Israelis.

Kook's definition of Jewish sovereignty contained within it the redefinition of religious Judaism.[38] The very existence of the State of Israel indicated that divine transformation was underway. Just as God had brought the epoch of exile to an end, so Jews had to dispense with the passivity associated with the Diaspora. In this incipient age, rabbinic admonitions against holy war and "storming the wall" to seize land and establish power lost validity.[39] Like Ben-Gurion and the founding generation, Kook announced an end to restraint in matters of conquest and settlement but went farther in declaring that Jewish law needed to adapt to the new situation. Rather than leaping over Jewish religious history to equate the biblical era and the political present, as had his secular predecessors, Zvi Yehudah Kook sought to change the religious structure itself. In this way, the religiously marginal book of Joshua that centuries of Rabbis had used as their counterexample for Jewish political behavior became the central text of Religious Zionism understood as both the record of what had happened and as an instruction manual of what to do in the present.

The outcome of the 1967 war affirmed Kook's vision of redemption and set the stage for its actualization. Israel's victory brought the main cities and sanctuaries of the Bible under Jewish control, which signaled to Religious Zionists completion of the first stage of conquest. This was to be celebrated and interpreted as a divine message to initiate the second stage of settlement. In a dramatic inversion of Jewish ethics, "the army and its might" became "something holy," "weapons became sanctified," and "the commandment to conquer the land of Israel acquire[d] a changed status . . . [as] a 'meta-commandment' that necessarily embodies a desirable war."[40] Those witnessing such momentous

38. When secular Zionists like Max Nordau pushed for a "Jewry of muscle," they meant that Jews should emulate Christian nationalists. Zvi Yehudah Kook, in contrast, perceived sovereignty as changing the religion itself. On both the gender and the political implications, see Daniel Boyarin, *Unheroic Conduct: The Rise of Heterosexuality and the Invention of the Jewish Man* (Berkeley: University of California Press, 1997).

39. On Religious Zionists' reorientations toward Jewish laws against taking the land by force, see Harvey, "Rabbi Reines on the Conquest of Canaan and Zionism," 394.

40. Avinoam Rosenak, "The Conquest of the Land of Israel and Associated Moral Questions in the Teachings of Rabbi Kook and His Disciples: Thoughts in Light of the Book *Herev Pipiyot Be-Yadam*," in Berthelot, David, and Hirshman, *The Gift of the Land*, 410.

events could not leave the victory incomplete. They needed to move to the newly conquered land, transform its demographics, and Judaize the landscape. Thus, the "meta-commandment" of settling the biblical land became for a select group the raison d'être of contemporary Jewish life. Military might factored as only half of the equation and only a partial redemption. God's plan, as outlined in the book of Joshua, required aggressive seizure of land and direct confrontation with the resident population.

By restoring God to the conquest, Kook provided his adherents with license for an unending war that by definition transcends legal norms and the social contract. Firestone defines the ideology as "the newly Judaized Zionism of the Settler Movement," in which Israel's wars "were re-imagined as expressions of divinely ordained military conquest."[41] The policy implications of settler ideology include the position that no inch of the biblical land seized in 1967 can be ceded to non-Jews. As for the Palestinians who own or dwell in the land in question, the State of Israel exercising its full sovereignty may determine whether or not they can remain in the land. Kook's interpretation of Joshua initiates a temporality that folds the violence of modern war and settlement into the biblical conquest, with events of the one resonating in the other to the point of nondistinction.

Joshua Land

Whereas the onset of messianic time is not clear to all beholders, settler interpretations of Joshua have undeniably transformed space. In the name of realizing the aims of Joshua, the burgeoning settler movement has focused its attention on claiming territory and establishing borders.[42] We can name the landscape that has emerged from settler-neoliberalism "Joshua Land" for several reasons. First, there is the Disney-like biblical reconstruction by way of settlement names, reenactments for settler children and Christian Evangelical tourists,[43] and the poverty enforced on proximate Palestinian communities

41. Firestone, *Holy War in Judaism*, 280.

42. To date, there is a network of about 125 settlements, "which, since the end of 2015 have been home to 588,000 Israeli citizens . . . covering about 9.73 percent of the total area of the West Bank." Michael Sfard, *The Wall and the Gate: Israel, Palestine, and the Legal Battle for Human Rights*, trans. Maya Johnston (New York: Metropolitan Books, 2018), 123.

43. At Shiloh, for example, the Gush Emunim Rabbi Yoel Bin-Nun selected his last name in order to claim the authority of Joshua Bin-Nun, who doled out tribal lands at Shiloh, and tours host "settlers dressed in biblical period costume." Eyal Weizman, *Hollow Land: Israel's*

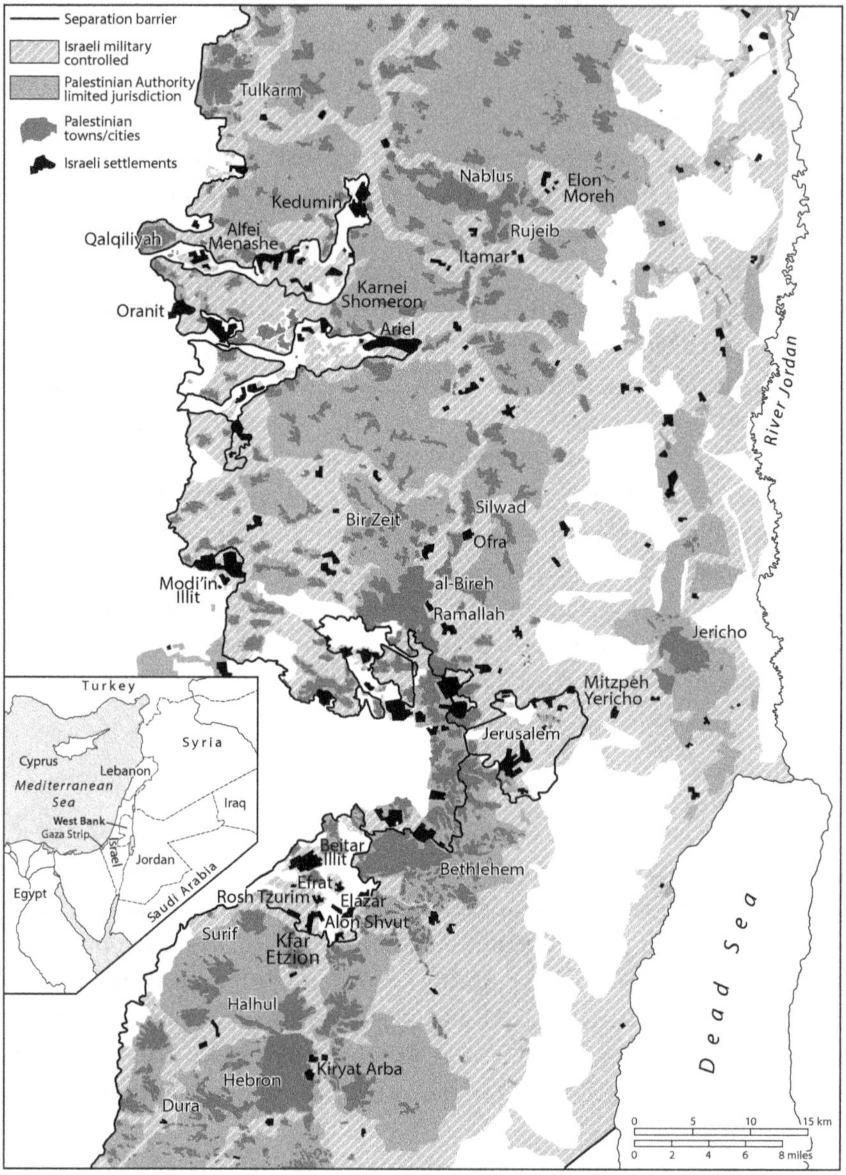

FIGURE 4.2. Map of Joshua Land. Blank areas within enclosed territory indicate Israeli controlled nature areas.

that ensures quaint anachronism visible to settlers and visitors. Beyond biblical simulation, the State of Israel has produced Joshua Land through sustained practices of conquest and settlement and by denying Palestinians territorial autonomy, thus turning the land itself into an incongruous patchwork of ethno-ideological enclaves in which Jews are interconnected by infrastructure like roads and water pipes and Palestinians are severed by blockades and barriers.

Architectural theorist Eyal Weizman describes how infrastructure instantiates the Occupation down to the smallest details like the narrowed area between turnstile arms at checkpoints. In a fragmented age, Ben-Gurion's aspiration for "the linear border . . . has splintered into a multitude of temporary, transposable, deployable, and removable border synonyms—'separation walls,' 'barriers,' 'blockades,' 'closures,' 'road blocks,' 'checkpoints,' 'sterile areas,' 'special security zones,' 'closed military areas' and 'killing zones.'"[44] The proliferation of boundaries and tenuous links forged across them reflects the erosion of the centralized state and diffusion of power among a range of actors. Thus, the infrastructural maze navigated differently by Israelis and Palestinians results from the interests of global corporations and construction firms, the settlers and rightwing government, US arms contracts, 1-percent influencers, Christian evangelicals, American Zionist organizations, and even, as Weizman notes, the humanitarian concerns of the international aid community. In addition, fragments of Labor Zionism, outdoor enthusiasm, and ecological restoration coexist with long-standing Palestinian cities and agrarian villages. The various iterations and combinations of these interests become visible in "multiplying archipelagos of externally alienated and internally homogenous ethno-national enclaves."[45]

Just as once-strong civic bonds have dissolved into the affiliations of competitive subgroups, so national territory now resembles the quixotic, overlapping claims of tribal patrimonies depicted in Joshua. The disintegration of Ben-Gurion's state began soon after the 1967 war, when the National Religious

---

Architecture of Occupation (New York: Verso, 2007), 136. On the Nazareth Village reenactment, see Rachel Havrelock, *River Jordan: The Mythology of a Dividing Line* (Chicago: University of Chicago Press, 2011). See also Yael Zerubavel, "Back to the Bible: Hiking in the Land as a Mnemonic Practice in Contemporary Israeli Tourist Discourse," in *Culture, Memory and History: Essays in Honor of Anita Shapira*, ed. Meir Hazan and Uri Cohen (Jerusalem: Zalman Shazar Center for Jewish History, 2012), 2:497–522 (Hebrew).

44. Weizman, *Hollow Land*, 6.

45. Weizman, *Hollow Land*, 155.

Party reestablished Kfar Etzion,[46] a Jewish outpost that fell in 1948, and a more confrontational group followed Rabbi Moshe Levinger into the heart of Palestinian Hebron, where they checked into the Park Hotel for Passover with no plans of exodus. The push to occupy the historical, densely populated Palestinian city (which, ironically enough, was known in the medieval and early modern periods as a site of religious coexistence) launched the Abrahamic phase of settlement with a focus on real-time performance of the first Hebrew's sojourns. Conceding as it tried to temper their zeal, the Labor government answered the Hebron hotel squatters by building a settlement near Hebron with the Abrahamically significant name of Kiryat Arba.[47]

Following Israel's humiliating 1973 war, the settler movement pinpointed its focus on colonizing occupied territories and splitting from the National Religious Party to become Gush Emunim (Bloc of the Faithful), headquartered in Kiryat Arba. As we look to Israeli military history and biblical texts to explain the phenomenon of the settler movement, we will also want to situate it within the arc of capitalism. In his 2018 book, *Can Democracy Survive Global Capitalism?* Robert Kuttner names 1973 "the end of the postwar social contract," which entailed the return to stagnant wages, gaping income inequality, and destabilizing economic lurches.[48] Such an environment of precarity and social cruelty, Kuttner contends, lays the groundwork for political fascism that promises to reconcile the exorbitant profits of select beneficiaries and the insecurity of workers by eliminating civic rights and freedoms.[49] The attendant income inequality exacerbates class differences to the point where national unity is possible only in a fascist key. As these global trends inevitably transformed Ben-Gurion's socialist, statist, militarized Jewish nation, they influenced—maybe even determined—the nature of the settler movement. As market economics destabilized civic space through the slashing of public

46. Following the return to Kfar Etzion in September 1967, the settlements of Alon Shvut (1970), Rosh Tzurim (1971), and Elazar (1975) were established.

47. As came to typify the settlements, Kiryat Arba was positioned on the hills above the Palestinian city. In 1979, Rabbi Levinger's wife, Miriam, led a group of women back into the heart of Hebron, where they took over a house and established what may be the most radical settler community.

48. Robert Kuttner, *Can Democracy Survive Global Capitalism?* (New York: W. W. Norton & Company, 2018), 76. Coincidently, Ben-Gurion passed away in 1973.

49. See also Caleb Crain, "Merchants of Doom: Is Capitalism a Threat to Democracy?," *New Yorker*, May 14, 2018, https://www.newyorker.com/magazine/2018/05/14/is-capitalism-a-threat-to-democracy.

funds and protections in the 1970s, the appeal to personal truth found in Scripture contributed to the notion of the individual—rather than the union of workers or the collective of citizenry—as a free agent able to negotiate the market and determine his fate. Many superwealthy recipients of so-called free market distribution noticed the power of fundamentalism to advance a moral vision that supports, rather than critiques, the stripping of rights and human dignity from large segments of the populace and, in turn, funded settlement projects. In conjunction with growing fundamentalist movements across the world, the settlers chipped away at state law and regulation as they provoked ethnic tension that necessitated greater investment in security and militarization. Such landscapes of conflict, as described by Middle East experts Timothy Mitchell and Toby Jones, enable the extraction of valuable resources by global multinational corporations, the privatization of the commons, and the swelling profits of arms manufacturers.[50] The specific case of Israeli settlers created a triumvirate involving settler leaders, Jewish North American billionaires whose fortunes tend to derive from the shadier side of late capitalism, and American evangelicals.[51]

Ariel (Arik) Sharon proved another canny interpreter of the political possibilities opened by the settlers, primarily a suspended state of chaos in which international laws of war and occupation could be evaded. Ceding the Joshua avatar to the settlers, Sharon preferred a cowboy image in constant circulation in the media. As Israel's defeat in 1973 eroded support for the Labor government of Golda Meir, Sharon made sure to emerge as "a youthful, energetic and anti-institutional alternative," who as a man could rightly ascend as "Arik King of Israel."[52] In effect, Sharon figured out how to reign amidst upheaval,

50. Timothy Mitchell, *Carbon Democracy: Political Power in the Age of Oil* (London: Verso, 2011); Toby Jones, *Desert Kingdom: How Oil and Water Forged Modern Saudi Arabia* (Cambridge, MA: Harvard University Press, 2010).

51. On the foundational relationships between the Jewish Underground, evangelical leaders such as Jerry Falwell, Senator Jesse Helms influenced by Ivan Boesky, and oil magnate Terry Risenhoover (who was sentenced in 1987 to four years in prison for selling worthless oil-exploration leases in Alaska), see Robert I. Friedman, *Zealots for Zion: Inside Israel's West Bank Settlement Movement* (New York: Random House, 1992), 142–152. On Ira Rennert, who funds settlers and lost his stockbroker certification in 1964 before "issuing millions in junk bonds to finance the purchase of dirty mining and industrial outfits," see Josh Harkinson, "Upper-Class Warfare in the Hamptons," *Mother Jones*, July/August 2012, https://www.motherjones.com/politics/2012/07/hamptons-ira-rennert-mansion-helicopter/.

52. Weizman, *Hollow Land*, 75.

fragmentation, and privatization by cultivating instability while perennially narrating a story of stability and strength on media outlets. Sharon, the settlers, and their economic supporters splintered Ben-Gurion's prized *Mamlahtiyut* (Statism) and then assembled the fragments for their own benefit.

Abraham, in a capitalist guise, remained a central figure as settlers approached the Palestinian city of Nablus (Joshua's Shechem) to establish an enclave where Sharon saw an opportunity in an abandoned station of the old Hijaz Railway. As the National-Religious Party organized "ascents" to the city by groups of wide-ranging ideologues, the point Sharon had marked on the map morphed into the site where Abraham experienced his first vision in the Promised Land at Elon (Terebinth) Moreh (Genesis 12:6–7). Moshe Levinger instigated the Judaization of this landscape by leading a group into the abandoned train depot where they busied themselves studying texts and refusing to evacuate. The Labor government's category confusion about the settlers—are they good Israelis expanding the reach of the state, or are they renegades at odds with the nation—emboldened the emerging leadership to pursue literal enactments of scenes from Joshua. As heads of Israeli institutions deliberated, Levinger led a march of twenty thousand Jews into Samaria, held aloft like a hero.[53] Levinger directed this "battle" of conquest, turning his tent into a "war situation room," where he negotiated with Shimon Peres.[54] No matter how true a successor Peres was to Ben-Gurion, the negotiations illuminated who had taken up the mantle of Joshua. Settler provocation of Palestinians and the Israeli government alike led to a victory in which Prime Minister Yitzhak Rabin allowed them to reside in a military camp in nearby Qadum. Some remained in Qadum, which eventually expanded into the settlement of Kedumin, as others set their sites on a hill near Nablus they identified definitively as Abraham's Elon Moreh. In 1978, these settlers decided to test the commitments of Menachem Begin's Likud government by squatting on the site. When "seven hundred dunams of land belonging to residents of the small Palestinian village of Rujeib" were seized and soldiers escorted the new inhabitants along the path of Abraham, Likud provided its answer on settlements.[55] However, a Supreme Court ruling blocked the expropriation of private land to establish the settlement, forcing the government to relocate the settler cohort to public

53. See Samuel C. Heilman, "Guides of the Faithful: Contemporary Religious Zionist Rabbis," in Appleby, *Spokesmen for the Despised*, 338.

54. Heilman, "Guides of the Faithful," 338.

55. Sfard, *Wall and the Gate*, 169.

land some five miles away. The settlers declared the new Elon Moreh as the actual site of Abraham's inaugural vision in the Promised Land.[56]

A Joshua phase of settlement soon extended the Abrahamic push. In addition to providing names for settlements like Gilgal and Gibeon and confirming that the relationship to non-Jewish neighbors should be hostile, the book of Joshua supports militarization of the settlement process by way of verses that castigate tribes for their failure to annihilate their neighbors. The reasoning goes that tribal settlement in Joshua's time was meant to extend and complete the conquest. Because failure to do so met with condemnation by Joshua and God alike, a settler line of interpretation maintains that causing full Palestinian displacement will exceed the accomplishments of biblical tribes and realize redemption of the entire Land of Israel. In this way, the book serves as a mandate to expropriate Palestinian land, uproot trees and crops, and precipitate Palestinian departure through persistent violence. It is important to note, however, that there is not a singular settler interpretation of Joshua. Counter to Ben-Gurion's dreams for the book, various Rabbis, leaders, and settlers themselves understand the precedent of Joshua differently. In place of a systematic reading, settler interpretation of the Bible depends upon its relevance to the particular situation of an individual or small group. This orientation, novel in the history of Jewish biblical interpretation with its focus on the collective, multiplies as hilltop youth and unauthorized trailer dwellers take verses more literally than their bourgeois predecessors in established settlements.

Gush Emunim named its first official settlement Ofra after a place that Joshua 18:23 lists among the tribe of Benjamin's territory. Like Nahalal (whose name comes from Joshua 19:15), the first moshav where Moshe Dayan roamed with Canaanites, Ofra marked an attempt to reenact tribal settlement in modern times. And, however incongruous the extremes of a socialist farming collective and postmodern fundamentalism in a suburb, both derived their settlement plan from Joshua more than European colonialism. Whereas Levinger's Abrahamic mode of settlement had been more openly confrontational, Gush Emunim activists snuck their way into Samaria by joining the work crew building an army base on lands belonging to the village of Silwad. Soon enough, the crew ceased retiring to Jerusalem in the evening and slept in the abandoned Ein Yabrud Jordanian army base. Simon Peres, again conciliatory, sanctioned

56. Recalibration of Abrahamic geography did not protect the lands of Rujeib. Four years after the evacuation, "a new settlement, Itamar, was built close to the village. It has expanded over the years and today includes some of Rujeib's land." Sfard, *Wall and the Gate*, 179–180.

the move with the caveat that the new settler base serve as a "work camp" and not a "community."[57] Gaining what is likely the most vital form of contemporary recognition, Ofra was connected to the national electricity grid in 1975. Plunk in the middle of Palestinian land, identical homes with sloped red roofs sprung up like a line of soldiers primed for battle. Ofra gained official recognition among Israeli communities when the Likud government assumed power in 1977.[58]

Ofra's moniker, "the mother of all settlements," further indicates how the book of Joshua functions as a settler handbook. In listing tribal towns and regions, later chapters of Joshua use the locution "town X and its daughters," which seems to describe satellite dwellings and farms that fell beneath the overarching jurisdiction of a specific town. When Gush Emunim activists dubbed Ofra the mother of settlements, they laid claim to the long list of places mentioned in Joshua while announcing the generative potential of their flagship settlement. This mother, they promised, would be most fruitful and multiply in settlements across Judea-Samaria-Gaza (Yesha). The book of Joshua provided the authority to build, expropriate, and antagonize while openly violating international law regarding occupied territories. The fact that the bulk of Ofra's land is illegally confiscated from Palestinian landowners has led to intermittent government sanction and demolition of homes, but the extreme acts of Gush Emunim have largely been normalized.[59] The mitzvah of settling the land, which many settlers purport to fulfill, expresses their sense of "symbolic reenactment of the conquering of the land in ancient times."[60] Zealous settlers hear God commanding them to seize the land in words spoken to Joshua and feel frustrated with the partial conclusions and aspirations for international acceptance by mainstream Israelis. This puts them at odds with society at large despite their

57. Nir Shalev, "The Ofra Settlement: An Unauthorized Outpost," *B'Tselem*, December 2008, 7.

58. One of Ofra and Gush Emunim's leading lights was Uri Elitzur, son of Yehuda Elitzur, the only religious member of Ben-Gurion's Joshua study group.

59. On Ofra's expropriations, see Shalev, "Ofra Settlement." Idith Zertal, Akiva Eldar, and Michael Feige analyze how illegal acts and fundamentalist motivations were made palatable to the general public through institutions like the monthly magazine *Nekuda*, iterations of dark Israeli humor, and governmental organizations like the Yesha council, a federation of settlement mayors. See Feige, "The Settlement of Ofra: Ritualizing Normalcy," in *Settling in the Hearts*, 181; and Zertal and Eldar, *Lords of the Land: The War Over Israel's Settlements in the Occupied Territories, 1967–2007*, trans. Vivian Eden (New York: Nation Books, 2007).

60. Feige, *Settling in the Hearts*, 68.

considerable political influence and deepens their sense of marginalization and defiance.

As national-religious institutions like yeshivas and the Bnai Akiva youth movement encouraged enlistment in the army, the settlers also took up arms to enforce their individual claims and establish local sovereignty through terror. Moshe Levinger introduced his own version of Joshua's holy war standards when he insisted that recruits to the *Machteret*—Jewish Underground—cell be "deeply religious, people who would never sin, people who haven't got the slightest inclination for violence."[61] In fact, the Jewish Underground aimed to do violence by attacking Palestinian leaders and blowing up the Al Aqsa Mosque and Dome of the Rock in Jerusalem. When the voters of Israel restored the Labor Party to power in 1992, Levinger again created his own parastate institution in the form of the *Ichud Rabbanim* (Union of Rabbis for the People and Land of Israel), whose charter declared, "It is a positive commandment to move to the Land of Israel, to settle there, to conquer it and to take possession of it."[62] The precedence of this commandment over others meant that those who would un-settle the land by restoring it to private Palestinian owners or to leaders of the Palestine Liberation Organization were sinners and enemies to boot.

At the same time that democracy was cast as an obstacle and proposals for violence became more outlandish, the movement pursued a suburban paradigm. American influence on the settlers along with the many American Jews in settler ranks and leadership helps to explain their consumptive land use and the relative lack of objection to their actions among American supporters of Israel.[63] The universal idiom of commerce provides settlers with another venue for normalization, a trend that becomes clear on the website of the Joshua-identified settlement Mitzpeh Yericho (the Jericho Lookout).[64] The section on the settlement's history begins,

61. See Heilman, "Guides of the Faithful," 343; and Robert I. Friedman, "The Messiah Complex," *Vanity Fair*, July 1991, 135.

62. Heilman, "Guides of the Faithful," 332.

63. See Sara Yael Hirschhorn, *City on a Hilltop: American Jews and the Israeli Settler Movement* (Cambridge, MA: Harvard University Press, 2017).

64. Weizman notes that the *Mitzpeh* (Lookout) settlement is a repeating type whose primary purpose is the directly stated act of surveillance. Like the landscape in question, surveillance becomes a diffuse "optical matrix radiating out from a proliferation of lookout points/settlements." *Hollow Land*, 132.

> As Joshua prepared for the conquer [*sic*] of Jericho, the area served as a temporary refuge for his spies; they fled up the hills to the west of Jericho after spying out the city—perhaps the hill upon which Mitzpeh Yericho is situated today![65]

The identification between the contemporary settlement and Joshua's spies is suggested gently with an unverified biblical reference that at once provides the very reason for Mitzpeh Yericho's location and existence. The history continues with academic research cited to substantiate the claim that the contemporary settlement revives both the conquest and an antique Jewish past with "the oldest known synagogue in Israel" located in the nearby Hasmonean winter palace. Illustrating the devaluation of non-Jewish history, the community chronicle next leaps to 1977, when the founding cohort camped near Jericho during the holiday of Sukkot before being moved first by the minister of defense and then by the minister of agriculture and settlement mastermind Ariel Sharon, who identified the possibilities of their current slope. In 1981, when Israel initiated its official program of settlement, Mitzpeh Yericho began formal development.

Along with themes from Joshua, the online story of Mitzpeh Yericho is an archetypal settlement tale incorporating stock elements of kibbutz founding stories. In categorizing the settlement of Mitzpeh Yericho, for example, language veers from Joshua with the term ישוב/*yishuv*, the name for communities within Israel's recognized borders or in the Jewish prestate society. The generic term for settlements within occupied territory is התנחלות/*hitnahalut*, from נחלה/*nahalah*—the tribal patrimonies doled out by Joshua. Referring to Mizpeh Yericho as a ישוב/*yishuv* rather than התנחלות/*hitnahalut* attempts to situate it as a natural, legitimate continuation of Jewish history. The other prominent theme characteristic of kibbutz origin stories is the eventual ideological split between community founders, although, in this instance, religion causes the rift.

> The religious residents remained in Mitzpeh Yericho, on the hill overlooking Jericho; while the non-religious established a new *yishuv*—Vered Yericho below, much closer to the town of Jericho.[66]

65. "About Mitzpeh Yericho," Mitzpeh Yericho: Overlooking the Cradle of Israel, accessed May 4, 2018, https://sites.google.com/site/mitzpeyericho/home.

66. "About Mitzpe Yericho."

The valuation inherent in the split comes across in the language of above and below—the religious faction remains perched above the Palestinian city, whereas the secular group resides below in much closer proximity. On the heights, "all families are expected to follow a religious lifestyle" and all "women to cover their hair." Along with seeking acceptance through analogy with an earlier generation of pioneers, the settlement's self-description mixes Joshua references—it is "part of the Benjamin Area municipality"—with local democracy: "the yishuv is run by an elected board of nine members."[67] But, ultimately, the aim of the settlement website is to sell real estate by emphasizing "breathtaking vistas of the desert" and a supportive environment for raising children. Personal interpretation of Joshua easily meshes with the promotion of private property (and plans for 1,200 new housing units along with a swimming pool). The conquest remains ever present at the same time that Mizpeh Yericho presents itself like any pious suburb in close proximity to a city characterized by large-scale disenfranchisement. For all its bluster and biblical nostalgia, the settlement enterprise achieves realization through state-sponsored privatization.

Whereas an individual's personal choice to adopt fundamentalist values is often described as a reaction to concurrent globalization, it is vital to investigate who invests in its infrastructure and ideological dissemination. Although shrouded in a good deal of secrecy,[68] much of the money supporting the settlement enterprise comes from casino moguls like the late Irving Moskowitz and Sheldon Adelson (and Meyer Lansky before them), who bolster parallel politics in the United States.[69] For those directly subsidized by the ultrarich or influenced by their media outlets, disenfranchised people constitute a threatening enemy who would take away their right to live as they do. Political liberals or other enfranchised groups who support the rights of the disenfranchised present no less of a threat. It was not out of step with Israeli culture to define

67. "About Mitzpeh Yericho."

68. Bradley Burston, "Who Pays for Israel's Settlements? It Could Be You," *Haaretz*, December 8, 2015, https://www.haaretz.com/opinion/.premium-who-pays-for-israel-s-settlements-it-could-be-you-1.5432838.

69. On Moskowitz and the parallel evictions in East Jerusalem and Hawaiian Gardens in Southern California, see Tim Elfrink, "Nikolas Cruz, Who Was Too Disturbed to Carry a Backpack, Legally Bought AR-15," *New Times Broward Palm Beach*, February 15, 2018, http://www.browardpalmbeach.com/news/nikolas-cruz-legally-purchased-ar-15-despite-long-history-of-mental-illness-warnings-9274747.

disenfranchised Palestinians as enemies, but the assignment of this label to liberal Jewish Israelis introduced new animosity into a state formed on the basis of shared ethnicity and history. As Labor Party leaders like Yitzhak Rabin and Shimon Peres accommodated the settlers and even absorbed them as part of Israel's security imperative, they failed to comprehend the hatred mounting against them. Fundamentalism appeared as a relic during the heyday of global liberalization in the 1990s that coincided with the terms of American president Bill Clinton and second act of Rabin and Peres. In Israel, as in conflicts across the world, the peace treaty with its promise of disarmament in the name of opening markets became a liberal political imperative.[70] Peres and Rabin saw their actions as fulfilling what Ben-Gurion had always intended—the swapping of occupied territory with its thorny demographics for more stable sovereignty and security. Prime Minister Rabin, who had participated in the expulsion of Palestinians from Lydda and Ramle in 1948 and served as IDF chief of staff in 1967, agreed to the Oslo Accords with Palestine Liberation Organization leader Yasir Arafat, shaking hands with his erstwhile enemy on the White House lawn on September 13, 1993. Gaza and the West Bank city of Jericho were the first sites of Israel's withdrawal in the name of creating space for Palestinian self-governance. Sovereignty, settlements, and government subsidy were subject to reassessment as the peace process revived the colonial idea of partitioning space into Israeli and Palestinian regions. British Mandate rule in the 1930s and 1940s had produced some crazy maps that cordoned land according to population clusters and the path of an oil pipeline, but they were no match for the contortions of Oslo drawn to confer territorial minimums for Palestine under the banner of the Two-State Solution.[71] Along with barriers and checkpoints, roads and bridges differentiating between settlers and Palestinians cut space into zones of access and restriction. Further diffusion results from the lettering of Zones A where Palestinian sovereignty is said to prevail, Zone B that alleges mixed control, and Zone C where Israel's dominance is declared, as well as from the nature of the settlement in question, whether secular, ultra-Orthodox, Religious Zionist, or purely inspired by economic subsidy.

70. On the peace treaty and open-market promises in 1990s El Salvador, see Joaquín M. Chávez, "How Did the Civil War in El Salvador End?," *The American Historical Review* 120, no. 5 (2015): 1784–1797.

71. On the pipeline and partition, see Rachel Havrelock, "The Borders Beneath: On Pipelines and Resource Sovereignty," *South Atlantic Quarterly* 116, no. 2 (2017): 408–416.

The settler movement framed the peace process as an assault on biblical patrimony in which the perpetrators were not Palestinians, but the elected government of Israel. The Joshua spirit soared in their enclaves as venom was redirected toward the very people who had reliably, albeit reluctantly, facilitated their program. In response to the peace process on November 11, 1993, Levinger's "Ichud Rabbanim settler rabbi group issued a rabbinic *psak*, a binding judgment based on halakha," which communicated their position on the land's boundaries and essential nature.

> All of historic Eretz Yisrael which is now in our possession belongs to the entire Jewish people past, present and future, and therefore no one in any generation can give away that to which he [alone] does not have title. Therefore any agreement to do so is null and void, obligates no one, has no legal or moral force whatsoever.[72]

However definitive the statement, the historic Eretz Yisrael in question was understood at once as spanning from the Jordan to the Sea or, basically, the post-1967 map and as reaching across the river into Jordan, which made the subsequent 1994 treaty with King Hussein almost as bad as the Oslo Accord.[73] Insisting with Joshua locution that "all" the land belongs to "the entire" Jewish people across all time, the ruling invalidated Israeli elections and rejected the authority of state representatives. No single person—read Yitzhak Rabin—has the right to negotiate the map because the only land deed that matters was granted by God and communicated in the book of Joshua. Under this premise, peace agreements are illegitimate and bind no one. The practical upshot of declaring peace agreements "null and void" was an injunction for settlers to refuse any government orders to evacuate, to continue their building even when illegal, and to resist the peace process.

The fourth decision of the ruling cited the Israeli government for flouting the laws of Torah, which forbid anyone "to relinquish the political rights of sovereignty and national ownership over any part of historic Eretz Yisrael to another authority or people."[74] Such laws, nowhere written in Torah or Talmud, exist only when Joshua's conquest functions as a "meta-commandment" that surrenders no sovereignty or "national ownership." The rabbinic ruling,

72. Heilman, "Guides of the Faithful," 351.

73. Rachel Havrelock, "Israelis and Jordanians on Their Peace Treaty," predissertation fieldwork in Jordan, Israel, and Palestine, December 1997–June 1998.

74. Heilman, "Guides of the Faithful," 352.

like most, generated many interpretations and applications. For example, former Ashkenazi chief rabbi Avraham Shapira identified the enemies at hand as Arabs, "communists that never recognized our right to Eretz Yisrael," "Jews [that] are part of the government," and "extreme leftists that never wanted a Jewish state but a binational one. They don't believe in the *Tanakh* [Scripture] and claim that the book of Joshua which describes how Joshua conquered Eretz Yisrael, should be expunged from the *Tanakh* that is taught in schools."[75] After listing expected rivals, Rabbi Shapira moved the battlefront inward against the Israeli government and Jewish leftists. Leftist crimes are not concrete, but rather relate to past hopes for binationalism and current dismissal of the book of Joshua. Their most objectionable transgression is the wish to omit the story of ancient Canaanite genocide from the secular high-school curriculum.[76] The former chief rabbi knew full well that Joshua influenced all Israelis and that settlers enjoyed significant state sponsorship, yet still spoke in terms of snares set by internal enemies. Fighting such enemies required extra vigilance. According to Rabbi Shapira's reasoning, so-called enemies of Joshua are the settlers' bitter enemies. His interpretive turn measures opposition with the yardstick of Joshua, the very book Ben-Gurion championed as fostering unity. By the 1990s, to love Joshua was to be a settler, and to hate it was to oppose the Occupation.

In 1994 Baruch Goldstein, an American-born doctor from Kiryat Arba, opened fire on Palestinians praying in the Hebron mosque that honors the burial place of Abraham and his immediate family, killing twenty-nine and injuring one hundred and twenty-five people. Rabin denounced the murders but did not move a single unauthorized outpost or redirect a penny of state subsidy. His continued conciliation did nothing to soften the opposition against him, which reached a religious crescendo in the ruling by three settler rabbis that declared the prime minister a *din rodef* (a pursuer of the defenseless). The implications were that Rabin, in negotiating with Palestinian leadership, was pursuing the destruction of the divinely inspired settlement program, leaving the settlers themselves defenseless. The Talmud, which limits justification for murder as well as for war, can be understood as sanctioning the killing of a *din rodef* in the name of self-defense. With a target on the back of the sitting prime minister, it took only a few weeks for Yigael Amir, a young ultra-Orthodox

75. Heilman, "Guides of the Faithful," 349.

76. On the educational debates, see Mazor, "Rise and Fall of the Book of Joshua," 35 (Hebrew).

law student taken with settler ideology, to enact the ruling and assassinate Yitzhak Rabin at a Tel Aviv rally for peace.

Ben-Gurion launched the twentieth-century Joshua narrative in conjunction with socialist economic conditions and a highly centralized state bureaucracy. He chose the story as a means of promoting national unity and elevating the military. Along with its significant contribution to public culture, the Joshua narrative stoked material aspirations for greater territory as achieved by Moshe Dayan in the 1967 war. During the book of Joshua's sequel in Israel, economic and social conditions radically changed as a result of inflation and the privatization of public goods.[77] As free market economics transformed the distribution of resources and services that had previously skewed socialist, the centralized state saw its power wane. Uneven distribution of resources exacerbated social differences, dissolving the tenuously unified nation into component groups based on class, ethnicity, and level of religious observance. The only institution in which social cohesion and national unity occasionally came into view was the military. Those groups for which globalization had a moderating influence dropped the Joshua narrative, and those among whom its conditions promoted extremism took up the Joshua story with a literalistic zeal unimaginable for the founding fathers. Ben-Gurion had proclaimed that there were no tribes in modern Israel, only units in a disciplined army, but from the 1970s onward, the term "Israeli" required hyphenation according to right or left wing; secular or orthodox (with its many splinter groups); Arab, Mizrahi, or Ashkenazi. Settlements developed their own militias, even publishing guides on how settlers should mete out their own standard of justice.[78] Prominent settler rabbis sanctioned the assassination of the democratically elected prime minister of the Jewish state and ruled that soldiers—those of their own persuasion in particular—were forbidden from following Israeli laws to dismantle settlements. Beyond the immediate effects of such novel forms of violence, settler initiative required response from other members of society and thus inspired further fracture into enclaves.

77. Wendy Brown links the trend with neoliberalism, which includes "deregulation of industries and capital flows; radical reduction in welfare state provisions and protections for the vulnerable; privatized and outsourced public goods; . . . replacement of progressive with regressive tax and tariff schemes; the end of wealth redistribution as an economic or social-political policy; the conversion of every human need or desire into a profitable enterprise; . . . and, most recently, the financialization of everything." *Undoing the Demos: Neoliberalism's Stealth Revolution* (Brooklyn: Zone Books, 2015), 28.

78. Friedman, *Zealots for Zion*, 55.

As in the book of Joshua, the capacious reach of Israel's national boundaries keeps everyone at war in highly localized battles. However, unlike Joshua's campaign that began with a falling wall, Israel's perpetual conquest has resulted in one of the more complex walls in human history. Plans for a unilateral, de facto border had circulated for decades, but only after the repeated suicide bombings of the Second Intifada was the Israeli public broadly supportive of a physical barrier to Palestinian movement. The security justification, however, frays when observing the massive expropriations of Palestinian land (10 percent of the total West Bank) enacted by the riverine twists of the wall and the compensatory connections for settlers to its east.[79] Approved by the Israeli cabinet in June 2002 and declared unlawful by the International Court of Justice in The Hague in July 2004, the Separation Barrier "is Israel's largest national project since the national water carrier."[80] Like Ben-Gurion's National Water Carrier, Netanyahu's Separation Barrier asserts Israeli sovereignty by unilaterally claiming resources through built infrastructure that forever remains a work in progress.

In a book about the phenomenon of wall building, Wendy Brown contends that intricate borders and militarized crossing points perform a kind of absolute state authority exactly as this power wanes.[81] More than an illusion, these walls are described by Brown as theatrical performances of persistence and strength by states hollowed out by private interests. In the twenty-first century, multinational corporations command more power than the nations whose resources, labor, and tax subsidies support them. It is this private sector, rather than state policy, that drives the movement of commodities and migration of labor. Yet exactly as the market overruns state sovereignty, the weakened states throw up spectacular borders to symbolize control over the bodies, goods, and wastes that regularly cross them. Such walls and checkpoints are largely unsuccessful in stemming the flows across them because they never aim to do so; rather, they exist to redirect national anxiety about economic disempowerment toward a group identified as threatening and alien. The state and its

79. Preventing Palestinians without an Israeli-issued permit from passing the wall has enabled Israeli employers to keep worker wages low in a system so precarious that simply being able to earn a day's wage represents a victory. This pressure on Palestinian labor has gone hand in hand with the expropriation of agricultural land of some 150 Palestinian communities. As a result of suits brought before the Israeli Supreme Court, about eighty-four gates that open according to the caprice of the Israeli military have been inserted into the wall.

80. Sfard, *Wall and the Gate*, 1.

81. Wendy Brown, *Walled States, Waning Sovereignty* (Brooklyn: Zone Books, 2010).

citizens have reason to worry, but less about Palestinians, Moroccans, Shiites, or Mexicans on the other side of a fence. According to Brown, the xenophobic rhetoric that justifies costly walls is the last gasp of the nation-state whose assets are largely privatized with benefits accruing to the heads of global companies and their local middlemen. The spreading precariousness of economic redistribution to the top is both denied and abated by conjuring up a more vulnerable group beyond a wall that allegedly poses an existential threat. Optics remain central—through fortification, the state appears to be in control, particularly of disenfranchised communities facing accelerated ecological degradation. But, in essence, the regulation of trade and wages in conjunction with the offshoring of waste remains largely in the hands of multinational corporations. In another twist of this operation, the corporations in question project images of tolerance and inclusion that seemingly contrast with the racist discrimination promoted by heads of state. Brown's larger theory about contemporary walls can be inflected in the specific case of Israel's wall, which marks the merger of state and corporation in an ongoing infrastructural project of dispossession.

The unilateral Separation Barrier perfectly illustrates the nature of a nonnegotiated border. Israel erects it where it desires in the name of keeping a maximum number of settlements inside the wall and the maximum number of Palestinians out. It blurs the internationally recognized Green Line and thus helps to disappear Palestine. A border whose two sides are controlled by the selfsame state, the wall asserts monolithic power at the same time that it unsettles the fundamental basis of the nation-state. If territory on two sides of a border belongs to the same state but has different regimes of law and politics, then what is the nature of the state itself? If Jewish settlements east of the wall belong to Israel but neighboring Palestinian cities do not, then the state lays claim to ethnic islands rather than contiguous territory.

In the West Bank, the Israeli revivification of Joshua reaches a literalistic apex where it harmonizes with Evangelical Christian interpretations. Hyperwealthy individuals and corporate persons stoke this Joshua fever because it creates a lawless context in which deregulation, extraction, and privatization can proceed apace. The wall abets these goals by placing the West Bank as a whole under Israel's auspices as it conceals exploitation, normalizes settlements through the absorption of those closest to the Green Line, and maintains a frontier scenario where individual settlers can determine the justice to suit them. Separated from the center of Israeli commerce in Tel Aviv, settlers can maintain the feeling of living in a biblical space where they possess *the* correct understanding of Judaism and Zionism atop ridges and mountains. However, as with Ben-Gurion's thorough militarization that never quite produced the desired nation-state, the settlers exert an increasing quotient of power in the West Bank at the same time that "the illusive Land of the Bible always eludes their grasp."[82] The more successful they are, the more olive trees and shepherds' flocks give way to suburban track homes, internal borders, and highways with private investors. A prevailing "architecture of claustrophobia" militarizes surrounding space, freeing up enlisted soldiers to monitor points of access and contact.[83] The central barrier, with its paved paths, barbed-wire fences, ditches, and concrete walls, spreads into ever more walls around Palestinian cities and settlements alike. All in all, the landscape looks like a version of Joshua in which rhetorical enmity is realized *in concreto*.

Against Joshua

The most stinging, enduring critique of Joshua came from an associate of Ben-Gurion and member of his party, who exposed the recurrent brutality folded into the conquest analogy. S. Yizhar, the pen name of Yizhar Smilansky, was an Israeli writer who applied his biblical sensibility and moral urgency first to the 1948 war and only later, in the more hopeful 1990s, to the book of Joshua. In the wake of 1948, Yizhar penned *Khirbet Khizeh*, a novella about a soldier's reluctant, interior witnessing of Palestinian expulsion as he follows orders to enact it.[84] Where Ben-Gurion had painted the victorious army in collective, mythic hues, Yizhar dwelled in the raw ambivalence of a singular soldier whose enemies do nothing to warrant the title.

In 1958, as the prime minister rehashed the war in his Joshua study group and Leon Uris stirred pathos with his novel *Exodus*, Yizhar published *Days of Ziklag*, a novel that reduces Israel's founding triumph to the moral quandaries plaguing a group of soldiers in a remote corner of the Negev desert.[85] Yizhar's

82. Feige, *Settling in the Hearts*, 82.

83. Neve Gordon has named this "the separation principle": "the abandonment of efforts to administer the lives of the colonized population while insisting on the continued exploitation of nonhuman resources (land and water)." *Israel's Occupation* (Berkeley: University of California Press, 2008), xix.

84. S. Yizhar, *Khirbet Khizeh*, trans. Nicholas de Lange and Yaacob Dweck (Ibis Editions, 2008).

85. Leon Uris, *Exodus* (Garden City, NY: Doubleday, 1958); S. Yizhar, *Yeme Tsiklag* (Tel Aviv: Zemorah-Bitan, 1996) (Hebrew).

work during Israel's first decade dramatizes the silent ethical objections of individual soldiers who act upon orders rather than their moral compass. The disjointed train of thought through which low-ranking fighters process their operations creates textual dissonance between the represented perpetration of violence and the reader's hope for humane intervention. Yizhar's were the earliest works of literature to grapple with the Palestinian dispossession at the root of the State of Israel, but, no matter how angry his fictional truth-telling made Israel's elites, he was shielded by his own elite status as a native-born member of a founding family and intelligence operative.[86] *Days of Ziklag* even won the prestigious Israel Prize in 1959, conceivably lending more urgency to the ongoing memorialization of the founding war at Ben-Gurion's study group. Perhaps owing to his unimpeachable status, not to mention the six terms he served as a member of the Knesset, Yizhar's fictional disclosure of Israel's founding abuses never turned him against the state or led to formal political outcry. However, in order for Yizhar to represent the country and to reanimate biblical language in modern literature,[87] he still needed to externalize and denounce the expropriations, the dehumanization, and the ritual of sending youth out to war. As settler actions intensified all dimensions of this constellation and hope stirred for a negotiated peace treaty with the Palestine Liberation Organization, Yizhar named Israel's problem Joshua and inveighed against it in a speech to the 1992 Conference on Humanistic Judaism in Jerusalem that was subsequently published in *Yediot Ahronot*, a leading Israeli newspaper.[88]

"Against Joshua" begins with ironic nostalgia for the biblical reveries of the prestate era: "the *Tanakh* was, of course, in the backpack of every trekker that would walk and read, walk and point . . . read it and excavate an ancient site . . .

86. Gabriel Piterberg points out that Yizhar's maternal uncle was Yosef Weitz, head of the Jewish National Fund and known to readers of this book for his role in creating the Village Files. Piterberg further understands *Days of Ziklag* as emerging "at the height of his commitment as an intellectual in the full Gramscian sense to Ben-Gurion's version of statism, known as *Mamlakhtiyut*." "Cleanser to Cleansed," *London Review of Books* 31, no. 4 (2009): 31–33.

87. On Yizhar's "public reticence" regarding dispossession and occupation and the failure of biblical rhetoric to produce a moral standard in Israel, see Shai Ginsburg, "S. Yizhar's *Khirbet Khizeh* and the Rhetoric of Conflict," in *Jewish Rhetorics: History, Theory, Practice*, ed. Michael Bernard-Donals and Janice W. Fernheimer (Boston: Brandeis University Press, 2014), 165–179.

88. The Conference was held on October 17, 1992 and the speech was republished as S. Yizhar, "Against Joshua," *Yediot Ahronot*, December 4, 1992 (Hebrew) and in *Sevivot* 31 (1993): 139–155 (Hebrew).

read the name of a hero and suddenly he'd manifest as a living symbol, here's Gideon, here's Samson, and, most certainly, here's David Son of Jesse. All of them were us in ancient dress."[89] The opening passage attests to how the modern landscape and Israeli identity gained legibility through biblical images, which allowed the actual features of place and backgrounds of people to go unseen.[90] The motif of return to an ancestral homeland brings Yizhar to Joshua, which he parses—but never names—as the central script of the modern state.

To his eyes, the book of Joshua's operative keyword is "possess" in the sense that "the size of your territory will match the scope of your ability to seize and to possess it."[91] Many meanings are folded into the biblical command to "possess," which Yizhar unpeels in order to expose the price of holding territory. Along with "possess" or "take possession of," ירש/*yarash* can also mean to "inherit" or to "dispossess." Emphasizing that possession depends upon force, Yizhar asks who bequeaths the land to Israel and who becomes dispossessed as a result. The answer to the question of inheritance may seem easy insofar as God promises Israel, like their ancestors before them, that they will inherit the land. But if the promise is so clear, then why must Israel seize the land by force and dispossess the Canaanites? Why must law and justice be suspended? Why must the dispossessed be disregarded on every front? War always requires the suspension of human morality, but divinely commanded dispossession forecloses any appeal to transcendent values. Should the blood of the dispossessed find its voice, like Abel's, and cry to heaven, "this time heaven commanded that all the voices be ignored." A God stripped of all ethics bequeaths territory that must be seized by force, "a taking of plunder here called inheritance."[92]

Yizhar confronts the God of Joshua who designates destruction and brutality as the proper way to serve Him with particular opprobrium. Challenging God certainly captures attention, particularly that of the Humanistic

89. Yizhar, "Against Joshua," *Sevivot* 31 (1993): 150 (Hebrew).

90. Mazor identifies this trend as central to the educational enterprise in both the pre and early state eras: "educators lifted up the images of early Israelite heroes, like Gideon and David, as symbols of national identification, the figure of Joshua served as one of them." "Rise and Fall of the Book of Joshua," 23 (Hebrew).

91. Yizhar, "Against Joshua," 151. Yizhar takes the command to dispossess from Haim Nahman Bialik's poem, "The Dead of Desert," see *Selected Poems*, ed. and trans. David Aberbach (New York: Overlook Buckworth, 2004), 60–63, in which Joshua urges, "Israel! Get up and dispossess," as much as from the book of Joshua itself.

92. Yizhar, "Against Joshua," 152.

Jews and secular Israelis first addressed by the piece, but Yizhar denounces God as a means of laying moral responsibility before Israel's political and military establishment. In the present, as in the book of Joshua, an unseen source issues the commands that Yizhar perceives as destroying enemy and soldier alike. By condemning the unseen issuers of commands, Yizhar tries to make them visible as primary agents. On this count, Yizhar's treatise functions like a parable that recasts a contemporary situation with anachronistic figures so that it becomes both legible and remote enough that the point can be absorbed before listeners throw up defenses. But Yizhar's parable also runs the risk of going uninterpreted and thereby lacking impact. When a parable employs foxes, fish, or mustard seeds, the need to locate human analogies is clear, yet when God is blamed for human horrors, one can simply accept that God is in charge or take it as additional evidence for disbelief. Nothing about the way in which Yizhar constructs the analogy ensures that the audience will unpack it or reach the point of condemning the individuals and state structures that necessitate repeated Palestinian dispossession and moral evacuation by Israeli soldiers. Thus, Yizhar leaves it easy enough to hate the book of Joshua without resisting a single command in the present.

Yizhar next unpacks the mode of seizure "by the sword." Refusing to allow the sword to function as mere metaphor, he reviews its potential material properties whether a sharp or dull blade that requires more intimate stabbing. How is the sword wielded in Jericho when "He says to kill by stabbing, by beheading, by slaughter not only the combatants, but also elders, women and children one after the other, not by shooting from afar, but rather by slitting neck after neck"?[93] The use of repetition—one after the other, neck after neck—echoes the cadence of Joshua as it seeks to make the scale of implied murder intelligible. Where the book of Joshua folds the mechanics of conquest into assurances that all the people of Canaan, every last one, fall before Israel, Yizhar insists on visualizing the details of such operations. Only after a relentless litany of Joshua's deeds does he conclude with military terms redolent of religious imagery: "then there remains cleared ground and total purification."[94] Achieving this goal, however, renders nothing but "scorched earth" that affords the conquerors "a clear inheritance without claimants." This "torah [law] of conquest, way of settlement" requires commitment to "might, might, and

93. Yizhar, "Against Joshua," 154.

94. Yizhar, "Against Joshua," 154.

more might, the sword, fire, blood, and utter destruction,"[95] external violence with internal repercussions. Conquest most certainly undoes the Canaanites and Amorites, whose only sin seems to be "that they did not want to give up what was theirs, the land of their fathers that their gods granted to them in days of yore," but it also ruins the conquerors who must, "as we know, shut off their humanity, shut off compassion, shut off consideration, shut off clemency."[96] The cost of inheriting "a land that does not desire additional guests, a territory without partners, in fact a land where it is necessary to destroy the previous inhabitants"[97] is blockage of any and all ethical responses.

After posing questions in a prophetic idiom, Yizhar pivots to literary criticism in order to discern why the book was written. He arrives at two possibilities: either the editor of Joshua made up its stories "to pander to hot-tempered fanatics who are always an inherent constituency among conquerors and settlers," or the events transpired as narrated, which "puts us in a very difficult place, which is hard to justify."[98] This difficult place supports the conclusion "that we are nothing but another set of conquerors among the countless many who have always been here. In our case as well there is no kind conquest and no righteous settlement. Indeed, we have wonderful excuses why it is permissible for us to conquer, destroy, not allow a soul to live, but such excuses don't turn the permissible into the tolerable or the impermissible to permissible." Dispensing with Jewish exceptionalism and the unique justification of the State of Israel following the Holocaust, Yizhar equates Israel with other conquests that have never been gentle or just. Without rehearsing the "wonderful excuses," he states bluntly that they do nothing to change the true state of affairs. Some people will simply accept that God has willed violent force as law and follow the book of Joshua as a manual, while others whose humanity remains intact will feel compelled to "speak out against this Joshua." In closing, Yizhar considers an additional function of the book as "a warning about what happens to a people that goes to conquer the land of another people, even with the very best reasons." As such, the purpose of Joshua is to produce trepidation. "True," Yizhar concedes, "not everyone is terrified, as is known, but, in any case, maybe some of the Jews who are sitting here are against Joshua."[99]

95. Yizhar, "Against Joshua," 154.
96. Yizhar, "Against Joshua," 154.
97. Yizhar, "Against Joshua," 155.
98. Yizhar, "Against Joshua," 156.
99. Yizhar, "Against Joshua," 156.

By outlining various possible responses to Joshua, Yizhar delineates social categories: there are fanatics motivated by the book's horrors, those hardened by accepting the apparent necessity of conquest, those whose humanity leads them to speak out against brutality, and those who might take the biblical book as a warning and join the outcry. Significantly, Yizhar sees the interpretation of Joshua as something that divides Israeli society internally such that standing against Joshua puts one in a moral minority, a complete inversion of Ben-Gurion's aspiration that Israeli interpretation of the book constitute a national narrative and manifestation of a collective bond. This prominent disciple inveighing against the Old Man's beloved book serves as yet another indicator of the dissipation of Ben-Gurion's imagined community. Furthermore, where Ben-Gurion dramatized the founding of the state in the language of Joshua, Yizhar holds the book up as a mirror in which Israelis should recognize themselves with consternation. The fact that most don't lends a sense of despair and isolation to his conclusion. Even a Knesset member who won the Israel Prize does not presume to speak to nation or party, but only to "perhaps a few" of the assembled. The largest group one can hope to persuade is "a few Jews" immediately present. It is notable that Yizhar speaks of Jews, rather than Israelis, suggesting that a moral compass might yet emerge from Diaspora communities in a reversal of Ben-Gurion's vision that a new "Torah will come out of Zion." In contrast to the collective produced by emulating Joshua, any group that might emerge against it is already factionalized and uncertain.

Considering the weight of his opprobrium, Yizhar's final thought that "perhaps a few of the Jews that are sitting here are against Joshua" seems modest. Why the resignation? Why not insist that Israel relinquish Joshua, cease its conquest in part or in full? Why limit the addressees to a few Jews presently in the room? It is highly possible that Yizhar hopes for opposition beyond that of the assembled audience, cuing it by the fact that "sitting here" in Hebrew also carries the meaning of "inhabiting this place." Yet, after Yizhar's prophetic condemnation of immorality, even the hope that a few Jews inhabiting the country oppose Joshua seems too limited. His deflection of the political may reflect a persistent compartmentalization in which he bore witness to Israeli ethical compromise in his fiction while leaving it unaddressed in his public political life.[100] Offering the benefit of the doubt, the address to "perhaps a few of the Jews sitting [dwelling] here" may extend the insight that just as the settlers, a minority group, achieve many of their goals by being pro-Joshua, so might an

100. See Ginsburg, "S. Yizhar's *Khirbet Khizeh* and the Rhetoric of Conflict."

even smaller number thwart their violence and expropriations by turning against it. Yizhar spoke to the issue more directly in a subsequent interview included with the republication of his Joshua diatribe, stating directly, "After the Six-Day War, Gush Emunim read Joshua as legitimation for 'possessing' with a strong arm. I believe that it is not the sword that creates rights, but rather justice that creates rights, justice that brings equal rights."[101] So, on the one hand, to stand against Joshua is to oppose the settlers and, on the other hand, it is to oppose the disenfranchisement of Palestinians. Yet Yizhar admits, "Our nation is still divided. A sizable portion believes in transfer [of Palestinians out of the land, usually to Jordan], brandishing the book of Joshua as justification, and a portion of us is against it."[102] Summoning all his might, Yizhar leads the charge to "rebel against Joshua." In the early 1990s, when it appeared that restrictive borders would melt away, Yizhar gestured toward an Israel of bridges, equal rights, and demilitarization. Getting there would require a turn "against Joshua," which he elaborated as a stance "against the Zionism of a drawn sword that negates the existence of the other nation because it has a big sword, against the awful Zionism whose symbol is an angel with a sword."[103] By pushing out the awful, violent Zionism, Yizhar assumed an unpopular stance at the same time that he tried to preserve a Zionism that is not awful. One always wishes to preserve the better aspects of one's country, and the 1990s promised a brave new world with open markets, electronic connections, and global circulation, but Yizhar left unanswered what would remain after "the Zionism of a drawn sword" was extirpated. What is Israel without Joshua?

Return of the Canaanites

As Israelis identified both positively and negatively with Joshua's soldiers and settlers, the role of indigenous Canaanites again dispossessed yet steadfast in their land was open to Palestinians.

Israeli enactments of conquest unwittingly placed Palestinians in the Canaanite position, but a Canaanite counterdiscourse has also developed as a manner of structural critique.[104] In the spheres of literary theory, biblical interpretation,

101. S. Yizhar, "S. Yizhar Now!," interview about "Against Joshua" *Sevivot* 31 (1993): 139–149 (Hebrew).

102. Yizhar, "S. Yizhar Now!," 140.

103. Yizhar, "S. Yizhar Now!,"149.

104. Nur Masalha describes both trends: "Zionist-Jewish zealots" who "have routinely compared Palestinian Muslims and Christians to the ancient Canaanites, Philistines, or Amalekites" and "secular Palestinian nationalists" who "have, anachronistically" seen in "Canaanites,

and genetics, academics and public figures have drawn connections between Palestinians and ancient Canaanites. Along with the sense of historical recurrence, Canaanite claims—like their Israeli counterparts—link political rights to an ethnic lineage that stretches back to early antiquity. The reasoning runs that the legitimate descendants of the Canaanites rightfully inherit their recorded property and sovereign rights. Indigenous claims blend with biblical figuration such that the biblical typology rings true to the present. Public voicing of the Canaanite position introduces a vital perspective not available in the biblical text into Israel's conquest complex. Furthermore, Canaanite discourse infuses ethics and justice into the brutality of ongoing war. At the same time, tragically, it supports the scenario of violent polarization and, thus, assures the endless replay of the Joshua plot.[105] One cannot help but wonder how to push the story onward to the decentralized home rule described in the second half of Joshua.

Edward Said articulated the "Canaanite reading" of conquest through a pitched debate in 1986 with political theorist Michael Walzer over "Exodus politics."[106] Their exchange remains iconic not only as a foretaste of the intractable issues that exploded one year later in the first Intifada, but also as an exemplary moment when would-be exegetes admitted to the twentieth-century stakes of interpreting Exodus. Walzer coined the term "Exodus politics" in his 1985 book *Exodus and Revolution* to describe the progressive "journey forward" that oppressed peoples take through the stages of liberation, transition, and state-building. From the relevant biblical books Walzer distilled a ritual structure (separation-liminality-return) and adapted it to a this-worldly political model, which neglected the commands to exterminate resident peoples, not to mention their execution. The ritual structure that informs the narrative order of exodus, wandering, and homecoming, however, is widely recognized as

Jebusites, Amorites and Philistines the direct forebears and linear ancestors of the modern Palestinians." See "Reading the Bible with the Eyes of the Canaanites: Neo-Zionism, Political Theology and the Land Traditions of the Bible (1967 to Gaza 2009)," *Holy Land Studies* 8, no. 1 (2009): 57–58.

105. As Nur Masalha phrases it in his reading of Henry Cattan's Canaanite claims, the attempt "to undermine the Zionist narrative" ends up "mirroring," "rehashing and appropriating the biblical narrative to construct a secular Palestinian narrative." *The Bible and Zionism: Invented Traditions, Archaeology and Post-Colonialism in Palestine-Israel* (London: Zed Books, 2007), 252.

106. Michael Walzer, *Exodus and Revolution* (New York: Basic Books, 1985); Edward Said, "Walzer's *Exodus and Revolution*: A Canaanite Reading," *Grand Street* 5, no. 2 (1986): 86–106; Michael Walzer and Edward Said, "An Exchange: 'Exodus and Revolution,'" *Grand Street* 5, no. 4 (1986): 246–259.

cyclic, whereas Walzer read Exodus as the linear unfolding of "radical social democratic politics."[107]

S. Yizhar, who had fought in Israel's war, externalized Joshua as the symbol of everything inhumane and thereby preserved the basic state structure, whereas the Jewish-American Walzer evoked stirring images of freedom and national rebirth without a word about the conquest. The privilege of Jewish-American ethno-national pride in Israel absent the military service and witnessing of Palestinian oppression often finds voice in such sanitized, attractive narratives, with other variations including Israel as the rebirth of Judaism, the little nation that could prevail against its encircling enemies, and the techno-apologetics at work in a term like "Start-Up Nation."[108] Walzer's version adds the theoretical appeal of linking Exodus with historical revolutionary movements and the flowering of true democracy through "an active and lively participation in religious and-/or political life . . . not from some of the people but from all of them."[109] In a side note, he confesses that the polity does not quite correspond with the resident population, "for the Canaanites are explicitly excluded from the world of moral concern."[110] Still, revolutionary zeal need not be tempered insofar as "the abominations of the Canaanites are their own work, human, all-too-human"—or, slightly rephrased, they invite their fate upon themselves. Israel's "reluctant warriors," who, at least "many of them, prefer peace," must live with the "tension between the concern for strangers and the original conquest and occupation of the land" in their enactment of a democratic Promised Land.[111]

Said's Canaanite response probed the nature of the state in which the "offending non-Jewish population is excluded from the world of moral concern."[112] Where scholarly reflections on Exodus may seem harmless enough, he wondered to what degree denial and elision sustain and regenerate exclusion and violence. Insofar as evidence-based histories of the nation-state simultaneously reveal its embedded exclusions, Said suggested that Walzer

107. Walzer, *Exodus and Revolution*, 109. See also John J. Collins, *The Bible after Babel: Historical Criticism in a Postmodern Age* (Grand Rapids, MI: Eerdmans Publishing, 2005), 65, on the apologetics at work in Walzer's study and centrality of the conquest to Said's reading.

108. Dan Senor and Saul Singer, *Start-up Nation: The Story of Israel's Economic Miracle* (New York: Twelve), 2009.

109. Walzer, *Exodus and Revolution*, 109.

110. Walzer, *Exodus and Revolution*, 142.

111. Walzer, *Exodus and Revolution*, 142–143.

112. Said, "Canaanite Reading," 93.

circumvented history in the name of redeeming the State of Israel through a transcendent analogy. Hardly alone in representing Israel absent its occupation, millions of disenfranchised residents, or the ever-deeper military penetration into Palestinian spaces, Walzer silenced these facts in his theoretical paradigm, which placed them beyond the scope of ethics. Said perceived the real story among the gaps: "how many extremely severe excisions and restrictions have occurred in order to produce the calmly civilized world of Walzer's Exodus?"[113] Certainly, Walzer admitted that the settlers and right-wing Zionists take inspiration from the conquest, but highlighted the deviant nature of a reading that dwells on "one moment in the Exodus story" that "plays only a small part."[114] Along the lines of what Roland Barthes called "Operation Margarine," in which a bit of wickedness is disclosed in order to preserve an overarching image of undeniable good,[115] Said viewed Walzer's denunciation of religious extremism as a way "to maintain Israel's image as a progressive and wholly admirable state."[116] Construed in this manner, Israeli extremists veer from—rather than extend or realize—the nature and purpose of the Jewish State, which Walzer insists is exodus rather than conquest.

Said's Canaanite reading would restore Palestinians to the world of moral concern and hold Israel accountable for its actions against them. It would also bring history to bear on examples of Exodus politics in order to understand them in their complex unfoldings. Walzer presented the Exodus story as living on in international struggles for liberation, including the Civil Rights Movement and Latin American Liberation Theology, yet Said observed how the model only gains full realization in Walzer's examples of Puritans and Zionists, two groups that took their example from God's call "to exterminate their opponents."[117] The Canaanite reading would reclassify what Walzer heralds as liberation movements as settler-colonial enterprises and attend to the fate of "the prior native inhabitants of the Promised Land."[118] Canaanite reading emerges as a method of unpacking the discourse of dominance and

113. Said, "Canaanite Reading," 89.

114. Walzer, *Exodus and Revolution*, 141.

115. Roland Barthes, "Operation Margarine," trans. Annette Lavers, in *Mythologies* (New York: Hill and Wang, 1972), 41–42.

116. Said, "Canaanite Reading," 97.

117. Said, "Walzer's *Exodus and Revolution*," 91. On the additional use of "the story of Joshua to equate Irish Catholics with the heathen Cannanites" in seventeenth-century England, see Masalha, "Reading the Bible with the Eyes of the Canaanites," 57.

118. Said, "Walzer's *Exodus and Revolution*," 93.

exploitation, which Said predicts will gain ground because "the more he shores up the sphere of Exodus politics the more likely it is that Canaanites on the outside will resist and try to penetrate the walls banning them from the goods of what is, after all, partly their world too."[119] He further anticipated that each attempt at penetrating the walls of conquest would cause them to be thrown up ever higher, but still offered a method to "more easily call injustice injustice, more easily speak directly and plainly of all oppression, and with less difficulty try to understand (rather than mystify or occlude) history and equality."[120]

In his response to Said's review, Walzer narrowed the universal/Western scope of his initial study to the debate among "Jewish supporters of Israel" about whether one should fashion the state after biblical conquest or rabbinic ethics.[121] The prevalence of biblical Hebrew in Ben-Gurion's Declaration of Independence renders this debate somewhat moot, but Walzer again exercised the Jewish-American privilege of supporting Israel while citing the higher moral standard of diasporic traditions. That said, his aim of showing "how later rabbinic interpreters of the text contrived to readmit the 'Canaanites' to the world of moral concern" marked a laudable exercise in political exegesis.[122] Yet how far can such moral readmission go when the state in question is mischaracterized and policies of occupation are buried in euphemism? To avoid such questions, Walzer switched the topic at hand from the Jewish state to "the entire religious tradition" of Judaism.[123] From this moral high ground, Walzer blasted Palestinian terrorism, "national liberation represented by a figure in a stocking mask," and Said's failure to condemn it.[124] Without ascribing any positive value to acts of terrorism, one should observe how Walzer disappeared Israeli militarism in his image of a national study house where Jewish values are continually debated; state power and its asymmetrical exercise simply evaporated. Walzer called out terror directed against the state and its citizens, but, because his model could not account for Occupation, he was unable to critique state violence. The fact of the matter was that "the Jews have a state." Walzer related to the state as a supporter of the liberal NGO Peace Now frustrated by the lack of Palestinian counterparts with whom he could have a

119. Said, "Walzer's *Exodus and Revolution*," 105.

120. Said, "Walzer's *Exodus and Revolution*," 105.

121. Walzer and Said, "An Exchange," 246–259.

122. Walzer and Said, "An Exchange," 249.

123. Walzer and Said, "An Exchange," 250.

124. Walzer and Said, "An Exchange," 252.

dialogue about peace. "I keep looking for a similar [peace] movement among the Palestinians."[125] The partner he needs is one who recognizes Jewish rights to the land without belaboring how such rights are executed in real time. Just as Walzer insisted that "people don't always get the political enemies they want," so he could not locate the desired Palestinian dialogue partner who could entertain Exodus politics without a Canaanite reading.[126]

Said's subsequent response, which faulted "Walzer's fantastic moral blindness" to the "difference between the connectedness of a critic with an oppressing society, and a critic whose connection is to an *oppressed* one,"[127] stated bluntly, "there is no Israel without the conquest of Canaan and the expulsion or inferior status of Canaanites—then as now."[128] This is the core of Said's argument and the subject that Walzer blocks. The rancor of their debate illustrates the modern stakes of interpreting the book of Joshua as it shows the limitations of casting politics in ethnic terms. The 2018–2019 Great Return March Friday protests in Gaza prove Said correct: caged people will inevitably "try to penetrate the walls banning them from the goods of what is, after all, partly their world too."[129] These goods have become increasingly basic, with the people of Gaza among the world's most undernourished and water-deprived.

After Said introduced the Canaanite reading, biblical scholars—particularly those associated with liberation theology or its critique—applied it to Scripture. Michael Prior, a biblical scholar and Vincentian priest, pointed to justifying "biblical land traditions" operative as Europeans settled in Latin America, South Africa, and Palestine. Likely because it constituted the site of his study and activism, Prior spoke directly to the role of such land traditions in Zionism, charging Deuteronomy as "a constitution suited to the religious ghetto" appealing "only [to] the introspective and xenophobic members of the 'national' group."[130] The balm is the Church, whose "christological and messianic interpretation" can refine the materiality of land traditions into pure allegory or, better yet, complete the "the imperfect and provisional" elements of the Old Testament with their "full meaning in the New Testament."[131] Catholic

125. Walzer and Said, "An Exchange," 252.

126. Walzer and Said, "An Exchange," 246.

127. Walzer and Said, "An Exchange," 253.

128. Walzer and Said, "An Exchange," 255.

129. Said, "Walzer's *Exodus and Revolution*," 105.

130. Michael Prior, *The Bible and Colonialism: A Moral Critique* (Sheffield: Sheffield Academic Press, 1997), 228.

131. Prior, *The Bible and Colonialism*, 284, 272.

liturgy, according to Prior, perfects the process by omitting or excising the horrors of conquest, such that "church-going Catholics encounter virtually none of the land traditions which are offensive."[132]

Prior correctly admonishes scholars and religious adherents for not contending with the conquest and the Occupation at once, yet the Church cannot gain absolution for its role in colonialism due to the beauty of Catholic liturgy. Moreover, the insistence that "South African Calvinists have repudiated and repented for their use of biblical legend to justify their treatment of the black and coloureds [and] the descendants of mediaeval Spanish and Portuguese colonialists and their victims struggle to repair some of the devastation whose effects perdure," while Zionists alone persist unchecked in their "exploitative intentions," is about as tendentious as it gets.[133] Settler-colonials have indeed marched to Joshua's tune, but it has usually been under the banner of Christianity, with Jewish nationalists as relative latecomers.[134]

For Naim Ateek—Palestinian scholar, Anglican priest, and head of the Jerusalem-based Palestinian Christian Sabeel Ecumenical Liberation Theology Center—the remedy to "the hostile language of Joshua" rests on a more spiritualized form of interpretation.[135] For Ateek, healing "the religious-political abuse of biblical interpretation" involves a two-pronged approach with avenues for Jewish and Christian Zionists.[136] Jewish Zionists would do better, Ateek advises, to recognize the repeated pattern in biblical narrative of drawing closer and being pushed away from God and community. Exodus and conquest, then, are not literal occasions to be instantiated in political life, but processes of learning through exile how to inhabit land, all of which—according to Psalm 24—belongs to God.[137] Ateek's advice to Christian Zionists, not surprising for an Anglican Priest, is more classically supersessionist in its celebration of the capacious kingdom of God, which "shatters any narrow

132. Prior, *The Bible and Colonialism*, 275.

133. Prior, *Bible and Colonialism*, 288–289.

134. See Jonathan Boyarin, *Palestine and Jewish History: Criticism at the Borders of Ethnography* (Minneapolis: University of Minnesota Press, 1996).

135. Naim S. Ateek, "A Palestinian Perspective: Biblical Perspectives on the Land," in *Voices from the Margin: Interpreting the Bible in the Third World*, 3rd ed., ed. R. S. Sugirtharajah (Maryknoll, NY: Orbis Books, 2016), 277.

136. Ateek, "Palestinian Perspective," 274.

137. A similar pitfall opens before Ateek, Prior, and Walzer: the conquest is implied in Jesus's battle with sin, in the exodus, and even in Psalm 24, which both declares God as sovereign over all the earth and to be "a war hero" (Ps 24:8).

concept of the land."[138] Both counterreadings seek to defang the conquest and to promote nonviolence in place of militarism, yet the operative binaries of biblical texts are left in place, albeit elevated in reaching toward the transcendent. There is still Hebrew and Canaanite.

Indigenous scholar Robert Allen Warrior, of the Osage Nation of American Indians, intervened more directly in the conquest narrative through his Canaanite reading. Warrior encountered the problem with the exodus narrative after first being moved by Dr. Martin Luther King Jr.'s stirring vision of the Promised Land and then realizing that "the obvious characters in the story for Native Americans to identify with are the Canaanites."[139] Liberation, he argued, could not follow from "a model of conquest, oppression and genocide for native Americans, Palestinians and other indigenous peoples." Warrior's approach, in contrast, was to "read the Exodus story with Canaanite eyes" and to address the narrative directly in a manner that qualifying scholarship cannot.[140] Warrior ponders how communities that receive the Bible can "differentiate between the liberating god and the god of conquest."[141] Since there is no guarantee that the god of justice will emerge from the narrative, Warrior insists that the conquest be acknowledged with each reading of the Bible, preferably with "the Canaanites at the center" as "the last remaining ignored voice in the text, except perhaps for the land itself."[142] His reading is not programmatic, but rather leaves the question of how Christians—indigenous Christians in particular—might embrace the text and struggle with the history of its interpretation through personal "theological reflection." In conclusion, Warrior suggests that a better "vision of justice, peace, and political sanity" might arise from indigenous communities themselves rather than texts disseminated through invasion. His Canaanite reading steps outside of the paradigm of Joshua.

Where archaeology once provided substantiation for collective origins, the evidence currently in vogue relies on DNA studies that locate primal genetic codes in contemporary groups. A carefully researched, much-reported 2017 study in the *American Journal of Human Genetics* heralded "the power of ancient DNA (aDNA) for addressing questions about population histories" as it

138. Ateek, "Palestinian Perspective," 280.

139. Robert Allen Warrior, "A Native American Perspective: Canaanites, Cowboys, and Indians," in Sugirtharajah, *Voices from the Margin*, 285.

140. Warrior, "Native American Perspective," 287.

141. Warrior, "Native American Perspective," 288.

142. Warrior, "Native American Perspective," 288.

presented evidence of genetic relationship between the bones of "five ancient individuals" found in the city of Sidon and dating to between 3,750 and 3,650 years ago and contemporary Lebanese residents near the burial site.[143] Just as the city name "Sidon" connects the ancient to the modern place, so the genetic research asserted "continuity in the Levant."[144] Beyond the "search for genetic signs that have *endured*," the study addresses questions of origin and how living populations might determine from whence they came. [145]

On this count, hypertechnical twenty-first century genetic research resembles the historical-geographic studies of the nineteenth and early twentieth centuries that strove to fix a point of beginning for various manifestations of human culture.[146] Genetic inquiries, in contrast, seem less interested in cultural products or processes than in some kind of ethnic essence that can be discovered only through the extraction of a buried code. The essence at issue here is Lebanese (potentially, by extension, Arab or Mediterranean), and its origin point is determined to be Canaanite. Bestowal of the Canaanite label shows the degree to which genetic research maneuvers within the ethnic categories of ancient literature.[147] They could have called the DNA from the soft petrous bone of the skeletons Sidonian, Mediterranean, Lebanese, or any number of titles, but instead gestured toward the sense of timelessness associated with the Bible. Because the scientific researchers named their subjects Canaanites, they quickly found themselves weighing in on questions of biblical interpretation.[148] Ancient DNA (aDNA) was mustered to answer the book of Joshua with the message that Canaanites still live. Not only was there no sudden, total extermination at the hands of the People of Israel, but Canaanites also transmitted their DNA over millennia.[149] A media blitz of "Canaanites found" and "Bible refuted" quickly followed.[150]

143. Marc Haber et al., "Continuity and Admixture in the Last Five Millennia of Levantine History from Ancient Canaanite and Present-Day Lebanese Genome Sequences," *American Journal of Human Genetics* 101, no. 2 (2017): 274.

144. Haber et al., "Continuity and Admixture," 277.

145. Nadia Abu El-Haj, *The Genealogical Science: The Search for Jewish Origins and the Politics of Epistemology* (Chicago: University of Chicago Press, 2012), 41.

146. This includes evolutionary biology, Abu El-Haj, *Genealogical Science*, 3.

147. This follows the axiomatic association of the biblical People of Israel with contemporary Jews; see Abu El-Haj, *Genealogical Science*, 63–108.

148. This follows from the trend in anthropological genetics, observed by Abu El-Haj, of reading DNA "as a historical document." *Genealogical Science*, 11.

149. Abu El-Haj, *Genealogical Science*, 275.

150. Kristin Romey, "Living Descendants of Biblical Canaanites Identified Via DNA," *National Geographic*, July 27, 2017, https://www.nationalgeographic.com/news/2017/07/canaanite

Let us stop to consider this form of interaction between science and the Bible. Beyond the discovery of genetic continuity between ancient skeletons and contemporary citizens of Lebanon, the team identified the skeletons as Canaanites whose "fate" was mischaracterized in the Bible. Not only is the veracity of the Bible's national characterizations taken for granted, but so is the relative historicity of its claims. Of course, contemporary biblical scholarship—not to mention the second half of the book of Joshua—yields the same conclusion, but the scientific study aims to correct perceived errors of culture as it relies on the selfsame cultural categories. In language reminiscent of the Tower of Babel story, the genetic study concludes, "different cultural groups who inhabited the Levant during the Bronze Age, such as the Ammonites, Moabites, Israelites, and Phoenicians, each achieved their own cultural identities but all shared a common genetic and ethnic root with Canaanites."[151] Several named nations of the Bible are linked through a common beginning, as if to locate harmony (or, at least, commonality) underlying the wars that consume ancient texts.

Nadia Abu El-Haj notes a difference between the race science of past decades, which understood biological difference as functioning to "*cause* cultural and cognitive differences," and contemporary anthropological genetics, which yield "'mere' indexes of ancestry and origins."[152] The authors of the Canaanite research certainly do not draw causal connections; in fact, they say nothing about potential links between Canaanites and Palestinians, but their indexing of ancestry according to the biblical record ends up reinforcing its represented national divides. According to their own conclusion, the skeletons could have just as easily been identified as Phoenician, Israelite, or—if the Bible did not place them east of the Jordan River—Ammonite or Moabite. They could also be named otherwise and not brought into any kind of relationship with the book of Joshua. The skeletons are christened Canaanite, it seems, not only to

-bible-ancient-dna-lebanon-genetics-archaeology; Lizzie Wade, "Ancient DNA Reveals Fate of the Mysterious Canaanites," *Science*, July 27, 2017, https://www.sciencemag.org/news/2017/07/ancient-dna-reveals-fate-mysterious-canaanites; Ian Johnston, "Bible Says Canaanites Were Wiped Out by Israelites but Scientists Just Found Their Descendants Living in Lebanon," *Independent*, July 27, 2017, https://www.independent.co.uk/news/science/bible-canaanites-wiped-out-old-testament-israelites-lebanon-descendants-discovered-science-dna-a7862936.html; Mira Abed, "The DNA of Ancient Canaanites Lives on in Modern-Day Lebanese, Genetic Analysis Shows," *Los Angeles Times*, July 27, 2017, https://www.latimes.com/science/sciencenow/la-sci-sn-canaanite-lebanese-genetics-20170727-story.html.

151. Abu El-Haj, *Genealogical Science*, 277.

152. Abu El-Haj, *Genealogical Science*, 22.

garner attention from the press, but also to establish an ur-ethnicity in the ancient Mediterranean from which all indigenes sprung. Is it not possible that various groups stemmed from different origins? Must there be a singular beginning, a pure lineage sullied by movement and diffusion? Other than substituting Canaanite survival for Canaanite demise, the genetic story does nothing to upend the pervasive conquest narrative.

A popular sense prevails that interior genetic truths make conflict, along with the politics of occupation and resistance, inevitable.[153] If both group connection and rivalry can be explained by inherited traits, then what good does examining entrenched political behavior and power distribution do? President Mahmoud Abbas and Prime Minister Benjamin Netanyahu regularly flash their Canaanite and Israelite credentials without belaboring their history. On July 7, 2019, Netanyahu's Twitter account lit up regarding a recent archaeological study of skeletons in the city of Ashkelon just north of the Gaza Strip. Based on evidence from DNA samples drawn from infant bones buried beneath the floors of "Philistine" dwellings, the study concludes that Philistines from the early Iron Age have roughly 14 percent more European ancestry in their genetic signatures than skeletons from the earlier Bronze Age. One coauthor of the study, Daniel Master, sees therein "direct evidence that the Philistines migrated from the west" and arrived late on the scene in the twelfth century BCE.[154] Another archaeologist of Philistine cities, Aren Maeir, cautions against ascribing such definitive origin stories on "'entangled' or 'transcultural' group[s]."[155] No fan of caution, Netanyahu gleaned from the links that "the origin of Philistines is in southern Europe," that "there's no connection between the ancient Philistines & the modern Palestinians," and the Palestinian

153. As much as biblical self-definitions lock Palestinians and Israelis in a feedback loop that turns politics into ethnicity, neither group initiated them. In broader terms, Abu El-Haj explains that "anthropological genetics is heir to race science, evolutionary biology, and populations genetics." *Genealogical Science*, 11. The biblical categorizing of ethnic groups dates to nineteenth-century colonial exploration and excavation when resident peoples were automatically viewed and represented as relics of the biblical past.

154. Michal Feldman, Daniel M. Master, Raffaela A. Bianco, Marta Burri, Philipp W. Stockhammer, Alissa Mittnik, Adam J. Aja, Choongwon Jeong, and Johannes Krause, "Ancient DNDA Sheds Light on the Genetic Origins of Early Iron Age Philistines," *Science Advances* 5, no. 7 (2019): 1–10. See Kristin Romey, "Ancient DNA May Reveal Origin of the Philistines," *National Geographic*, July 3, 2019, https://www.nationalgeographic.com/culture/2019/07/ancient-dna-reveal-philistine-origins.

155. Romey, "Ancient DNA May Reveal Origin of the Philistines."

presence in the "Land of Israel" cannot be "compared to the 4,000 year connection that the Jewish people have."[156] Questions regarding how an infant skeleton or the ruins of a building can be definitively identified as Philistine shrink before Netanyahu's takeaways that antiquity confers no legitimacy on Palestinian claims to property and rights, which cannot, in turn, even be considered in the same breath with the ineffable Jewish "connection" spanning millennia.

Faced with Donald Trump's recognition of Jerusalem as Israel's capital and its implicit triumph for settlers and their economic sponsors, President Abbas asserted that Palestinians predate the Jews in the Holy City as the "original Canaanites." Abbas proved a deft political exegete—no Philistine he—at the same time that he tacitly accepted Israeli claims to the land based on Scripture and group lineage. If the Jews have a right to Jerusalem on the basis of antiquity, Abbas implied, then how much greater is the Palestinian right to the city due to Canaanite ancestry predating Joshua and even Abraham. The fact that the Palestinian president's delegitimizing of the Israeli claim operates within its logic attests to the totality of the conquest paradigm. In addition to claiming sovereignty based on primacy, Abbas's Canaanite statement signaled the persistence of irreconcilable conflict in a form resembling the early chapters of Joshua. This was not an incidental point on his part, but a manner of exposing the absence of a fair broker in the United States and declaring the end to the era of peace negotiations—"the Oslo accords are dead."[157] Neither nationalism nor globalization has offered a paradigm for Israeli-Palestinian relations other than conquest.

156. @netanyahu, Twitter, July 7, 2019, 6:08 a.m., https://twitter.com/netanyahu/status/1147824702360100864.

157. Jack Khoury, "Abbas Rips into Trump: Palestinians Are Original Canaanites, Were in Jerusalem before the Jews," *Haaretz*, January 17, 2018, https://www.haaretz.com/middle-east-news/palestinians/abbas-palestinians-are-canaanites-were-in-jerusalem-before-jews-1.5743576.

CONCLUSION

End This War

WE HAVE SEEN the book of Joshua's imprint on politics, geography, and culture in Israel, so, in closing, let us consider how modern militarization in biblical garb has impacted the land itself.

To what degree are war, nationalism, and social fragmentation reflected in the environment? In what ways do the resulting environmental conditions secure the status quo as they portend a bleak future? How does perennial war prevent moves toward sustained survival? Our consideration of such questions is not exhaustive, but instead returns to the conundrum faced by Achsah in the book of Joshua of how to live on land with no water. The twenty-first-century instantiation of the scenario takes us to contemporary Gaza, eerily similar to the autonomous Philistine region that Joshua could not subdue. Today, the Gaza Strip is a 140-square-mile stretch of Mediterranean coastline tucked between Israel and Egypt where a population of over two million people lives confined under a blockade. Israel restricts basic materials from entering Gaza, either in retaliation for hostile acts or under the principle of their possible dual-use in munitions. The Coastal Aquifer that runs beneath Gaza and serves as its primary source of drinking water has collapsed.[1] A harbinger of what is likely to come in many regions of the world where warming temperatures and overextraction strain water systems beyond their capacities, the aquifer's collapse is rarely mentioned in reporting on Gaza.

As an event in its own right, the demise of the Coastal Aquifer signals political failure extreme enough to have destroyed ancient waters held beneath the earth since prehistoric times. By virtue of aquifer collapse and lack of sanitation

1. United Nations Special Coordinator for the Middle East Peace Process, Gaza in 2020: A Livable Place?, August 2012, https://www.unrwa.org/userfiles/file/publications/gaza/Gaza in 2020.pdf.

infrastructure, a report by the United Nations roundly declares the Gaza Strip uninhabitable, yet no plans to relocate residents or supply them with potable water have been formulated.[2] Although I cannot predict precisely what will occur when over two million people restricted to 140 square miles of land have nothing to drink, no positive scenario comes to mind. The present situation gains complexity along with a bizarre twist when we widen the lens to see how aquifer collapse intersects with the desalination of water near Israel's beaches. The meeting of these waters should not be taken as incidental, but rather as components of a single system. The broader point here is that the privatization of water (or other resources for that matter) occurs in tandem with the erosion of the human right to water or alienation from it in the form of high pricing, restricted access, or diminished quality.[3] By reading the blockade of Gaza, the collapse of its aquifer, the migration of waste, and the for-profit industrial production of drinking water at desalination plants as parts of a system, we can see how the daily encounter with toxins experienced by disenfranchised communities radiates outward to ultimately form a new polity of the damaged. Like all historical polities, the denizens of these polluted republics have particular experiences based on their race and class standing, made all the more extreme in the situation of perpetual war. Harm is disproportionately allocated to the poor and the marginalized, yet all residents lose aspects of physical well-being and sovereignty over resources as private corporations secure ownership of local assets and rights to pollute. I will argue not only for a reformulation of the public as those who draw from a common water source—rather than as ethnonational subjects—but also that addressing sites of the most compromised water *first* is the best way to reclaim privatized water for this public.

In appraising how the absence of water infrastructure interacts with one of the more sophisticated examples of producing water, we will lean on the concept of the hydrosocial cycle, as coined by Jamie Linton and Jessica Budds, to account for the mutually constitutive way in which water shapes human life and human endeavors determine the quality and quantity of available water. Moving from the idea of the hydrological, a naturally circulating course for water, to that of a hydrosocial cycle marks "a shift from thinking of relations *between* things—such as the impacts of humans on water quality—to the relations *constituting* things—such as the cultural, economic and political

2. United Nations Country Team in the occupied Palestinian territory, Gaza in 2020.

3. See Maude Barlow and Tony Clarke, *Blue Gold: The Fight to Stop the Corporate Theft of the World's Water* (New York: The New Press, 2002).

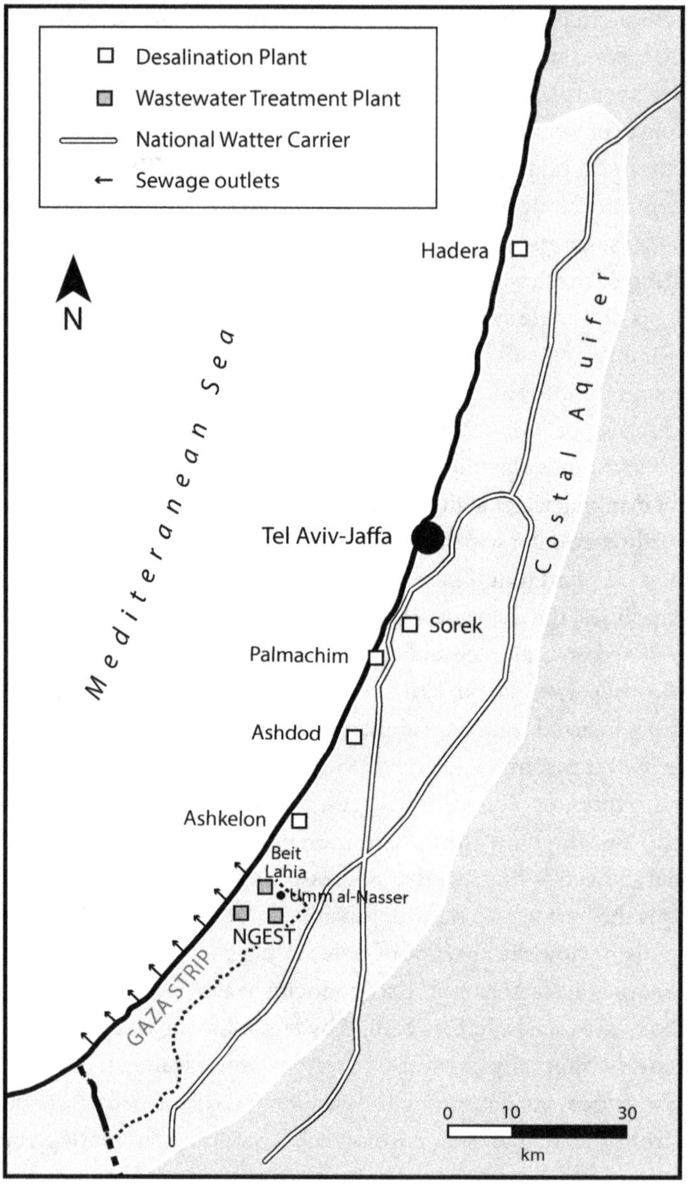

FIGURE 5.1. Map of the Coastal Aquifer, Israeli Desalination Plants on the Mediterranean, and Sites of Wastewater Treatment in the northern Gaza Strip, Roni Blushtein-Livnon.

processes that constitute the particular character of desalinated water, treated drinking water or holy water."[4] The hydrosocial cycle means that water and society are interlinked such that one cannot point to distinct "preformed entities (like 'water' and 'society')" or recognize them as independent processes thereafter.[5] The availability of water mirrors social relations that, in turn, affect whether drops of water will evaporate, become contaminated, or spend eternity twisting through labyrinthine pipes. Eric Swyngedouw insists on attending to "the fundamentally socially produced character of such inequitable hydro-social configurations" such that we do not declare a place to be water scarce without looking to how water is extracted and to whom it is distributed.[6] The water system, Swyngedouw shows, "is increasingly articulated via the financial nexus and organized through market mechanisms and the power of money, irrespective of social, human or ecological need."[7] We can distill his statement: water flows toward money.

Financialized water perfectly describes what now moves through the vast network of pipes commissioned by David Ben-Gurion as the National Water Carrier, the hardware behind his movement to "make the desert bloom." The irony of privatized water moving through a socialist network probably causes Israel's founder to turn in his desert tomb, yet his ethno-nationalism, in effect, fertilized the field for private investors. Ben-Gurion's 1959 Water Law even nationalized the rain as the jurisdiction of the state. As if to concretize a longstanding Judaic analogy between water and Torah, Ben-Gurion initiated the infrastructure of national water in 1958, the very year he nationalized Torah at his Joshua study group.[8] Neighboring states reacted to Israel's siphoning of water with a refusal to ratify binding allocation agreements while taking inspiration about how dams and other diversionary structures could be constructed without regional consultation.[9] Sabotaging the National Water Carrier

4. Jamie Linton and Jessica Budds, "The Hydrosocial Cycle: Defining and Mobilizing a Relational-Dialectical Approach to Water," *Geoforum* 57 (2014): 173.

5. Linton and Budds, "Hydrosocial Cycle," 173.

6. Eric Swyngedouw, "The Political Economy and Political Ecology of the Hydro-Social Cycle," *Journal of Contemporary Water Research and Education* 142 (2009): 57.

7. Swyngedouw, "Political Economy and Political Ecology of the Hydro-Social Cycle," 58.

8. It is also the year Ben-Gurion's order to drain the Huleh Lake and wetlands in the Jordan River watershed was accomplished; see Yael Zerubavel, *Desert in the Promised Land* (Stanford: Stanford University Press, 2019), 160.

9. Miriam Lowi, *Water and Power: The Politics of a Scarce Resource in the Jordan River Basin* (Cambridge: Cambridge University Press, 1993).

constituted the inaugural acts of the Palestine Liberation Organization and served as a key motivation for Syria in the 1967 war.[10] Still, the Water Carrier endured, exemplifying how pipes can pinpoint a certain set of beneficiaries no matter their distance from a source, and laid the groundwork for Israel's orientation toward water.

As Samer Alatout has shown, national infrastructure brought with it a concept of scarcity that required citizen conservation of water and a drive for better technologies.[11] Since every drop was deemed vital to the survival of the state, Israeli citizens related to water beyond the framework of personal consumption. This drive along with funding streams earmarked for security led to famed Israeli water technologies such as drip irrigation, water recycling, precision agriculture, and the reverse osmosis membranes that made the desalination of water more cost-effective.[12] As Israel markets them as part of a global communication strategy intended to divert attention from the Occupation, these technologies are adopted across the world in the name of conservation or climate change adaptation.[13] Taking seriously the global extent of the hydrosocial cycle would suggest that the technologies themselves bear the imprint of ethno-national exclusion and militarization.

The Coastal Aquifer spans southern Israel, Gaza, and a portion of Egypt's Sinai Peninsula, serving only Gaza as a source of drinking water. Its sheer existence has allowed waves of Palestinian refugees to dwell in the Strip, which in the 1990s became, along with Jericho, the first site of recognized Palestinian

10. For a sophisticated analysis of the power constellation around water in the Middle East that eschews the notion of water wars, see Mark Zeitoun, *Power and Water in the Middle East: The Hidden Politics of the Palestinian-Israeli Water Conflict* (London: I. B. Tauris, 2008), 68–71.

11. Samer Alatout, "From Abundance to Scarcity (1936–1959): A Fluid History of Jewish Subjectivity in Historic Palestine and Israel," in *Reapproaching the Border: New Perspectives on the Study of Palestine/Israel*, ed. Mark LeVine and Sandy Sufian (New York: Rowan Publishers, 2007), 199–220; and "'States' of Scarcity: Water, Space, and Identity Politics in Israel, 1948–1959," *Environment and Planning D: Society and Space* 26, no. 6 (2008): 959–982.

12. Data cited by Zeitoun on Israeli withdrawals from aquifers in which "abstraction–and over-abstraction . . . is thus determined through Israeli pumping alone," supports a conclusion that the technologies in question serve as the means of controlling water, *Power and Water*, 52.

13. Seth M. Siegel even lauds Israel for supplying its "neighbor"—the Palestinians—with water as he champions the use of public money for private water tech companies and blames "inter-Palestinian political rivalry" for "recent politicization of water" that has led to the Gaza crisis; see *Let There Be Water: Israel's Solution for a Water-Starved World* (New York: St. Martin's Press, 2015), 176.

Authority within historical Palestine. Israeli settlers with military cover began to arrive in 1970 and remained in Gaza until Israel's unilateral withdrawal in 2005. The evacuation proved traumatic for Israel, deepening political rifts as the scenes of Israeli soldiers forcibly removing Jewish settlers seemed to bring war inward, yet not much changed for Gazans. Israel continues to control the airspace, the coastline, and crossing points of what Avi Shlaim, among others, has called the "biggest open-door prison on Earth."[14] The 2006 electoral victory by the Islamist resistance party Hamas helped assure militarized opposition and the continuation of Israeli besiegement and unrelenting war. The launching of missiles with steadily extending range from the Strip—many intercepted by Israel's Iron Dome—and the bombardment of Gaza's packed neighborhoods follow an almost ritualistic pattern, as if to assure all vested parties that the war rages on. Explosion, invasion, withdrawal, and cease-fire repeat with no change in politics or social relations with interim periods devoted to rearmament and generating media that confirm fundamental enmity. The military technologies available to Israel through funding from the United States and those available to Gaza through more sporadic funding from Qatar and Iran ensure that the local antagonists also enact regional and international disputes.

The Gaza Strip tends to be characterized in terms of its explosive skies or untenable population density. When observers do look underground, they mostly see the extensive tunnels that run to Egypt and enable a literally underground economy. The world hears little about the collapse of the Coastal Aquifer or what it means when a source of drinking water becomes nonviable. There seems to me no more precise gauge of financialized nationalism's endpoint. A report filed with the United Nations Office for the Coordination of Humanitarian Affairs describes how the aquifer provided a stable source of water until the 1990s, when its decline began. At the report's 2018 posting, 97 percent of water from the aquifer was deemed unfit for human consumption based on World Health Organization (WHO) standards.[15] Israeli targeting of sewage and drinking water infrastructure during military operations has

14. Avi Shlaim, "Ten Years after the First War on Gaza, Israel Still Plans Endless Brute Force," *Guardian*, January 7, 2019, https://www.theguardian.com/commentisfree/2019/jan/07/ten-years-first-war-gaza-operation-cast-lead-israel-brute-force.

15. UN Office for the Coordination of Humanitarian Affairs, "Study Warns Water Sanitation Crisis in Gaza May Cause Disease Outbreak and Possible Endemic," *The Monthly Humanitarian*

imperiled any natural replenishment of the aquifer as it meets the needs of two million people. Extraction from the aquifer occurs at three times the rate of its recharge by rain or tributary flow, which opens up large gaps in the porous rock that holds water. These open spaces are then filled by other sources, which, in this case, consist mainly of seawater and sewage. Around Gaza, seawater and sewage are largely one and the same, so the lapping of the Mediterranean into the empty aquifer both salinizes and contaminates any fresh water it might contain. Other vacancies are filled by seepage of human waste or runoff from gardens and farms that often carries fertilizer and pesticide chemicals. Diversion of sewage and runoff from the aquifer is hobbled by the absence of functioning infrastructure and an insufficient energy supply—recurrently cut as a punitive measure by Israel—to run existing plants.[16] This comports with Sophia Stamatopoulou-Robbins's observations of how Palestinians experience "infrastructural abandonment" that "yields uncomfortable and sometimes disastrous proximities to waste."[17]

The people of Gaza know that their water is bad and turn to private suppliers whenever possible. A solid indicator of how markets operate in crisis, this water comes at prices "10–30 times more expensive than piped water."[18] Even at such a steep cost, there is little guarantee that this water, largely produced through the small-scale desalination of inland waters, is safe to drink.[19] Permanent blockade does not leave people in the financial position to pay such high rates, so Gazans are often left to dig for the contents of the aquifer. The lack of water and its unsuitability for consumption contributes to about a

---

Bulletin, October 2018, https://www.ochaopt.org/content/study-warns-water-sanitation-crisis-gaza-may-cause-disease-outbreak-and-possible-epidemic.

16. "Community Based Problem Solving on Water Issues. Cross-Border 'Priority Initiatives' of the Good Water Neighbors Project," Ecopeace Middle East, November 2016, http://ecopeaceme.org/wp-content/uploads/2017/03/Community_Based_Problem_Solving_Nov_2016_Final.pdf.

17. Sophia Stamatopoulou-Robbins, *Waste Siege: The Life of Infrastructure in Palestine* (Stanford: Stanford University Press, 2020), 211. Because states have traditionally built and maintained infrastructure and thus mediated different encounters with waste—when infrastructure works, waste disappears, and when it doesn't, waste becomes a crisis—exposure to waste becomes "diagnostic of the nature of governance" (4).

18. UN OCHA, "Study Warns."

19. Zafrir Rinat, "Ninety-Seven Percent of Gaza Drinking Water Contaminated by Sewage, Salt, Expert Warns," *Haaretz*, January 21, 2018, https://www.haaretz.com/middle-east-news/palestinians/.premium-expert-warns-97-of-gaza-drinking-water-contaminated-by-sewage-salt-1.5747876.

quarter of all diseases in Gaza, with other infectious diseases that negatively impact the growth of children resulting from insufficient water for hygiene.[20] The hydrosocial cycle turns in a constant state of war that reverberates in a spoiled aquifer and chronically ill bodies.

When addressed, solutions to the collapsed aquifer entail Israel supplying Gaza with water or energy to treat wastewater, pump out salinized water, and disinfect drinking water. Strategies for shared Israeli-Palestinian water management and governance around Gaza have dissipated behind the drums of war.[21] Ongoing war means that Israel has not made plans to pipe water into Gaza, despite the potential to monetize the extreme water need. Due to the advocacy of the trilateral Jordanian-Palestinian-Israeli NGO Ecopeace Middle East, Israel increased the delivery of electricity to Gaza in June 2016 in order to power the Northern Gaza Emergency Sewage Treatment (NGEST) plant established by the World Bank.[22] However positive (not to mention necessary) it is to build a sewage treatment plant, the word "emergency" (sometimes dropped from its name to normalize the project) expresses the crux of the problem. The northern Gaza plant was born of emergency when sewage lakes caved beside the crumbling Beit Lahia plant and inundated the proximate village of Um Al Nasser, causing death, injury, and considerable loss of property.[23] A flood of life-threatening effluent represents a common nightmare, yet response to the emergency was slowed by Israeli blockage and procedures of global finance. Construction materials for industrial plants of any scale are classified as dual-use, meaning that they could be weaponized and are therefore restricted by Israel. But even before the materials could cross into Gaza, they needed to be purchased, which globalized the pointedly local emergency. Despite the fact that Gaza ratepayers will ultimately foot the bill, no direct loan

20. UN OCHA, "Study Warns."

21. On strategies for shared management of the Coastal Aquifer, see E. Weinthal et al., "The Water Crisis in the Gaza Strip: Prospects for Resolution," *Ground Water* 43, no. 5 (2005): 653–660.

22. "Gaza Water and Sanitation Crisis: Gaza's Water and Sanitation Crisis and Implications for Regional Stability," EcoPeace Middle East, accessed June 10, 2019, http://ecopeaceme.org/projects/water-the-peace-process/gaza-water-sanitation-crisis. In the interest of full disclosure, I am a member of the Ecopeace Middle East International Advisory Committee. See also Stamatopoulou-Robbins, *Waste Siege*, 1.

23. "North Gaza Communities Will Finally Benefit from Sewage Treatment Services," Report from World Bank, March 12, 2018, https://reliefweb.int/report/occupied-palestinian-territory/north-gaza-communities-will-finally-benefit-sewage-treatment.

was available to the Hamas government because it is labeled as terrorist. Israel had no intention of financing the project. The impasse brought in the World Bank, which wrangled European countries to put up financing.[24] Delayed by military flare-ups and damage done to the Beit Lahia plant, which was targeted during Israel's 2014 Protective Edge war on Gaza, the NGEST plant took ten years to construct. Its standing has not tempered the emergency. The electricity to power the plant secured by Ecopeace still fluctuates with escalation of conflict, as well as competition among sectors in Gaza with equally extreme needs. Ecopeace insists that the plant needs its own power line, but that this should serve as an interim measure rather than an enduring dependency on Israeli energy supply.[25]

The problem of Israel controlling the energy supply is redoubled by the fact that operating funds tied up with global capital can disappear at any point.[26] The World Bank financed the NGEST plant and stands as its owner of record, but transferred its daily operation to the Gaza Coastal Municipalities Water Utility.[27] This seems appropriate on the surface, but belies the fact that the Gaza utility is expected to locate funds to run the overleveraged plant and secure cost recovery for its investors. The Palestinian finance ministry in Gaza committed to finance the plant's operation and management until the end of

24. The actual cost was US $81.54 million, exceeding the estimate of $43.05 million; prepared by Kavita Mathur; reviewed by J. W. van Holst Pellekaan; ICR Review Coordinator, Christopher David Nelson, Implementation Completion Report Review, Independent Evaluation Group, GZ—North Gaza Emergency Sewage Treatment, 4, accessed June 3, 2019, http://documents.worldbank.org/curated/en/589751556300443166/pdf/West-Bank-and-Gaza-GZ-North-Gaza-Emerg-Sewage-Treatment.pdf. Robert Kuttner speaks to how institutions like the International Monetary Fund, World Bank, and World Trade Organization "have been substantially captured by financial elites." *Can Democracy Survive Global Capitalism?* (New York: W.W. Norton & Company, 2018), 238–239.

25. A similar power line to the Beit Lahia plant existed until it was damaged during the 2014 war; see Mathur, North Gaza Emergency Sewage Treatment, 4.

26. On the troubled dynamics of international donors to Palestinian sewage treatment as part of strategies for protecting "shared waters" with Israel, see Stamatopoulou-Robbins, *Waste Siege*, 187–206.

27. The World Bank leveraged its own West Bank & Gaza Multi-donor Trust Fund and administered joint cofinancing with Belgian, European Commission, and Swedish International Development Funds. Parallel financing came from the European Investment Bank, French Agency for Development, and PLO. "North Gaza Communities Will Finally Benefit from Sewage Treatment Services," reliefweb, March 12, 2018, https://reliefweb.int/report/occupied-palestinian-territory/north-gaza-communities-will-finally-benefit-sewage-treatment.

February 2020, when the Coastal Aquifer is slated to meet its official death. By March 2020, Gaza municipalities need to configure financing for the plant while confronting its sizable deficit, rendering the entire project precarious in nature.[28] The independent assessor of the project foresees the funding shortfall as likely to bring "the inevitable outcome" of "deterioration" and "costly reconstruction or rehabilitation."[29] In the face of acute sanitation needs and the high prices Gazans are willing to pay for drinking water, the private sector got a sewage treatment plant built but lacks the ability or the will to keep it operational. The debt will likely hover over northern Gaza even when the plant stops working and begins to crumble.

Slightly curbed for the time being, wastewater evades the blockade to stream into the Mediterranean Sea.[30] Due to strong northward currents, this waste lands at Israeli beaches.[31] Like those throughout the world, Israel's beaches are highly valued sites of recreation, leisure, and tourism. What sets them apart is that many double as sources of drinking water industrially produced at desalination plants. Israel's internationally celebrated solution to the desiccation and degradation of its watersheds has been the desalting of seawater through high-tech reverse osmosis membranes. Desalination provides about two-thirds of Israel's domestic water supply with built-in provisions to upscale in short order. As the viability of the Coastal Aquifer reaches its end and the operation of the NGEST treatment plant faces an uncertain future, the State of Israel plans to increase its desalination capacity to somewhere between 1.1 and 1.2 billion cubic meters a year. Returning to the idea of the hydrosocial cycle, we can see how uncertain World Bank funding, no provisions for a structurally oppressed population to procure drinking water, and the expansion of private equity control over water are key turns in its Israeli-Palestinian instantiation.

Although Mekorot, the Israeli state water utility, remains publicly held, it increasingly serves as operator of pipes with diminishing jurisdiction over water sources whose funds seed private companies.[32] Private equity has

28. See Mathur, North Gaza Emergency Sewage Treatment, 11.

29. See Mathur, North Gaza Emergency Sewage Treatment, 19.

30. Ecopeace has recorded seventeen wastewater pipes carrying over 108,000 cubic meters a day of slightly or entirely untreated sewage into the Mediterranean. We can estimate that additional seepage occurs beyond that of the pipes.

31. "Community Based Problem Solving on Water Issues," EcoPeace Middle East. In July 2017, the Zikim beach in Ashkelon closed due to high levels of wastewater washing ashore.

32. Siegel celebrates the erosion of a publicly held utility through some of the classic rationalizations of water privatization. He tells a story of "the pro-business, pro-innovation

eclipsed the utility's power largely through the development of desalination.[33] Because of its socialist underpinnings and early alienation from fossil fuel markets due to Arab boycott, Israel came late to global capitalism in the 1990s, but then more than made up for lost time. Prime Minister Benjamin Netanyahu has played a starring role in Israel's process of privatization, yet desalination belongs to the Israeli oligarch Yitzhak Tshuva. Tshuva's corporate avatars include IDE Technologies, Israel Chemicals Limited, and Delek, an energy conglomerate with sizable shares in the natural gas fields on the Eastern Mediterranean seabed. Tshuva's water monopoly alongside his ownership of natural gas constitutes a form of vertical integration in which the tycoon controls an energy source and a downstream market—desalination—that requires copious amounts of energy.[34] The scenario subverts Ben-Gurion's 1959 Water Law that designated all water as commonly held and controlled by the state. Those who applaud the market for eliminating the inefficiencies of government through competition should address both the absence of competition and waning citizen water rights. Those who champion the market as the way to overcome the restrictive nature of nationalism should observe how, to date, the global trading of desalination shares has changed little about the availability of water to Palestinians. Everyone should pay closer attention when private sector spokesmen lament the social contract in which the state bears

---

government of Ariel Sharon" transforming a "change-averse, once innovative organization" by sharing information about state water supply with "inventors and entrepreneurs" who received "seed capital" and promises of implementation from Mekorot only to "retain the intellectual property rights to the solutions and benefit from the commercial exploitation of it." *Let There Be Water*, 153. He never considers that the engineers and technology experts in question might become unionized employees of the utility (rather, Mekorot senior executives donated "as much as thousands of hours" to private companies [245]), that public water and the data about it might be safeguarded from the private sector, or that the so-called entrepreneurs might acquire their own capital. In Siegel's water world, no Israeli Occupation exists and the sole problem rests with truculent Palestinian "neighbors" slow to adopt Israeli-born technologies that, he insists, would solve the basic problem of access.

33. Ironically, private capital was initially heralded as a means "to undermine the monopoly power of the national water company," yet resulted in a near water monopoly in the hands of one oligarch. Amidst the transfer from the public to a handful of men, the secondary goal of undercutting "organized labor" was achieved. Eran Feitelson and Gad Rosenthal, "Desalination, Space and Power: The Ramifications of Israel's Changing Water Geography," *Geoforum* 43, no. 2 (2012): 273.

34. The price of desalinated water is pegged to energy costs.

responsibility for providing safe, affordable water, as well as humanitarian ideas about the universal right to water, as barriers to privatization.[35]

The introduction of market mechanisms into the production and delivery of water tends to make bad situations worse due to lack of incentives for serving poor communities, cutting costs at random to increase investor dividends, and leaving customers to dirt and thirst when they cannot pay rates set as collateral for large loans leveraged by the latest buyer. In enumerating these degradations, one cannot lose sight of the most dramatic change of all: the loss of sovereignty over water. When private equity takes over, citizens and the state alike lose price controls, access, and oversight of water, as they become customers of, rather than sovereign over, water sources. Palestinian experiences of this shift only intensify the earlier loss of water sovereignty to the State of Israel, meaning that it is Palestinian alienation from water (rather than jurisdiction over) that becomes financialized. Total Israeli state control of water has leant itself to the smooth transfer of assets to the private sector while maintaining its association with security.[36] Even as state sovereignty erodes and public rates increase, statist discriminations hold and deepen amidst the monetization of water. In addition to being a crisis in its own right, the

35. This is the very argument in a conference paper entitled "Implementation of Build-Operate-Transfer Schemes: Obstacles & Solutions," presented at a conference by IDE Technologies Ltd.'s Executive Vice President for Special Projects, Fredi Lokiec, and authored by Lokiec and R. Meerovitch, accessed June 12, 2019, https://www.ide-tech.com/en/white-papers/implementation-of-build-operate-transfer-schemes-obstacles-and-solutions, which also instructs companies building infrastructure in developing countries to rely "on bilateral financing institutions such as the World Bank group" and "international commercial banks" (8).

36. Breaches in this security are becoming increasingly evident. For example, the Hong Kong based Hutchison Water, a Chinese multinational corporation, remains in the running for the Sorek B desalination plant despite tensions in the so-called United States-China trade war (Amos Harel, "Despite U.S. Pressure, Chinese Firm Closing in on Highly Sensitive Israeli Location," *Haaretz*, September 7, 2019, https://www.haaretz.com/israel-news/.premium-despite-u-s-pressure-chinese-firm-closing-in-on-highly-sensitive-israeli-location-1.7805466); its proximity to an Israeli Air Force base and Sorek Nuclear Research Center (Amos Harel, "With Its National Security at Stake, Israel Takes Sides in U.S.-China Trade War," *Haaretz*, May 26, 2019, https://www.haaretz.com/us-news/.premium-u-s-china-trade-war-israel-takes-sides-national-security-1.7280881); and a cyber-attack perpetrated against Israeli competitors for the selfsame tender (Yaniv Kubovich, "Israeli Firm Vying with Chinese for Highly Sensitive Plant Hit by Cyberattack," *Haaretz*, November 19, 2019, https://www.haaretz.com/israel-news/.premium-israeli-firm-vying-with-chinese-rival-to-build-key-plant-hit-by-cyberattack-1.8127227).

Palestinian water scenario serves as a bellwether for how private capital treats public health emergencies. One wonders how extensive the resemblance will be when Israel becomes totally dependent on desalinated water and the question of who receives and who is severed from water is traded on the market as another set of risks.

Israel's very first desalination factory on the Mediterranean coast was built in Ashkelon, just over ten miles from the Beit Lahia treatment plant in Gaza. Inbal, a government-owned corporation with a public private partnership department that attends to financing for the State of Israel's Water Desalination Authority, entered into a public-private partnership with Veolia (at that time called Vivendi Environnement)—the global corporation implicated in several of the world's more famous water crises—in 2001 to construct what was then the world's largest desalination plant.[37] Nothing better represents the inseparability of energy and desalinated water—what Toby Jones has described as oil turned to water through "a political enterprise"[38]—than the placement of the Ashkelon desalination plant on the premises of the Europe Asia (aka Eilat Ashkelon) Pipeline Company. Ashkelon hosts considerable petroleum storage capacity built to accommodate the Iranian-Israeli oil partnership of yore that brought tankers through the Red Sea to Eilat in southern Israel and filled a pipeline to Ashkelon to meet domestic Israeli needs and feed tankers on the Mediterranean bound for Europe. When the partnership collapsed following the 1979 Iranian Revolution, the company added a line to receive imports at the Ashkelon port and direct oil to Eilat. Housing the desalination plant on the pipeline company premises offered compatible zoning and ensures immediate, constant energy supply.[39]

37. On Veolia, see Maude Barlow, *Blue Future: Protecting Water for People and the Planet Forever* (New York: The New Press, 2013), 23. For Veolia's role in the Flint Water Crisis, see the court case *State of Michigan v. Veolia North America, Inc.*

38. Toby Jones, *Desert Kingdom: How Oil and Water Forged Modern Saudi Arabia* (Cambridge, MA: Harvard University Press, 2010), 3.

39. The project includes an IPP (independent power producer) with a capacity of 80 MW. The IPP was also built as a Public Private Partnership project to provide the plant's electricity. In addition, the IPP sells excess capacity to private clients via the national grid. The pipeline company itself is shrouded in secrecy and possible tax dodges; see Haaretz Editorial Board, "The Time Has Come for Israel to Expose Its Most Secret Firm," *Haaretz*, September 18, 2016, https://www.haaretz.com/opinion/the-time-has-come-for-israel-to-expose-its-secret-firm-1.5437187; Israel Ministry of Finance, "Ashkelon Desalination Plant," accessed June 11, 2019,

VID Desalination acquired a twenty-five-year concession for the Ashkelon desalination plant according to a Build-Operate-Transfer (BOT) model, which holds that the plant will be transferred to the government of Israel upon expiration of the concession. It will certainly be worth watching whether or not the transfer will occur in 2026 and if the government of Israel at that time will be an entity separate from private capital secured by a public army. The main players in desalination are the aforementioned oligarch Yitzhak Tshuva, the equally titanic tycoon Idan Ofer, and the Veolia corporation (which itself has investors, including Idan Ofer). Each assumes different avatars in the game of profiting from resources, switching shares as if playing cards. In 2001, VID Desalination, which obtained the concession, was owned by IDE Technologies[40]—jointly held by Israel Chemicals Ltd (Ofer) and Delek Group (Tshuva)—(50 percent), Vivendi/Veolia (25 percent), and Ellern Industries (25 percent) held by the Dankner family, tycoons who lost their wealth and met with disgrace and jail time.[41] In 2002, the Israeli government awarded a second contract to VID Desalination, which had in the meantime become a split partnership between IDE Technologies and Veolia. Lifting the private equity curtain further shows how Tshuva gained an even greater share over Ashkelon's water by purchasing a 50-percent stake in Idan Ofer's Israel Chemicals Limited in 2002.[42]

---

https://mof.gov.il/en/InternationalAffairs/InfrastructuresAndProjects/Projects/Pages/Project_DesalinationPlant-Ashkelon.aspx.

40. IDE Technologies began as Israel Desalination Engineering, which Ben-Gurion funded to explore whether desalination was possible. An early partnership with Fairbanks Whitney (subsequently called Colt Industries) later morphed into a government business in which Israel sold its "desalination know-how." "IDE was merged with another Israeli-government business in the 1980s, and as part of the privatization boom in Israel in the 1990s, the company was sold." Siegel, *Let There Be Water*, 114.

41. As Israeli tycoons meet around desalination deals, they intersect at other junctures such as the crazy project at the New Frontier hotel and casino on the Las Vegas Strip in which Tshuva and Nochi Danker blew up the hotel and casino in order to reproduce Tshuva's New York Plaza Hotel only to leave an empty lot yawning during the 2008 housing crisis. See Amotz Asa-El, "Demise of Israel's Tycoons: Billionaire Nochi Dankner's Collapse Underscores the Demise of a Whole Class of Tycoons and the End of an Economic Era," *Jerusalem Post*, February 4, 2017, https://www.jpost.com/Jerusalem-Report/The-harder-they-fall-477139.

42. The relationship between Tshuva and Ofer remained tense, with the two fighting over "the proper valuation for the company, once in 2010 when Tshuva sought to take the company public but didn't due to ICL opposition, and another time in 2011 when Delek sought to sell its stake to ICL and again IDE's valuation thwarted the agreement." Yoram Gabison, "Israel

Veolia's involvement in Ashkelon and the Israeli water sector at large seemingly came to an end in 2005—the year that the Ashkelon Plant opened—when the Boycott, Divestment, and Sanctions movement, which seeks an end to Israel's Occupation and its normalization, successfully campaigned against Veolia for its central role in the Jerusalem Light Rail that crosses into occupied territory.[43] Veolia's suite of water holdings was then acquired by the Los Angeles-based firm Oaktree Capital. In 2010, due to the unmatched success of the Ashkelon plant, it was expanded by nearly 20 percent to 392,000 cubic meters of water a day. Because desalinated water profits always flow toward Yitzhak Tshuva, his Delek Automotive division bought Oaktree Capital's share in 2018 for $288 million.[44] In 2011, Israeli State Comptroller Micha Lindenstrauss sounded the warning about price gouging for desalinated water due to the vertical integration of natural gas, electricity, and water all controlled by Delek and Israel Chemicals/Israel Corporation, that is, Tshuva and Ofer. With the desalination market expanding, Lindenstrauss noted that, at the time, IDE held 75 percent of desalted water flowing through Israeli pipes, stressing the need for competition as new plants were built.[45] Israel Chemicals' eyes turned eastward to the sizable market for desalted water in Arab countries, which makes up about 60 percent of world demand, so put its half share of IDE Technologies up for sale in 2014 (to unload Israeli assets in order to compete in the Arab world), completing the sale in 2017 for $167 million with a capital gain of approximately $40 million.[46]

Chemicals Puts Desalination Unit Up for Sale," *Haaretz*, November 12, 2014, https://www.haaretz.com/israel-news/business/.premium-israel-chemicals-puts-desalination-unit-up-for-sale-1.5328000?=&ts=_1559234312692.

43. An article in the Israeli newspaper *Haaretz* on October 11, 2007, reports that Veolia Environment has worked in Israel for fourteen years with plans of expansion, owns 25 percent of the Ashkelon desalination facility, and continues to own 20 percent of the light-rail project in Jerusalem. The thrust of the article follows Oligarch Idan Ofer's 3.5-percent stake in Veolia through which he earned $800 million. Avi Bar-Eli, "Idan Ofer's Midas Touch: Veolia Stake Doubles in Value," *Haaretz*, October 11, 2007, https://www.haaretz.com/1.4983971.

44. Delek Automotive's CEO, Gil Agmon, was arrested in 2007 on suspicion of bribing a civil servant on a municipal planning and construction committee. See Sharon Shpurer and Arnon Ben-Yair, "Delek Motors CEO Gil Agmon Arrested on Bribery Suspicion," *Haaretz*, September 5, 2007, https://www.haaretz.com/1.4971362.

45. Itai Trilnick, "Comptroller: State Quailed before Tycoons, so Water Will Cost More," *Haaretz*, May 2, 2012, https://www.haaretz.com/israel-news/business/1.5218625.

46. Gabison, "Israel Chemicals Puts Desalination Unit Up for Sale."

The acquisition of public sector assets by a few hustle-capitalists is not restricted to water, but follows a structure in which public projects lose funding (often the lost funding goes back to investors in the form of both subsidies and tax abatements), the institutions that have had their funding cut are deemed inefficient and thus in need of private capitalization, an investor obtains an enormous loan to purchase the institution, usually citing rate payers or remnant government funding as collateral, slashes costs and fires employees, pockets a significant portion of the loan, then looks to sell.[47] In the case of Israeli water, the state-run Israel Water Commission morphed into the Israel Water Authority in 2006 in order to introduce private investment to the sector.[48] In employing this language, I wish to note the disparity between what most people think when they hear such a phrase—that capital enters into a specific sector—and what actually occurs—that capital is extracted or leveraged, leaving the operation in demonstrably worse shape or requiring higher rates from users. Desalination showcases a unique variation of the process because the potable water produced does not exist prior to the tenders, financialization, and construction. Some degree of desalination is certainly necessary amidst climate change and consumption patterns in Israel, as well as in other parts of the world. However, the loans and windfalls of tycoons around the delivery of daily water are enormous, the water in question partially commodified such that the goal is to find bulk customers rather than support life or conserve, and water sources are degraded either through the offloading of excess brine back into the sea or by weakened freshwater basins, where low-tech conservation falters because people have come to believe that a technological silver bullet will eventually fix their water too. The energy-intensive nature of industrial water facilities further fuels the warming planet and its negative impacts on water.

The concession holder for a desalination plant runs no such risks, but rather can rest assured that the state will purchase a set quantity of water throughout the franchise period, with more to be purchased should a plant expand. The position of the state thus shifts from that of supplier to customer as public campaigns to treasure every drop morph into construction of fountains in city squares. As illustrated by the scandal in which the Sorek and Palmachim desalination facilities falsified reports to conceal dangerous levels

47. Kuttner, *Can Democracy Survive Global Capitalism?*, 111–113.

48. The Treasury sought to break up Mekorot, the state company, with a discourse of achieving efficiency through competition; see Feitelson and Rosenthal, "Desalination, Space, and Power," 278.

of chloride far exceeding those specified in their franchise agreements,[49] governments forfeit the responsibility to regulate water quality and safeguard public health when they privatize their water systems.[50] Israeli state rhetoric insists that the public benefits by the record-low rates for processed sea water provided by IDE, but this must be weighed against how IDE lowers prices primarily as a barter chip for the option to build cogeneration power stations alongside desalination factories.[51] Profit multiplies because the power stations are subsidized to supply the water plants and can sell the excess energy to other customers through the national grid. Even more public revenue filtered into IDE when Alpha Water 2 Limited Partnership acquired Israel Chemicals' share in IDE Technologies. Because the structure of desalination concessions prevented Tshuva from obtaining a complete hold of IDE, he anointed Avshalom Felber, CEO and president of IDE, as a partner.[52] Felber then lined up two insurance firms and the Israel Teachers' Union educational funds' group to finance his Alpha Water Partnership.[53] In this way, public

49. Chloride is the main ingredient in sea salt. Hiding the chloride content in the water produced at the plants saved them around $3.4 million. Sue Surkes, "Two Desalination Plants Faked Water Quality Data to Cut Costs," *Times of Israel*, September 3, 2019, https://www.timesofisrael.com/two-desalination-plants-faked-water-quality-data-to-cut-costs-report/.

50. The Administrative Affairs Court briefly "suspended the tender" for IDE Technologies and Hutchison in conjunction with Sorek B after it came to light that they falsified and concealed water quality reports to save money. Bini Aschkenasy, "Israeli Court Freezes Desalination Tender, Forcing State Scrutiny of Bidders," *Haaretz*, November 5, 2019, https://www.haaretz.com/israel-news/.premium-court-freezes-desalination-tender-forcing-state-to-reexamine-status-of-bidders-1.8084744. By December 2019, the companies were restored to the tender competition, facing no criminal investigation and a symbolic penalty of 30 million cubic meters of desalinated water to be supplied free of charge for the public, Sue Surkes, "Desalination plant that lied about salts to save cash escapes criminal probe," *The Times of Israel*, December 12, 2019, https://www.timesofisrael.com/desalination-plant-that-lied-about-salts-to-save-cash-avoids-criminal-probe/.

51. Amiram Barkat and Sonia Gorodeisky, "Tshuva Must Sell Desalination Plant to Bid for Sorek," *Globes*, August 23, 2018, https://en.globes.co.il/en/article-tshuva-must-sell-desalination-plant-to-bid-for-sorek-1001251043.

52. Felber and Alpha are poised to gain a greater share of IDE; see "Alfa Partners Set to Increase Its Stake in IDE," *Global Water Intelligence*, January 2, 2019, https://www.globalwaterintel.com/news/2019/1/alfa-partners-set-to-increase-its-stake-in-ide. Tshuva often motivates his CEOs by cutting them in on large deals where his control hits legal limits.

53. This sale is a microcosm of privatization. Not only did the Teachers' Union funds become wrapped up in the gamble of finance, but the two insurance companies have fully penetrated the realm of benefits and pensions. Behind Clal Insurance Enterprises Holdings is a 45-percent share held by the firm ruined by former oligarch Yochi Danker and 10 percent by Israel's Bank

funds to support the advanced training of teachers became bound up in privatization of the water sector.

IDE was ready to surrender its first-born plant in Ashkelon to run the bigger market around Tel Aviv. In 2018, IDE exercised its right of first refusal to absorb the 49-percent share in the Sorek A plant that serves the populous Tel Aviv area from Hutchison Water, a Hong Kong-based firm, becoming its sole owner and majority holder of Israel's overall desalination capacity.[54] Then the real prize appeared on the horizon: plans for Sorek B, which promises to surpass its sibling as the biggest and best desalination plant in the world. IDE made known its intentions to bid on the Sorek B tender and to use its record to beat out other bidders.[55] Tshuva/Delek's steps toward monopoly in both energy and desalinated water triggered the interest of Michal Halperin, the latest head of Israel's Antitrust Authority. Although her report provided the usual rationale for the privatization of water, she determined that if IDE wanted to bid on Sorek B, then it needed to sell its 100-percent share of Sorek A.[56] The fact

---

Hapoalim, with other shares traded on the Tel Aviv Stock Exchange. "ICL Completes the Sale of Its 50% Share of IDE Technologies for Approximately $167 Million," *PR Newswire*, December 10, 2017, https://www.prnewswire.com/news-releases/icl-completes-the-sale-of-its-50-share-of-ide-technologies-for-approximately-167-million-300569365.html. Another microcosm of this hydrosocial cycle is that Ayalon Insurance Company's general partner is controlled by Avshalom Felber—meaning that Felber/IDE owns shares through IDE itself and a subpartner.

54. "IDE Pays $53.3 Million for 49 Per Cent of Sorek Desalination Plant," *water: desalination + reuse*, June 13, 2018, https://www.desalination.biz/news/0/IDE-pays-533-million-for-49-per-cent-of-Sorek-desalination-plant/9038/. Siegel speaks of Hutchison Water as "a Chinese-Israeli water company" led, in part, by Ronen Wolfman, Mekorot's former CEO; *Let There Be Water*, 118.

55. The other bidders: GES, of Israel; China's Hutchison, and PMEC; and the European Suez, and Acciona together with Israel's Allied, and Aqualia with WPI of Israel. See "Bidders Line Up for Sorek 2, as IDE Agrees Put Option," *water: desalination + reuse*, October 9, 2018, https://www.desalination.biz/news/0/Bidders-line-up-for-Sorek-2-as-IDE-agrees-put-option/9120/.

56. Halperin's report cites the State authority as the ultimate recipient of desalination concessions (in the case of Sorek A in 2037) and negotiator of water prices. "The Participation of IDE in the Planning, Building, and Operation of an Additional Desalination Facility at Sorek," State of Israel Antitrust Authority, August 23, 2018, https://www.gov.il/BlobFolder/unit/centralization_decrease_committee/he/Vaadot_ahchud_CentralizationDecreaseCommittee_opinion2018_IDE.pdf (Hebrew). See also "Bid Lined Up for Soreq 1 Plant in IDE Desal Antitrust Deal," *Global Water Intelligence*, October 18, 2018, https://www.globalwaterintel.com/global-water-intelligence-magazine/19/10/general/bid-lined-up-for-soreq-1-plant-in-ide-desal-antitrust-deal.

that receiving the tender for Sorek B was supposedly not assured by offloading Sorek A led to much extolling of IDE and its "voluntary sale" of such a significant asset. Angling for the newest contract, IDE sold Sorek A to the capital arm of the Dan Public Transportation company for between $146 and 149 million.[57] Even as IDE divested equity and ceded its Sorek A operation and management contract, it still aced its private equity scorecard with 2018 net profit increased by 275 percent and conditions cleared to own the world's largest desalination plant that will be able to outproduce competition, should any arise.[58] The degradation and fraud surrounding Sorek A's water supply, discovered in the summer of 2019, may yet hobble IDE's monopolistic aims and mark an exceptional chain of events.[59]

It remains the case that desalination plants could supply water to the Gaza Strip. Plans for the expansion of desalination at Sorek B include a production increase slated for depleted river basins,[60] so it is not outside the realm of possibility that the Coastal Aquifer could be replenished by desalinated water. A combination of Gazan ratepayers and international aid dollars could even increase Tshuva's growing fortune, if this is indeed the price of water. Ultimately, the impediment to scenarios like these is the very structure of Occupation fixed in place through biblical projections and their political instantiations. As relatively easy as it would be to pipe freshwater into Gaza and redirect pipes of waste from the sea to operative treatment plants, it is safe to say that it will not happen absent fundamental social change. Despite doubt that such change can occur, it remains necessary to imagine that eroding rights, damaging environmental conditions, and restrictive pricing can lead somewhere other than twenty-first-century versions of political fascism. I would like to suggest that such change might occur by taking water out of the parameters of

57. Formally Dan Capital Investments and Infrastructures Ltd. "Dan Capital Will Purchase the Sorek 1 Desalination Plant from IDE for More Than NIS 540 Million," *Israel Financial Insider*, October 7, 2018, http://www.ifi.today/agriculture/226-Dan-Capital-will-purchase-the-Sorek-1-desalination-plant-from-IDE-for-more-than-NIS-540-million.html.

58. "Bid Lined Up for Soreq 1 Plant"; and "IDE Sees Profits Jump as Capital Recycling Ticks Up," *Global Water Intelligence*, April 4, 2019, https://www.globalwaterintel.com/news/2019/14/ide-sees-profits-jump-as-capital-recycling-ticks-up.

59. Bini Aschkenasy, "Israeli Court Freezes Desalination Tender, Forcing State Scrutiny of Bidders," *Haaretz*, November 5, 2019, https://www.haaretz.com/israel-news/.premium-court-freezes-desalination-tender-forcing-state-to-reexamine-status-of-bidders-1.8084744.

60. Environmental groups maintain skepticism about mixing desalinated and fresh water, particularly after two plants were shown to have falsified reports of chloride levels.

privatized nationalism and recategorizing it as a sovereign claim of all the people inhabiting a watershed.

A watershed is an area defined by where rain falls and how it drains into particular streams, rivers, and lakes. The flow of water etches the boundaries of the watershed and ties together all who inhabit it in the shared interest of continuous, clean hydration. The movement of rain through a watershed displays the interconnectedness of waterways and land; it also reflects the ecological health of a region in the sense that water picks up minerals, toxins, and byproducts as it crosses social boundaries. When we think in terms of the watershed rather than the nation-state, issues of working infrastructure, decontamination, and conservation move to the forefront. Engineered watersheds like those created by industrial desalination present a certain challenge to this conception of socio-environmental regions, but, as we have seen with the Coastal Aquifer and desalination plants, they remain integrated nonetheless. Even in the world's many manufactured watersheds, common interest in preserving safe, affordable, and accessible water persists.

The book of Joshua, paradoxically enough, offers a precedent for emerging watershed politics and charts the course for moving beyond conquest and toward inhabitation. Its second half presents a mix of peoples, tribes, clans, and households present in shared regions. The picture is not utopian—skirmish and competition continue—but a decentralized system with loose alliances and variant sites of sovereignty is justified by Scripture as much as militarized Occupation. In conjunction with the second half of Joshua, the book of Judges attests to the variegated social order of ancient Israel. Ancient and modern conjoin in the very name of the Sorek desalination enterprise after the brook of Sorek where the biblical Delilah dwelled, allowing us to jointly interpret the two places and times. Despite interpretive associations with a prostitute and a Philistine from Timnah, two other women who also factor in Samson's life, nothing about Delilah's story explicitly renders her as either. True, she lives alone like Rahab of Jericho and accepts money from Philistine princes to undo Samson, but she is identified only as "the woman from the valley of Sorek" (Judg 16:4). In light of the book of Joshua, the phrase communicates quite a bit. Significantly, Delilah is not identified as Philistine, Judahite, or a member of the Tribe of Dan. Whereas her tribal and political affiliations remain amorphous, she is pointedly an inhabitant of the Sorek Valley, opposed to a violent strongman upsetting its mix of peoples. If she is a Philistine, then Delilah collaborates with her kinspeople to bring down a serial disrupter of peace and fertility. If she is a Danite or Judahite, then Delilah works across boundaries to maintain the social balance around her watershed. But Delilah cannot be pinned to any ethnic or political group because her affiliation is with a stream and its valley. Her example, like those of Rahab and Achsah, offers a vision of multiple groups inhabiting shared space and how they might resist those who seek to introduce war.

Following the example of these figures today involves attending to social balance and equitable water distribution through practices of bioregionalism. Bioregionalism advocates for the overall health and future viability of watersheds as it empowers all inhabitants through jurisdiction and oversight of their water. A bioregional council, such as those formed by Ecopeace Middle East's Good Water Neighbors program, convenes local politicians, community leaders, educators, scientists, artists, and youth to collectively study the watershed, the sources of its impairment, and its modes of distribution.[61] This collective approach builds trust and allows for policies and practices in the broad interest of the watershed. Decentralization, unfortunately, is likewise a beloved word of privatizers, working as code for breaking up state control, so constant effort must be exerted to keep water in public hands no matter how prolonged addressing the variant needs of different groups can be. Fully remediating damaged parts of the watershed, addressing the areas not serviced by a pipe, or balancing sites of underinvestment are not acts expressing inefficiency, but rather the only way to ensure uncontaminated water for residents throughout a basin. Bioregional decentralization devolves state power to localities while maintaining and expanding public control.[62]

61. I refer to a similar method as Source-Path-People that involves learning about the source of water, the path that it takes to reach you, and whom it interconnects, on the *Freshwater Stories* digital storytelling site, Rachel Havrelock and Sharif Ezzat, "Get Involved," *Freshwater Stories*, uploaded November 15, 2017, http://freshwaterstories.com/get-involved.

62. The Israeli-Palestinian Joint Water Committee (JWC) established as part of the Oslo II Agreeement does not represent a good example because it never established a principle of Palestinian water sovereignty as it stipulated that approval of any infrastructure in Palestinian communities or the settlements required committee consensus (1995, Annex III, Article 40). The Oslo Agreement further established a scenario in which local forms of Palestinian water delivery became subject to Israeli veto. Practically, the consensus requirement meant that Palestinian members of the JWC had to approve settlement infrastructure in order to gain the votes approving any water procurement. Although Palestinian members submitted more proposals for approval, more water infrastructure for settlements overall gained approval. Whatever the committee votes, Israeli governments have shown readiness to build the pumps and pipes for settlements. See Mark Zeitoun, "Bargaining Power—The Joint Water Committee," in *Power and Water in the Middle East*, 99–109. After years of frustration and worsening water conditions in

The first step in any collective strategy for protecting common water should be addressing the trouble spots, which entails confronting how marginalized groups tend to have the least access, greatest impairment, and most expensive water. In addition, it is vital that leadership come from impacted communities. There may be plenty of engineers, researchers, and investors who think they hold the solution, but in order to be durable and effective, new systems of water procurement and remediation must align with the priorities of the resident community. This constitutes one of the reasons why the stakeholder model that equates the interests of residents, polluters, and capital fails to protect the watershed and those who draw from it. In our case, this means that Israel cannot unilaterally solve Gaza's water problems without reciprocity and elevation of local water leaders. In conjunction, the key push must be redistributive—redirecting the subsidy of corporations and private equity to Palestinian beneficiaries. The massive loss of Palestinian property and its absorption by Israel and Israelis has yet to be addressed in legal or economic terms. Although it would not resolve this question, equitable distribution of water under Palestinian sovereign oversight would move in the right direction while likely conferring the benefits of remediated public water on all. Because corporations and capitalists have successfully implanted a truism that objects to "handouts" to disenfranchised groups while viewing massive subsidies to the wealthy as generating "jobs," the outwardly radiating benefits of prioritizing water crises must be emphasized at every turn.[63] Allowing Gazans to address the sewage problem, for example, would protect northern beaches and the Israeli water supply.

However vital it is to maintain municipal control over water where it still exists, such a move is not sufficient. Structures like the National Water Carrier, after all, were built at a scale reflecting national confidence about public

---

the West Bank as settlements mushroomed with an increasing supply of water, Palestinian representatives formally refused to continue meeting as part of the Joint Water Committee. From 2010 to 2017, no meetings occurred. With Palestinian water supply plummeting to crisis levels, the Trump administration's Middle East envoy Jason Greenblatt negotiated an increase of Israeli water sales to the Palestinian Authority with the caveat that the Joint Water Committee needed to convene. No matter their stance of political resistance, Palestinian members of the JWC simply needed to provide their constituents with the water to live.

63. During my own 2019 visit to the Sorek A desalination plant, I was struck by how few workers were present, which reminded me more of the refineries than the water treatment plants that I have toured. I was unaware of the chloride contamination of the water when I saw and drank it.

funding that no longer exists even as they continue to manifest discriminatory forms of distribution. Not only should municipal systems expand and equalize their service, but they also gain a perfect justification for remaining public when they offer the best service to the highest number of people. Insofar as the number of rate payers and the rates that they can sustain serve as collateral in the loans obtained by private enterprise, public systems should look to similar financing to improve and expand.

The barriers to a confederation of watersheds in a hotly contested, water-challenged place cannot be denied, yet the depletion of national and international plans to end the conflict and the horizon of energy-intensive, privatized water amidst punishing climate change also set ideal conditions for the rapid adoption of watershed politics. Resource sovereignty is the perfect intermediate step between the current state of war and political resolution. Whereas full resource sovereignty, including gas, oil, and mineral rights, is ideal, beginning with water is somewhat easier due to its long, international history as part of a commons and existing legal frameworks of public trust and regulation. In the blended land of Israel-Palestine, establishing parity through shared water sovereignty could be a perfect end run around the current impasse. For Palestinians, an established claim of water sovereignty could address the distributive imbalance as it set up jurisdiction over the sizable aquifer beneath the West Bank, as well as surface water and parts of the Mediterranean coastline from which sea water is drawn. In trying to redress historical injustice, it seems paradoxical that marginalized groups restricted from national self-assertion should attain sovereignty over resources only at the point where they are imperiled, but it is also the case that those who have suffered the most at the hands of extant systems likely have the best sense of how to transform them. Extending the principle of resource sovereignty to a portion of the Eastern Mediterranean gas fields (the very ones owned by oligarch Tshuva and his American friends at Noble Energy) could confer even greater benefits, like providing both the funding and the energy for development in Gaza, including waste water treatment and desalination. In turn, this would ensure a higher quality of desalted Mediterranean water and fewer threats of Israeli beach closure. Finally, I can think of no reason why Yitzhak Tshuva needs to be further enriched as two million people—and likely others to join them—go without drinking water.

Israeli-Palestinian resource sovereignty could be scaled to a full de-escalation strategy. Observing the status quo, four regions become apparent. There is a mixed Jewish-Arab population in the Galilee. Extending an equitable policy of resource access and services to the enfranchised Palestinian citizens of Galilee and vesting their representatives on the existing regional councils could form the basis for bioregional governance. A similarly mixed group populates the Negev, where desalination plants and incipient alternative energies could serve all residents while generating revenues long due to indigenous Negev Bedouin for expropriated land. Nationalist aspirations could find fulfillment in the Jewish-majority "Israel" along the coastline and Arab-majority "Palestine" in the West Bank. The guarantee of mutual minority rights and representation could avert a costly and complicated population transfer.

Bioregional governance bodies overseeing resource distribution could further be federated in the name of integrated policies. The flow of water already provides the perfect system theory. In Eyal Weizman's words, "The hydrological cycle of the Jordan Valley basin, of which Israel/Palestine and the surrounding states form part, is a system of cyclical flows that cuts through the area's political and security borders."[64] Such reconfiguration of authority over water requires the permanent disbanding of the Joint Water Committee, whose overall effect has been to enact Israeli occupation over Palestinian water sources while seeking Palestinian imprimatur.[65] It might also immediately address some of the primary injustices of current water distribution, including the Israeli claim of 80 percent of West Bank water, the exorbitant rates Palestinians pay for water that flows beneath their feet, and the lack of potable water in Gaza.

Why would the truculent Israeli government agree to support Palestinian water sovereignty? One reason is that working with water instead of territory implicitly maintains that more recent arrivals are as sovereign over their watershed as historical communities. This means that, should they more equitably distribute the copious water made available to them, Israeli settlements need not be entirely dismantled. Along with those already covered in this book, the problem with the settlements from the perspective of watershed politics is not entirely that they are there, but rather how they orient space and commandeer resources. Despite the elaborate theatrics of Joshua Land, Israelis and Palestinians—further clustered by class, religious observance and political affiliation—are copresent between the Jordan River and the Mediterranean Sea. Their water sources are one and the same. The multiplication of restrictive barriers attempts to override this and to enforce a myth of Jewish

64. Eyal Weizman, *Hollow Land: Israel's Architecture of Occupation* (New York: Verso, 2007), 18.

65. Jan Selby, "Cooperation, Domination and Colonisation: The Israeli-Palestinian Joint Water Committee," *Water Alternatives* 6, no. 1 (2013): 1–24.

separation on a conflicting reality. So, what if we consider the demographics not in terms of national struggle, but in terms of the water resources necessary to sustain the population at current and future junctures? What if resource management formed the basis for regional social and political institutions? Finally, what if the British colonial map with its ethnic partitions was dropped once and for all and instead we began to think—as did Ben-Gurion and King Faisal in the 1920s, not to mention tribal leaders like those reflected in the book of Joshua—of sustainably federated regions? What if the conquest reached its end and the land grew quiet from war?

INDEX

A NOTE ON THE TYPE

This book has been composed in Arno, an Old-style serif typeface in the classic Venetian tradition, designed by Robert Slimbach at Adobe.

CPSIA information can be obtained
at www.ICGtesting.com
Printed in the USA
JSHW031914020222
22479JS00004B/4

9 780691 235622